# facing Frankenstein

## Defeat Your True Opponent in Sport

# facing Frankenstein

## Defeat Your True Opponent in Sport

*Featuring*

### The Six Pathways To

### Mental Toughness Programme[©]

## Dr. Mark S. Elliott

DAVID JAMES PUBLISHING

First published in 2011 by

David James Publishing

www.davidjamespublishing.com

Copyright © 2011 Dr Mark S. Elliott

www.drmarkselliott.co.uk


Cover illustration copyright © 2011 Adrian Lutton

Cover Design copyright © 2011 Nick Stokes

**ISBN: 978-0-9568816-5-6**

To the loves of my life,

Alison, James and Matthew

&

For Karen

# Contents

## Afterword:

## Appendices                                                503

# Foreword

## By **Rory Best**, Ulster and Ireland

It is a privilege to write the Foreword to Mark's book. Mark is one of the best sport psychologists around and has been instrumental in my rise through the ranks of professional rugby union. It is not an exaggeration to say that my progress was dramatic

Within weeks of my first meeting with Mark, in June 2005, I had progressed from being back-up hooker with Ulster to holding down a regular place in the team. What's more, in November that year, I won my first international cap for Ireland! It was at Lansdowne Road against the All Blacks, no less, and was the realisation of a boyhood dream. It was a truly special occasion, one that I never expected to come round so soon. But when you're mentally tough, anything is possible. I have since gone on to represent Ireland 47 times, including playing in the 2007 World Cup, and have captained Ulster for the past four seasons.

Without doubt, working with Mark was the turning point in my career. I consulted him because of his strong reputation as a no-nonsense, yet warm individual who had achieved amazing results with athletes and teams. He was also the leading psychologist with the Sports Institute Northern Ireland.

My main goal in engaging Mark's services was to become psychologically tougher. Despite being relatively new to the world of professional rugby, I realised that the top players in the sport were not necessarily the most technically skillful.

However, they were always the most mentally tough. They were in control of their thinking and their emotions, had solid self-belief, exceptional focus and responded to critical moments in matches with brilliance. In other words, they had learned to master their inner opponent. With their inner game under control, their outer game flourished.

A major part of Mark's teachings is to blow apart a host of human illusions. He explains that we have learned to see the world in ways that are far from helpful and particularly destructive in performance settings. One of these myths is to see external events, such as making a mistake during a match, as the *cause* of a negative emotional reaction or a loss of focus.

This insight changed everything. It was incredibly empowering. It meant that I was creating my own stress and was therefore my own worst enemy. It also meant that I held the reins to my emotional and mental state at any one moment.

To whet my competitive juices, Mark suggested I saw my negative thoughts, feelings, images etc. as the weaponry of a nasty internal saboteur who wanted me to fail. We called this internal parasite my *mental monster* in reference to the way *Frankenstein* created his monster, only for it to turn on him. I liked this analogy as it provided an easy-to-understand and motivating rationale for the mental training I had to do.

I successfully followed Mark's *Six Pathways to Mental Toughness* programme, which is tailor-made to overcome this Frankenstein Factor.

*Facing Frankenstein is* a terrific book that goes right to the heart of the mental game by making you accountable for your own emotional state and readiness to perform.

Part One of the book explains how and why you get in your own way and then in Part Two you have the outstanding *Six Pathways to Mental Toughness* programme. This training will help strengthen your resolve and self-belief. You will begin to think more clearly and constructively, while also learning to silence your mind when the situation requires it. You will discover some incredible mental game secrets and have at your disposal numerous practical tips and techniques. Real examples from the world of elite sport are used to illustrate the many learning points in the book.

I cannot emphasise enough the value of *Facing Frankenstein*. You need to read it. Mark's insight into how athletes sabotage their preparation and performances is unique. His words inspire and educate in equal measure and his training is second to none. And I should know. Thanks to Mark and his methods, I am now playing and performing on the world stage. You too can reach your sporting potential by following the advice and learning the techniques in his book.

I can assure you that before long you'll be mentally tough and performing at your peak on a regular basis!

**Rory Best**

*Ulster and Ireland*

July, 2011

# About the author

**'Dr. Mark Elliott is Northern Ireland's best-known sports psychologist'** *Green and White Army: The Northern Ireland Fans*, Ivan Martin 2008, p.90

For the past 20 years, Dr. Mark Elliott's mental training expertise has been helping teams, individual athletes and coaches across the world, international, professional and elite amateur levels perform at their peak.

Mark is a chartered sport psychologist and runs his own sport psychology and counselling consultancy.

He possesses a Doctor of Psychology degree (PsyD) as well as both a master's and bachelor's degree in psychology. He is also an Associate Fellow of The British Psychological Society.

Mark has worked with performers from over twenty different sports. Amongst his clients he lists: European Tour golfers; International and British & Irish Lions' rugby players; Olympic and Paralympic athletes; professional footballers and clubs; pro ice hockey teams; boxers and mixed martial artists; and, senior county teams and individual performers from Gaelic sports.

He has also acted as sport psychology consultant to the Sports Institute Northern Ireland (SINI).

Considered Ireland's top sport psychologist, Mark has helped his clients to break records and to win tournaments at national, international and world levels. He has gained considerable coverage across the national print and broadcast media and regularly conducts seminars and workshops in sport psychology. It is telling that many of his prominent clients have publically endorsed his work.

Wherever there's a performance setting, Mark is there to help. Accordingly, he has also been consulted by entrepreneurs, business executives, sales people, fire-fighters, lawyers and physicians.

Mark feels privileged to have worked with some of the best performers on the planet. He has learned so much from his clients, and the writing of *Facing Frankenstein* has been inspired by these incredible people. He wants to give something back, to pass on essential knowledge and a practical know-how that really works and endures.

# Praise for Mark's work

'Without doubt, working with Mark was the turning point in my career.' **Rory Best, Ulster Captain and Ireland international.**

'I have a lot to thank Mark for. I was having a tough time in my rugby career when I met him and he listened to my problems. He helped me to set goals about how to get myself back playing good rugby and force my way into the Ireland team. I still use his ideas in preparing mentally for games.' **Tommy Bowe, rugby wing: Ospreys, Ireland, and the British and Irish Lions.**

'I have been playing top level sport for the past 11 years and I can say, without hesitation, that Mark Elliott is the best sports psychologist I have encountered. His analogies and his insights are masterful and he knows his craft inside out.' **Paul Brady, World Number 1 handball player.**

'I have worked with Mark since 2004. A specific example of Mark's positive impact on my mental game was seen in my playoff for the 2009 Portuguese Open – which became my first win on the European Tour. It would have been easy for me to get ahead of myself and to think that my opponent, Gonzalo Fernandez-Castano, who was undefeated in previous playoffs, against Lee Westwood and Henrik Stenson, would produce the goods again against me. But having understood that I can only control my own game, I took the pressure off myself, realising that it wasn't the end of the world if I was to lose. I focused instead on one shot at a time and staying in the moment. I stuck to this feeling of being 'in the now' throughout the playoff and didn't waver when I hit poor shots. This learned mentality enabled me to make three good recoveries and eventually to win the tournament. Before hitting my winning putt I said "just put your best stroke on it and accept". That's a good approach to golf.' *Michael Hoey, European Tour golfer and winner of the 2009 Estoril Open de Portugal and the 2011 Madeira Islands Open. Former Walker Cup player and British Amateur Champion.*

'Working with Mark has taken my mental game to a totally new level. Thanks to his training system, I have high levels of self-belief and trust. I have confidence in my boxing ability and have developed a level of resilience that has helped me cope with some very tough times and to keep going despite them. My focus on the job at hand has improved greatly and skills like visualisation have proved invaluable in my preparation for training and fights. Mark's mantra with me is "Lead with the Mind and the Body Will Follow", advice that has helped me win British and European belts and put me in world title contention.' *Brian Magee, Professional Boxer, Interim WBA World super middleweight champion and former European champion.*

'Mark is both a true expert in his field and a really good bloke; the combination of which shines through in his work. His ideas, techniques and words are powerfully emotive and bring with them great focus and confidence.' *Simon Danielli, rugby wing: Ulster and Scotland.*

'Mark worked with me when I was playing professionally for three years and I can honestly say that I had my best three seasons when we were working together. Athletes spend so much time preparing physically, but I have seen the biggest and strongest players crumble under pressure or not be able to bounce back from a bad game or a bad play. Mark helped me focus on the little things and to be aware of the situations when I let negative emotions take over. I completely buy in to the importance of training your mind as well as your body and now that I am running a professional sports team, I believe in it even more. You can see when emotions or the mental side of the game is playing a part in success or failure, and being able to control it, and better yet being able to use it to your advantage, is a competitive edge that no truly dedicated athlete should let pass by. I still use the skills Mark taught me in my business and personal life and I can honestly say that working with Mark over the years has proven to be invaluable to me and to my team.' **Todd Kelman, General Manager, Belfast Giants.**

'Mark has proven himself to be one of the top men in his field. He has worked with many players and teams I have coached. His commonsense and fun approach gives every athlete the chance to reach his BEST!' **Martin McElkennon, Renowned Elite Trainer and Coach, Gaelic Football.**

'While head coach for the Belfast Giants, I was fortunate to work with Dr. Mark Elliott. His expertise in sport psychology provided me and my players with highly effective mental skills and methods to improve individual and team performances. Mark's contribution ultimately resulted in the capture of championship and league titles. I continue to use his methods today in my current coaching role with The Pursuit of Excellence Hockey Academy in Kelowna, Canada.' **Dave Whistle, top ice hockey coach.**

'Being a starting goalie in the Elite League is not an easy task as you're playing 60 to 70 games a season, with lots of ups and downs. I was on a mental down slope and in a rut until I started to work with Mark. Thanks to him I was able, that same season, to go on and win 2 championships with the Giants and have never looked back since. Mark guided me back up to the top of my game. I still use his methods today.' **Stevie Lyle, ice hockey netminder:**

*formerly of the Belfast Giants and now with the Cardiff Devils and Team GB.*

'I have used the services of Mark Elliott during my brief spell as first team manager of Larne football club. Larne were bottom of the Irish Premier League and the confidence in particular was at a very low ebb. Mark was able to help me with ideas and psychological benefits that would help the players' state of mind. Mark offered help with building the chemistry of the group; he gave me some very good advice on supporting the players individually and collectively. There were players who struggled with many different issues, these included such things as: Coping strategies, emotional imbalances, managing difference, peer pressure and loss of momentum. During my time at Larne, Mark proved to be a fantastic support mechanism which was a contributing factor in the club achieving a 12th place finish, a remarkable turnaround.' *Kenny Shiels, Manager, Kilmarnock FC.*

'Every rugby career has ups and downs. I was lucky to have Mark to see me through the lows and to keep me grounded during the highs. It has been a pleasure to work with him.' *Ryan Caldwell, Bath.*

'Having been the first to introduce sports psychology into the Irish Premier League through Mark Elliott, I know only too well the benefits of mental preparation for enhanced performance. Mark's work with me at Lisburn Distillery FC was immense in this area. I am indebted to him. Many thanks, Mark.' *Paul Kirk, top football coach - UEFA Pro Licence holder.*

'Thanks to Mark, I gained an awareness of how my mind works; and what was once my weakest area, my mental game, I believe is now my strongest. Working with Mark has been an essential part of my development as an athlete and has brought me closer to reaching my full potential.' *Lisa Kearney, Elite Judoka (48kg): 2010 World Cup gold medallist and London 2012 contender.*

'As the first Irish player to sign for the Belfast Giants, there was intense media interest on how I would fair in the upper echelons of British hockey. This speculation reached a crescendo when it was announced that I would make my first professional start against Basingstoke Bison in the Elite League. It was all the more stressful as our other goalie had been suspended and my backup for the match would be an untried youngster. I was, in reality, on my own. I consulted Dr. Mark Elliott, the Giants' sport psychologist, for mental training sessions. By teaching me several mental game methods and tricks, Mark helped me to take control of my inner game before and during the Bison's match. We won the game; I had a shutout and was named Man of the Match. I can say with every certainty that the pivotal factor in achieving this level of performance, in this game and in the remainder of my career, was the new mental training I undertook.' *Chris McGimpsey, Pro ice hockey goalie, formerly of the Belfast Giants.*

'Working with Mark has made me approach, not only my competitive surfing in a different manner, but also the way I train. Mark has taught me that the mind is your most powerful tool to achieve an excellent performance. With the techniques I have learned, my surfing is at a new level which, without Mark, it wouldn't be. It has been an honour to work with Mark and continues to be so.' *Ronan Oertzen, Surfer, Ireland International.*

'Mark has helped me so much with getting rid of my fear and letting my talent shine through on the course. Since working with Mark I also feel I get a lot more enjoyment from the game and as a result I put in better performances.' *David Leathem, USA Jaguars' Golf Team.*

'High Performance sport reflects the full gamut of life. The roller coaster of emotions attached to performing at the highest level cannot be underestimated; the joy and adulation to the long hours of often lonely and selfish preparation. Both the athlete and coach need support to guide and prepare them for that journey. I have been very fortunate to meet Mark; he has given me the skills, the sound practical advice plus unwavering support to help me keep a healthy balance in my life. From the Olympic environment to the support needed to keep my family life stable. Mark has been empathetic and at times challenging; his sense of perspective and of good old-fashioned values has helped me make critical and important decisions to develop a world class coaching practice.' *Stephen Maguire, Athletics Coach: Coach to Jason Smyth, Gold Medal Paralympian, London 2012 Olympic prospect and potential history-maker.*

'Mark has worked for the Sports Institute as a consultant supporting athletes and coaches from a range of Olympic and Paralympic sports. His approach emphasizes the importance of identifying realistic goals and facilitates self-awareness of underlying barriers to goal achievement.

The Six Pathways to Mental Toughness training programme, presented in this book, provides the key skills necessary to help individuals gain a competitive advantage.

The material is written in a user friendly manner and aims to equip athletes with more effective thinking and behavioural skills. Mark has helped many an athlete and coach and now has captured his principles in a manner that is accessible to all who have an interest in gaining the edge on the competition. Be proactive – open the book and make a start – let Mark show you how to attain high level performance consistently.' **Peter McCabe, Athlete Services Manager, Sport Institute Northern Ireland.**

'Mark is the complete professional who has that rare gift of being able to quickly take in the whole picture whilst maintaining a meticulous eye for detail.' **Dr Dave Williams, Retired Senior Lecturer, Dept of Psychology, The University of Hull.**

'Being aware of many of the teams and individuals that Mark has worked with and knowing the record of success that they have had, I have no doubt of his ability to help produce results in the sporting arena. I have recommended him to contacts of my own and would have no hesitation in doing so again as there is real evidence of results – tangible too, with trophies and medals collected along the way.' **Stuart McKinley, Sports Journalist, The Belfast Telegraph.**

# **Acknowledgements**

Olin Miller was right when he said that *"Writing is the hardest way to earn a living, with the possible exception of wrestling alligators."* And not only is it an arduous task, but also writing can be a very lonely pursuit. However, this is where I have been very lucky, blessed indeed. For helping me to wrestle this book from the jaws of capitulation has been a team of amazing people.

At the outset, I want to offer my heartfelt thanks to my beautiful wife Alison and to my two big sons, James and Matthew. Without their love, support, understanding and utmost patience, I would never have written this book.

Alison, it seems that you knew me before I did. When we met in 1986, I was a lost soul, a shadow of my true self. You have loved me unconditionally and provided the unerring support and belief that has enabled me to grow. It is no coincidence that my greatest achievements, both professional and personal, have occurred over the past twenty-five years.

And it makes my heart skip a beat every time I see your spirit, resilience and humour in our two boys.

What can I say Matthew and James? Well, for one, I love you both to bits and always will. In terms of my book, I want to say a big thank you for your steadfast support and tolerance. That neither of you ever played the 'it's just not fair' card is a sign of your maturity and understanding.

Instead, you took to the book and its content from the get-go, especially when you discovered that it involved some sort of monster!

To this day, I still have my Lego Frankenstein's monster sitting on top of my PC. Thanks for this Matthew. And keep up the golf young fella. You mightn't know it, but you're our Pension Fund!

James, your advice and support belied your tender years. I will never forget our late night chats when you would entice my mind away from such trivialities as sentence construction and onto much more meaningful matters. While I couldn't shed a great deal of light on the whys and wherefores of Creation, I hope I left you in no doubt that you and Matthew should appreciate life, always be true to yourselves and strive to be everything you can be.

Oh and by the way, James, many thanks for coming up with the book title. Great choice!

I wish to thank the thousands of people I have counselled and trained over the past twenty years. It has been a privilege to work with and meet each and every one of you. All the while you were learning from me, I was learning from you. Be in no doubt, there would be no book without you.

In particular, I want to thank, from the bottom of my heart, the following fantastic athletes and coaches who have contributed to this book and brought it to life with real-world insights: Rory Best, Tommy Bowe, Paul Brady, Ryan Caldwell, Simon Danielli, Michael Hoey, Brian Irvine, Lisa Kearney, Todd Kelman, Paul Kirk, Dave Leathem, Stevie Lyle, Brian Magee, Stephen Maguire, Peter McCabe, Martin McElkennon, Chris McGimpsey, Ronan Oertzen, Kenny Shiels and Dave Whistle.

Special mention must go to Ulster captain, Ireland star and absolute gentleman Rory Best who very kindly penned the Foreword to the book. Thank you so much Rory!

I was delighted when I was signed-up by David James Publishing (www.davidjamespublishing.com). They are a cutting edge, progressive Publishing House headed up by David Stokes and Jim Montgomery. Their expertise, inspiration and passion for publishing helped shape my manuscript into a book ready for the world to see. David and Jim, thank you so much. Your professionalism is second to none; your support and patience absolute.

My thanks go to long-time friend and top sports journalist, Stuart McKinley. Stuart, we met in the early 2000s and you have played a key role in publicising my work and spreading the word about the benefits of sport psychology. On numerous occasions you went that extra mile to help me out. This is what true friends do for each other. I hope that we continue to work together for many years to come.

Special thanks also go to psychologist, former business partner and friend Heather Whistle who encouraged me several years ago to share my mental training methods with a wider audience.

Well Heather, I have at last followed through on your advice – better late than never - and I deeply appreciate the confidence you have always shown in me. Although you have moved back home to Canada with Dave and the boys, the impact of your enthusiasm for life, sport and psychology will remain with me always.

My doctorate supervisor was Dr. Dave Williams of The University of Hull. Dave, you are a very special man. Your advice has always been wise and has enabled me to navigate the rugged landscape of academic and professional life. Your confidence in me and my work has been instrumental in the writing of this book. My gratitude for your support and friendship is beyond measure.

Last, but by no means least, my gratitude and admiration goes to childhood friend and illustrator-extraordinaire, Adrian Lutton, who has brought the mental monster to life in a truly remarkable way. I am sure you'll agree that his artwork is exceptional. Thank you so much Adrian. Athletes who read this book can now see their true opponent in the 'flesh'.

The one drawback about the 'Acknowledgements' section is that you cannot thank everyone all at once. Instead, you have to draw up a list, which suggests a hierarchy of gratitude. This couldn't be further from the truth. I thank everyone equally for the completion of this book.

As long as I have breath in my body I will never forget this period in my life; a time when so many talented and generous people helped me realise my dream. These are people who didn't let society degenius them.

*Genius is nothing more or less than childhood recovered by will, a childhood now equipped for self-expression with an adult's capacities.*

**- Charles Pierre Baudelaire**

*I am convinced all of humanity is born with more gifts than we know. Most are born geniuses and just get de-geniused rapidly.*

**- Buckminster Fuller**

*We are all geniuses up to the age of ten.*

**- Aldous Huxley**

# Introduction

## THE DAY I QUIT

It was a quirk of fate, I suppose, that I became a qualified sport psychologist. After all, I had lost the mental battle myself and with it my dream of becoming a professional footballer. And it wasn't a pipe-dream either. I had a chance.

I was sixteen when I quit football, packing my goalkeeping gloves away for the very last time. I can be even more specific if you like, not that I think about it often!  It was twenty past six on Saturday the 23rd of February 1980, when I arrived home in tears after a match.

I stormed past my bewildered parents, ran upstairs to my bedroom, ripped down my posters of goalkeeping greats Pat Jennings (sorry Pat), Alex Stepney, Ray Clemence and Sepp Maier, scrunched them up and stuffed them in my wardrobe, along with my green, pimpled Sondico goalie gloves. They remained there untouched for the next twenty years, lying snuggly against a pile of *Shoot* Christmas annuals at the back of the wardrobe.

Several weeks of careless goalkeeping had culminated that day, in winter 1980, in a car crash of a performance. I couldn't take it any longer.

Fed-up, embarrassed and disillusioned, after I had committed another horrendous mistake to cost my team the match, I gave up, never returning to goalkeeping again.

Yet not too many months earlier, I had been a promising goalkeeper who'd had a Northern Ireland Schoolboy trial, and been invited to train with an Irish First Division club.

It had all looked pretty good. As far as I was concerned I had a chance of making real strides towards a future in professional football. Little did I know then, of course, that it would be as a sport psychologist and not as a player.

While I had been aware at the time of some sort of internal scuffle for power going on in my mind, I hadn't the knowledge at sixteen to explain what it was.

I simply thought I was a useless keeper, that I had lost my ability, and that I had been foolhardy to consider a career in football was ever a possibility for little old me.

Though life took over - school exams, university, girls, bars and cars – one question remained unanswered in my mind, irritating me like an unreachable itch: How come I had been a better goalkeeper at 12 than I was at *16*?

## MY MONSTER

Three psychology degrees, several years of professional practice and hundreds of clients later I had finally given the itch a good old scratch.

I had answered the question - though what emerged was disquieting, to say the least. In fact, my sense at sixteen that some sort of skirmish for supremacy was going on in my mind was right on the money.

The reason why I morphed from schoolboy trial hero to quitter status zero was because I had unknowingly manufactured a type of evil twin, a monstrous other self, whose sole aim was to hijack the true, unpolluted self I was born with.

This synthetic self, this mental monster, realised its ambition, for I changed from a living-in-the-moment happy kid, bursting with unqualified joy and sporting promise into a sixteen year-old youth who'd grown to hate the sport he loved so much. My inner saboteur did a great job on me, rendering my goalkeeping ability ineffective and extinguishing my sporting dream.

It was an insidious process. Over time I started to think, feel and behave in ways that generated mental and emotional interference. Before, during and after matches I began to think far too much about the wrong stuff. Negative thoughts would emerge from left field and instead of evicting them, I let them make a summer house out of my mind – then they moved all their relatives in and stayed for years. My mental monster became the squatter from hell!

I bathed in the psychological acid bath of defeatist interpretations, foreboding images and negative memories. Worry, doubt, distraction and a crushing self-consciousness all coalesced to eat into my technical ability leaving it anaemic. My goalkeeping ability was eaten up from the inside-out. It was all over.

As my mental monster was part of me, it went wherever I went. Consequently, it spread its influence way beyond sport. Not content with ripping up my sporting ambition, my inner monster also came to life in other situations where I felt under scrutiny. For example, my so-called social life became very stressful.

Mixing with girls became a mental minefield that I tiptoed through. A stinging self-consciousness saw to that. It pervaded what should have been enjoyable, fun times – the best years of my life, as the saying goes.

I became adept at finding threats in my environment. Not physical ones, but those that threatened my ego. I started to shun social invitations, finding it less stressful to avoid outings than to put myself in the spotlight. I was overly concerned with what other people were thinking about me. It almost goes without saying that these were not happy and productive times.

I now know that I had succumbed to a flaw in the human condition, a flaw which emerges as childhood innocence ends. It is a flaw I have named the *Frankenstein Factor*© – AND YOU HAVE IT TOO. And it is solely because of this Factor that you need a mental game for sport. It is *not*, as you've been told up to now, because sport is psychologically demanding!

I know it's a radical statement, but it's true all the same. Playing sport competitively, even at the very top table, has never of itself been a strain on the psyche. It is the Frankenstein Factor that places tension on the mind; but that's a *human* thing, not a sport thing!

The parallels with Mary Shelley's story-bound scientist will be revealed very soon in Chapter 1, but for now I'd like to stress that the majority of athletes I work with find the analogy extremely useful and insightful.

In terms of sport not being mentally demanding, well my clients initially become a bit slack-jawed at the enormity of the claim, before then listening to the rationale backing it up.

Once I explain the claim fully, it's like a wake-up call for them and for the first time they see things for how they really are. They understand the real reason why they need a mental game and it motivates them like crazy to become mentally tough. After all, there's a monster chasing them!

When I discovered the Frankenstein Factor and learned the truth about the nature of reality, I was initially pretty angry. I was cross that I had to spend years uncovering it for myself and subsequently for my clients. I wondered why I had never been taught it at school. However, this annoyance was soon replaced by a desire to find a way to defeat my mental monster. It was time to face up to it; time to live life fearlessly for a change and to make something of myself.

To do these things, I had to understand the monster more fully, to study it closely. I had to know my enemy to be able to defeat it. And defeat it I did. I overcame the Frankenstein Factor by first designing and then following to the letter, *The Six Pathways to Mental Toughness*© programme. I designed this training system over a period of eight months several years ago. After some pruning and refinement it became the most powerful of mental game systems, helping me turn my life around and transforming my clients into world beaters.

On a personal level, I progressed from being a socially anxious, self-conscious, poorly performing doom merchant in my teens and early twenties, to become a Doctor of Psychology; a successful practitioner with two practices; and according to one media source, to be 'Ireland's leading sport psychologist'. In terms of the latter, I couldn't possibly comment, of course!

In all seriousness though, you can appreciate these achievements all the more when I tell you that my teachers at school didn't view me as university material. In fact, not even as A-Level material! (A-Levels exams are taken in the final year of High School in the UK). Basically, my teachers saw me as incapable of making any great strides in the world.

But by taking back control of my mind, I was back in the box seat running my thoughts, emotions and behaviour. By developing real and durable mental toughness, I was no longer a slave to my mind.

I returned to my natural state, the way I was meant to be. Accordingly, I grew in confidence. I started to believe in myself; good things could come my way after all. It wasn't just for the chosen few. It was for *anyone* willing to put him or herself out there, take risks, persist through adversity and keep focusing on the process.

I learned the obvious – success doesn't come knocking on your door. You have to do stuff!

## Work-In- Progress

Now let's be clear about one thing here, in case it all sounds like Pollyanna. My transformation from being a victim of my inner monster, to being its master, was blooming hard work.

Progress ebbed and flowed. But I kept at it, as I was highly driven to run my own mind for a change. I wanted to live life properly from the inside-out and to experience pleasure and success. I continue to work at it every day. But isn't that what life is – a work-in-progress? You keep learning and growing. The moment you think you have licked life, is the moment it has licked you! So I keep practising what I preach.

Although my mental makeover has been significant, it doesn't mean that life is now dead easy and stress-free. It isn't. That would be wholly unrealistic and rather strange, I would've thought. We are all part of nature and therefore, like nature itself, are subject to the unavoidable and truly upsetting.

Now, to be upset by life's inescapable tragedies is one thing, but to create your own upset is something else entirely. This book acknowledges the former and helps you desist from the latter.

## If Only

This is the book I wish I'd had as a teenager. It would have helped me understand my difficulties and could have prevented me quitting football. Who knows how far I could have progressed in the game, if I'd had access to the *Six Pathways* programme back then.

What pleases me most right now though, is that *you* have access to it. You have in your hands a mighty book, one that will raise your mental game to world class level and improve your performances like never before.

## Who Is The Book For?

*Facing Frankenstein* is for the athlete who wants to become a total athlete. It is for athletes across all sports and at all levels of ability. The terms 'athlete' and 'performer' are used throughout the book to cover all sportspeople, from the casual amateur participant, right through to the professional elite and world-class. I use the male pronoun only for ease of writing.

I am hopeful that the book will challenge the mental game sceptic, as much as it refreshes and nourishes the enthusiast. The book should also be read by coaches and parents, as well as by the curious and intrigued.

You do not have to be at your wits' end to get the most out of this book, but it will benefit those who have hit some 'fed-up' point in their sporting progress. So, perhaps you have come to this book exasperated by inconsistent performances, or your all too frequent defeats to lower-ranked opponents, or an inability to close out victory. Or maybe you're haunted by fear of failure or burdened by a mind that incessantly churns out defeatist thoughts, memories and images. It could be that over-anxiety is suffocating your preparation and performance and that this book represents a last attempt to resurrect your performances and to regain mental control.

Whatever your reasons, sporting background or ability level, you are very welcome to the book. It's good to see you here.

## What The Book Is

*Facing Frankenstein* is a straight-talking, accessible and practical book. It is designed to accommodate and meet *your* needs, and what it teaches you will endure. It directs you to become active in overcoming your inner monster and in building up your mental skills portfolio.

The book covers the journey to mental toughness that all athletes need to take. You will begin by attaining massive awareness in Part One, before moving on to Part Two where, by following *The Six Pathways to Mental Toughness* programme, you will end up with a rock solid mental game.

While it can be expensive to consult a sport psychologist, this book offers you the very knowledge and guidance you would receive from many face-to-face sessions. What this means is that you are only one book away from breakthrough performances and sporting success.

Now that is an awesome deal!

## 20 Years' Experience

I have had the privilege over the past two decades to work with some of the best sports performers on the planet. I have been hired by teams and individual athletes across the world, international, professional and elite amateur levels. I've also worked with and advised top coaches. The job I have is wonderful. I have learned so much from my clients; and the writing of this book has been inspired by these incredible people. I want to give something back, to pass on essential knowledge and a practical know-how of what really works.

Not only do I thank those from within sport, but also I need to acknowledge all of those people who have consulted me from various other performance settings. My work with entrepreneurs, business executives, sales people, fire-fighters, lawyers and physicians has also infused me with massive knowledge and human insight.

It is from this wealth of personal and professional experience that I have concluded, without hesitation, that as humans we are complicit in our own psychological and emotional angst. That, for reasons of socialisation and education, we have become caged in our left brains, proficient at self-sabotage and adept at tripping ourselves up.

And it is purely because of this tendency that athletes need to be mentally tough; we all need to be. And this book shows you how. Let's take a closer look.

## FORMAT AND CONTENT OF THE BOOK

*Facing Frankenstein* is organised into two parts, with each part fortifying the other.

**Part One, Mental Game Awareness and Assessment**, represents the beginning of your journey to mental toughness. You will come to understand why you need a mental game, what the mental game of sport actually is, what mental toughness looks like and why it is essential to attain it.

You'll also be able to assess your own level of mental strength.

There are three chapters in Part One, each building towards the training programme in Part Two. Let's take a brief look at each of them.

In **chapter 1**, you will meet your true opponent in sport – your mental monster.

You will learn about:

- What the *Frankenstein Factor* is;
- How it developed during your formative years; and,
- The powerful influence it can have over your sporting performances.

At last you will understand the real reason why you need a mental game and be taken aback that it's got nothing to do with sport itself. You will also discover that *sport psychology* is a misnomer, and that performing well and succeeding in sport is down to the psychology of *being human*.

YOU WILL BE ASTOUNDED BY WHAT YOU READ IN THIS CHAPTER. The information it contains is mind-blowing. You will find out that you have been misled about the true nature of reality, and that you've unwittingly been living and performing under the jackboot of your mental monster for years.

In **Chapter 2**, you are given the keys to your mental game arsenal, to the psychological artillery that will enable you to overcome your mental monster. This weaponry can be summed up in two words – *mental toughness*.

It is therefore the purpose of this chapter to describe what mental toughness is, its characteristics and how you can attain it.

The six key strands of mental toughness will be set out and brought to life through real examples from some of the best athletes in the world. By the end of the chapter, you will be left in no doubt that mental toughness is crucial to peak performance.

**Chapter 3** invites you to rate the current status of your own mental game using the *Pathways Profiling* system. This assessment will enable you to gauge how mentally tough you are right now. It will also provide a baseline against which you will chart your progress, as you work through *The Six Pathways to Mental Toughness* programme in Part Two. You will find that very few mental training books offer an assessment and monitoring system as comprehensive as the one contained in this chapter.

Chapter 3 will also introduce you to the six pathways to mental toughness. You will learn how each of these six training modules can raise your mental game in remarkably effective ways. This will set you up perfectly for the second phase of your journey.

**Part Two**, **Mental Game Action**, is the doing part of the book. It consists of six chapters, one for each of 6 Pathways. While each of the pathways is a standalone training course in its own right, it is the combined effect of the pathways training that leads to mental toughness

The six modules cover numerous mental skills and techniques, and are jam-packed with over 80 practical exercises that will enable you to attain powerful mental game ability.

So whenever you see a 'Pathway Pit Stop', you should fetch your pen and a notebook (head this up as a *Mental Game Journal*) and complete the set task.

At the beginning of each Pathway chapter you will find a section headed up '**MONSTER WATCH**'.

This section describes the specific ways in which your mental monster sabotages and toys with the mental game area relevant to the chapter. These descriptions should drive you on to make the most of the training on offer.

The six chapters in Part Two are:

**Pathway to Motivation and Momentum** (Chapter 4)

**Pathway to Total Self-Belief** (Chapter 5)

**Pathway to World Class Thinking** (Chapter 6)

**Pathway to Effective Focus** (Chapter 7)

**Pathway to Imagery Control** (Chapter 8)

**Pathway to Emotional Control** (Chapter 9)

## Pathway Pledges

Put the work into Part Two of the book and you will become mentally tough, guaranteed. Specifically, you will:

- Become self-driven to attain massive progress in your sport, and to enjoy the journey.

- Develop unflinching belief in yourself and your ability to master situations.

- Develop the ability to think constructively at all times and to create your own reality.

- Learn how to attain a quiet but focused mind during competition.

- Discover how to prepare for competition in the most powerful way possible.

- Perform with poise, having the ability to control your emotions, before, during and after performance.

## 6 Ways to Make the Pathways Programme Work for You

To maximise the opportunity presented to you in the book, it is important for you to do six things:

### – Form A Partnership With Your Mind

One of the first steps in advancing your mental game for sport is to make friends with your mind. Stop neglecting it. You'll be amazed at the benefits accruing to you from treating your mind as a partner in your sporting journey.

Even Homer Simpson has conceded to this. From the episode 'The Front', we see Homer preparing to sit his final exam to, at long last, graduate from High School:

> **Homer:** *"All right brain, you don't like me, and I don't like you. But let's just get me through this, and I can get back to killing you with beer"*
>
> **Homer's brain**: *"It's a deal!"*

Your partnership with your mind should, of course, be much more friendly, effective and enduring than dear old Homer's short-lived rapprochement with his.

### – Be Compassionate (To Yourself)

When I quit football I didn't know that I had learned a set of destructive mental habits. In fact, I didn't know that I didn't know! I simply thought I was born with insufficient ability and that the sporting gods had chosen other people for sporting glory.

I now know, of course, that the Frankenstein Factor was behind my demise; it wasn't my genes. I had learned to sabotage my efforts to progress.

Once I discovered this, I absolved myself from all guilt and regret and became compassionate towards my younger self. It is important for you do the same. Be fair to yourself. Be compassionate.

### – Start With A Clean Slate

You can only start out from where you are now, and as you are reading this book you are already beginning to rectify the situation.

That's all that can be asked of anyone; accepting where you are now and plan for forward motion. So, well done!

### – Be a Participant, Not a Passenger

Although advancing your mental game is very much a journey, your role is not to be an impatient passenger: "Are we there yet?" "Am I mentally tough yet?" "Are we there yet?" Aaahhhhh!!

Rather, it's best that you become a participant. I'll do the 'driving' for a while, but in the end, your mental game needs and goals will dictate the speed at which we travel and the landscape we cover.

Ultimately then, *you* set *your* goals, *you* shape the route and *you* do the work. Commit to this now.

## – Seek Out Travelling Companions

I would encourage you to garner support for your journey to mental toughness by bringing your coach on board. It would also be useful to disclose your goals to your parents, partner and best friend.

In other words, to people who care about you, who want the best for you and who will be there for you whenever times are difficult.

A strong support team will add an extra motivating dimension to your efforts. While you should want to improve for your own sake, having someone else rooting for you reinforces your commitment to your goals.

## – Dismiss The Myth Of The Quick Fix

Personal change takes time. There are no quick fixes! They do not exist, no matter how appealing some of the slick marketing is out there (you know the type - 7 days to this, that and the other!).

Remember, it has taken time to arrive at where you are now and it'll take time to cultivate new and constructive habits.

Moreover, you need to appreciate that mental skills are just that, skills. As such, you acquire them in much the same way as you acquired your physical and technical skills. And you know from experience, that this took dedicated practice over a protracted period.

It is essential, therefore, that you allow time for the absorption of the new mental habits you'll learn along each Pathway. Work hard and be patient. There is no shortcut to mental skill proficiency.

But I can assure you that the end result will be worth it.

## Real-World Examples

Throughout the book, you will find real-world examples from the top athletes and performers I have worked with over the years.

Many of these guys are household names and they offer you numerous illustrations of mental toughness in action from the hotbed of elite sport.

I believe you'll find their comments and experiences extremely enlightening.

You will also meet Rick, Aaron, Taylor, Iain, Natalie and Grant, who offer you six great case studies.

These athletes begin their stories of mental game difficulties in Chapter 3, before then providing the solutions to their problems throughout Part Two of the book.

## If Not Now, When?

I strongly recommend that you sharpen your mental skills now, and to do so with the same vigour as you sharpen your technical and physical skills. Become a total athlete, a performer who prepares both body and mind.

Without a strong mental game you will not reach your potential. If you truly want to understand and address your psychological barriers to performance, to attain mental mastery, and to realise your sporting promise, then *Facing Frankenstein* is the book for you. It is an essential tool for today's ambitious athlete. It's an opportunity not to be missed.

Be assured, the days of being stalked by your mental monster are almost over!

# Part One

## Mental Game Awareness and Assessment

*We Western people are apt to think our great problems are external, environmental. We are not skilled in the inner life, where the real roots of our problems lie. The outer distractions of our interests reflect an inner lack of integration of our own lives. We are trying to be several selves at once, without all our selves being organised by a single mastering life within us.*

**- Thomas R. Kelly**, *A Testament of Devotion*

# Chapter 1

# THE FRANKENSTEIN FACTOR©

## *The **real** reason why athletes need a mental game*

I beheld the wretch - the miserable monster whom
I had created.

- Victor Frankenstein in, **Mary Shelley's** *Frankenstein*

I have never seen a greater monster or miracle
than myself.

**- Michel De Montaigne**

I'm not afraid of anyone, but sometimes I'm afraid
of myself.

**- Justine Henin**

In this chapter you will:

■ Meet your true opponent in sport - your Mental Monster.

■ Discover how it sabotages your potential for greatness, by using all sorts of cunning tricks and illusions.

■ Find out how to defeat it.


For many years now, it has been a passion of mine to tell it like it is to as many athletes as possible around the globe. I want to place on record a truth that no other sport psychology book has ever sufficiently acknowledged. I want athletes to know the *real* reason why they need a mental game. And I can tell them right now, it's *not* because competitive sport is mentally demanding.

That's right! Playing sport *ISN'T* mentally demanding. Rather, it is athletes themselves who are mentally demanding.

And they are like this because of the *Frankenstein Factor* and its malevolent spawn, the monster within.

It's the case then, that the plain and simple truth is this: **You need a mental game because the Frankenstein Factor exists, not because sport exists.**

Now I realise this will sound a bit strange to you, which is entirely understandable. After all, you've just read the word 'Frankenstein' in a sport psychology book and been told something about the mental game of sport that goes against everything you've been taught.

However, even though you have been told for years that sport itself creates the mental challenge, the truth is, it doesn't. *You* create it! The source of your stresses and strains lies much closer to home. It's an inside job; always has been. To varying degrees, we all have difficulty coping; not with sport or life, but with *ourselves*. Yet it was never meant to be this way.

We are born with fantastic genetic gifts and limitless potential. With the positive nurturing of what nature has bequeathed us, we should all be guaranteed a successful, rewarding and contented life.

Straightforward isn't it? Well you'd think so. However, this simple formula for fulfilment doesn't take account of the single greatest blemish in the human condition – the Frankenstein Factor.

> *We are born princes and the civilizing*
> *process makes us frogs.*
> **- Eric Berne**

## THE FRANKENSTEIN FACTOR DEFINED

**The Frankenstein Factor is a metaphor for the human tendency to self-sabotage. Self-sabotage is a human habit shaped by our mental game neglect, together with the lop-sided way we are educated and the negative messages we receive from parents, peers and society itself.**

As you can see from this definition, there are three things that coalesce to produce the Frankenstein Factor; three ingredients that shape our propensity for self-sabotage:

1. Mental game neglect

2. The one-dimensional education system

3. Society's narrow messages about what to think and how to behave.

We'll now examine the three elements in turn. In doing so, you will begin to understand, perhaps for the first time, why playing sport competitively is so challenging for athletes.

And remember, it's got *nothing* to do with sport itself. It's a HUMAN thing.

# 1. Mental Game Neglect

## Watch This, Shut Up!

We have evolved a remarkable brain, jam-packed with awesome systems that, if harnessed properly, can make life's journey pleasurable, meaningful and fulfilled.

We can develop real, loving and trusting relationships; be at peace with ourselves and others; become intrinsically motivated to engage in meaningful activity; set massive goals and meet them; remain healthy for longer; and live life, rather than merely exist for seventy-odd years and then die.

ALL OF THIS is within the reach of ALL OF US. But here's the rub: no-one has taught us how to use our brain for a better life; how to play the mental game effectively.

The human brain is the seat of all learning and behaviour, constructive *and* destructive. Its systems are remarkable genetic gifts and portals to all things good *and* bad, depending on how you use them.

For instance, the brain's analytical and imagery systems provided the blueprint for both the H-Bomb *and* the defibrillator. The former is life-taking, the latter life-saving.

The same constructive/destructive dichotomy exists across all of life's endeavours, including playing sport.

However, as a result of not being educated on how to employ the full wealth of our brain's capabilities, many of us simply fumble in the dark trying our best to manage life. Without systematic instruction and direction we inevitably end up playing the mental game badly; we slip to the destructive side of the constructive/destructive divide. We end up using our brain's super systems poorly, but unknowingly so. The lack of formal mental game guidance is a shocking oversight in our education system.

I mean, here we are, an advanced species, with a supercharged mental system between our ears and nobody has bothered to tell us how best to use it!

Tellingly, sports journalist Brendan Gallagher wrote the following piece under the heading *The Great Sporting Secret*:

> **"All the great coaches in all the major sports are agreed on one thing: the most important part of an athlete's body is the top three inches of his head. The brain is a wonderful and infinitely versatile tool - it controls everything - and is at the very heart of how sportsmen and women perform around the globe. A fit brain is worth a million press-ups or thousands of hours ploughing up and down the pool every morning."**
>
> *- BBC SPORT, Raise Your Game*

The magnificence of such an asset should never be kept secret, should it?

As an interesting aside, the perceptive American stand-up comedian and social commentator, the late Bill Hicks, believed that no government would want its subjects to be in charge of their own minds, as this could lead to creative thought, challenging the authorities and onwards to anarchy. Best therefore that we minions become distracted by other more frivolous things, like keeping up with the Joneses, debt, drinking beer, popping pills and watching television every night. To Hicks this was the unwritten "Watch this, Shut up!" government policy.

Hicks may have a point of course, but as I don't want 'The Men in Black' (and I don't mean Richie McCaw and his teammates) battering my door down, I'll leave any hints of premeditated neglect to the conspiracy theorists. But whatever its genesis, be it conspiracy or ignorance, mental game neglect has left many of us as unintentional Victor Frankensteins. And before you recoil at the suggestion, the analogy with Mary Shelley's fictional scientist *is* entirely appropriate.

## You Are My Creator, but I am Your Master – Obey. *The Monster*, *Frankenstein*

Victor Frankenstein, not being God, didn't know the rules of creating life. You'll know the story. Setting out to play God himself, Frankenstein stitched together bits and pieces of body parts, eventually bringing to life his worst nightmare. The monster he created was finally brought to life by a flash of electricity.

Now, it was while rereading Shelley's work that I noticed the distinct parallels between Baron Frankenstein's destructive works and how we go about things as humans.

I realised that as we don't know the rules of the mental game, due to the neglect referred to above, we 'do a Frankenstein'.

That is, we suture together a whole series of negative messages, beliefs, thoughts, images, memories, emotions and behaviours into a powerful body of destructive mental habits. In doing this, we are no different to the Baron. We end up creating something hideous - something that will destroy us, from the inside-out.

We end up crafting our very own *mental* monster. Which, just like Frankenstein's fiend, is also brought to life by electrical impulses – those that flow through our brain.

## Many of us do a 'Frankenstein'
## with our minds

Mental game neglect has left us all exposed to self-sabotage, a situation fed by the messages we receive from the world around us and by the ways in which we are educated.

## 2. Education: A Game of One Half!

### Left-Brain Bias

Well, we go to school and have the left hemisphere of our brains stretched like a taut stomach, while our derelict right brains remain slack and underdeveloped. As the worlds of academia and employment are geared to the left-brained individual, it makes sense for the education system to prepare us for life after school. But the fact that the world is set up for left-brainers is a different thing altogether. It is unusual. Why not right-brainers? Why not whole brainers? Why the left tendency?

I'll leave those questions hanging. What's more important, is that you realise that the left hemisphere of the brain is about logic and facts; words and language; analysis, structure and detail; the past and the future; and being separate from our environment. Put simply, our educational rearing teaches us to think, think and think again. To analyse to the $n^{th}$ degree and to live anywhere except in the present moment. You can see the problem for the athlete in this can't you?

By the way, if you don't believe we're obsessed by detail then I've only one thing left to say to you on the matter, and it's this... *twitter*!

## 3. Socialisation

### Society's Messages

But, is such left brain training necessarily a bad thing? Surely there's nothing wrong with learning language and developing the capacity to think and analyse? Well of course there isn't. Not until you find out that society has been 'telling' us *what* to think and *what* to analyse...and that it hasn't always been good for us!

# School trains us HOW to think

# Society tells us WHAT to think!

In subtle and not-so-subtle ways, significant others (parents, peers, politicians, teachers and the mass media) send us messages about what is acceptable to them and society, and what is not.

They define the narrow boundaries of success and failure, of possibility and impossibility, of perfection and imperfection and of happiness and discontent. They hint at our vulnerability in the big bad world and at our unlikelihood to cope effectively.

And feeding this process, to obese proportions, is the advertising and celebrity media. This social machine preaches *inadequacy*. It tells us that *we are nothing without* certain accoutrements.

As such, self-worth, happiness and success are promoted as a product of perfect looks, a six pack, a great house, an expensive car and so on. Fall for this fantasy and you sell your soul to consumerism.

Inadequacy and anxiety are therefore bred into us. We are 'trained' to feel worthless, restless and disgruntled. We fret about what other people are thinking about us, with ridicule and embarrassment peddled as the mastodons and sabre-toothed tigers of modern times.

Not a great base from which to forge a rewarding life, let alone a sports career!

The negative messages that bleed from the educational, societal and familial domains congeal over time creating a mental clot that interferes greatly with our capacity to be our true selves.

As a result, a ceiling is placed on the unbelievable potential we were born with.

## BIRTH OF THE FRANKENSTEIN FACTOR

### A Monstrous Conception

So, there you have it! Like an egg being fertilised, our mental game neglect is pollinated by the way we are socialised and educated.

And before we know it, we've given birth to a bouncing baby ...MONSTER!

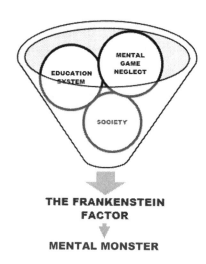

**Figure 1:** The Birth of the Mental Monster

Now if the mental monster didn't exist, if athletes didn't create their own mental interference, then there would be no need for a mental game. But it does, they do, and there is! And you need to accept this fact, before then fighting back with all your might.

The first step in overcoming *your* mental monster is to understand its modus operandi; to learn how it exploits the ways in which you have been educated and socialised, to spin you a story about the nature of reality.

Even though it's all complete nonsense, the monster is incredibly convincing.

But then, aren't all illusionists?

## YOUR MENTAL MONSTER, MASTER OF ILLUSION

Your inner monster knows that its reign of oppression will be over, the very moment you realise who you truly are and that you are capable of being and achieving ANYTHING you want to.

To ensure this doesn't happen, the monster does all it can to keep you sidetracked from working this out. But how does this mental gadfly do this?

Well, with some jiggery-pokery that's how.

# Magician of the Mental Underworld

## 4 Key Illusions -

## 1) The Illusion of Separateness

Your mental monster insists that YOU are separate from the world around you. By doing this, it keeps your focus away from recognising the magnificence of your authentic self. It convinces you that the physical environment is *all* that exists. In this way *you* forget that *YOU* exist.

By seducing you with the outside world, your inner saboteur whets your appetite for material gain. It fools you that true happiness and contentment can only to be found 'out there' through such rewards as possessions, social status and adulation.

By turning your motivational compass to 'external', your monster has set you up for a lifetime of frustration, anxiety, low self-esteem and ultimately, emptiness. By doing this, it significantly *reduces* your chances of attaining your goals in sport and life.

The myth of separateness also fools you that external events govern your emotional and mental states. This is why you have been convinced that sport is psychologically demanding. This is why you believe a missed putt, or some other sporting faux pas actually *causes* you to lose your temper, feel anxious or become distracted. But it doesn't. You're doing it to yourself.

While some athletes I work with have initially recoiled at the 'you're doing it to yourself' message, they concede fairly quickly that reactions, such as anger, anxiety or self-blame, are not caused by the triggering incident (e.g., a poor refereeing decision, playing in front of the national selectors, or slicing a drive).

They soon realise that the gateway to their unhelpful reactions is the negative meaning they ascribe to the event, and *not* the event itself.

This has to be the case; otherwise all of life's events would impact upon all humans equally. But they don't.

> *A human being is a part of the whole called by us*
> *"the universe", a part limited in time and space.*
> *He experiences himself, his thoughts and feelings,*
> *as something separate from the rest - a kind of*
> *optical illusion of consciousness. This delusion is a*
> *kind of prison for us*
> **- Albert Einstein**

## Mankind's Brutality

You can see how the illusion of separateness has led to the 'them and us' mindset that pervades all of humanity. This learned mentality has directly led to wars, racism and all sorts of other prejudices, violence and injustices. It also produces the human propensity to place people, including oneself, into neat little boxes, with neat little labels.

"He's a jerk!!", "I'm useless", "I'm a loser", and so on.

## 2) The Illusion of Time

Here's another beauty! By fooling you that time exists, your mental monster persuades you to focus your mind in two places that are non-existent – the past and the future. In doing this, it encourages you to waste energy living anywhere but the present moment.

This illusion is solely responsible for your tendency to flip and flop between such destructive emotions as regret and worry. Yet ironically, these two activities take place in the present.

When you dwell on an error, you're doing so *right now*, and when you forecast a poor performance, you also do so *right now*. There is *nothing* that exists, other than the present moment.

NOTHING!

It's what you do in the moment that counts. And if you're worrying or regretting, you are wasting valuable energy.

## 3) The Illusion of Fixed Ability

In its efforts to prevent you from fulfilling your potential, your inner monster can spin you the lie that ability is fixed at birth. That your capacity to excel in sport and life is pre-determined. If this is happening to you, then you'll probably view talent as some sort of genetic 'rabbit's foot' that propels certain lucky people on to success. You will believe that talent is preset and static and therefore not open to change.

By infiltrating your belief system with this self-limiting myth, the mental monster sabotages your motivation and snuffs out your dreams. Research by Stanford University professor, Carol Dweck, confirms that those who believe in this genetic model of success are less inclined to view training as useful and tend to quit before their potential is realised.

## 4) The Illusion of Self-importance

Here your mental monster convinces you that you're at the centre of everyone else's universe; that you're *oh so important*, so special.

By spinning you this seductive line, it steals your focus away from reclaiming your authentic self and instead places it on to other people. And so begins a lifelong preoccupation with what others are thinking about you.

Wow! Your mental monster is a very clever creature. Think about it.

There is no better way to tie you up in knots than by intertwining your self-worth with the (perceived) opinions of those around you!

By doing this, there is a veritable feast of worry ready for you to get your teeth into. You can now fret about a myriad of people and their views of you and your performance.

I can tell you now, this myth is a human curse. It fans the flames of fear. Fear of being ridiculed. Of being thought of negatively. Of not being liked. Of having your puffed-up ego burst.

The Illusion of Self-importance, or *specialness*, also creates the '*Do you not know who I am?*' mentality. Such conceit ensures complacency and as you'll know, complacency is the enemy of success.

Being absorbed with other people can lead to bouts of resentment and jealousy, when friends or rivals do well.

You find that as you start to judge yourself in comparison to others, you no longer exist as you. You become you *relative* to significant others. As such, you open up a Pandora's Box of frustration, self-criticism, despondency and low self-esteem. It means that you can only feel good about yourself whenever others are doing less well than you.

It also means that you are only ever in one of two emotional states: you are either feeling superior or inferior to other people. Either way, you are not being yourself, your *true* self. It's a false way to live.

## The Mother of All Destructive Beliefs

From my sport psychology and counselling work, and simply from listening to family, friends and colleagues talk and behave, I have concluded, without hesitation, that chief amongst our self-sabotaging beliefs is this one:

> **"I must be highly thought of by other people at all times."**

It is the mother of all unhelpful beliefs and for the sportsperson is a massive impediment to peak performance. After all, his focus should be on the task-at-hand, not on other people's opinions of his efforts. **It is impossible for you to reach your true potential with one eye on other people's opinions**.

## An Inability to Accept What Is

An offshoot of the illusion of self-importance is that we can feel so special to the extent that we actually believe bad stuff shouldn't come our way. And this 'bad stuff' can include such relative trivialities as sporting errors. This belief leads to an inability to accept *what is* and to dwell on *what should have been*.

The ensuing distraction is just what your mental monster wants. But not what your performance needs. Being unwilling to accept that life is a shade of grey, rather than black or white, is the hallmark of perfectionism.

And perfectionism is a landmark on the road to hell. I have seen it tear many a mind and spirit asunder. Not surprising, as it's about expecting flawless performances and that life goes your way, AT ALL TIMES.

Such unrealistic expectations set the perfectionist up for perceived and actual failure, despondency, self-criticism and often, depression.

Perfectionism is self-sabotage at its purest.

## The Prison without Walls

The vast majority of the Western world's population are fooled by these four illusions. Consequently, they end up incarcerated in a prison of the mind. The cell is not one with four walls, but rather is one made up of four letters: **F.E.A.R.**

We fear failure and we fear success. We fear losing face and we fear being ridiculed. We fear loss of status and reputation and we fear change and discomfort.

All of these are real threats to many of us in today's 'Frankenstein-Factored' world.

## I'm An Athlete...Get Me Out Of Here!

## - Out of My Mental Prison that is!

The reason why I say it's a prison *without walls* is because we can liberate ourselves simply by 'walking' out of it any time we like.

But, of course, this presupposes two things:

- You know you're in the mental prison in the first place; and,
- You know how to liberate yourself by becoming mentally tough.

This book enables you to accomplish both of these things. Part One of the book describes the prison and offers you the chance to assess how incarcerated you are, while Part Two shows you the way back to your authentic self through a mental toughness training programme.

Right, let's zoom-in even further on how your mental monster weakens your mental game. On how it specifically dismantles your ability to deliver high level performances on a consistent basis.

## Malevolent Puppeteer

As destructive as Shelley's fictional beast, our inner fiend rampages through our minds, exploiting our fantastic brain systems for its own nefarious ends.

By commandeering our imagery, language, emotion, attention and memory systems it attacks us where it can exert maximum influence. In doing so, it seizes control of SIX key mental game areas: motivation, self-belief, thinking skills, concentration, mental rehearsal/imagery and emotional control.

By seizing these areas, your mental monster has, in effect, taken control of your sporting career. Clever monster indeed, as these six areas represent the bedrock of mental toughness.

When I look back over my own sporting collapse, the enduring memory is one of helplessness. I had no power.

My negative thoughts, images and emotions appeared to be controlled by some sort of mental manipulator. I was a marionette to a malevolent puppeteer; a force that I couldn't quite put my finger on.

Let's have a closer look. Let's go back to a time in my life when I was overwhelmed by the Frankenstein Factor.

## Me 0-1 **Mental Monster**

As I have already described in the introduction to the book, I quit football at sixteen, leaving my dreams behind me. It was a really tough time.

I had always trained hard, had a desire to progress and even had an international schoolboy trial. But these beacons of advancement were usurped by something inside of me that was pulling the strings to my emotions, thoughts and actions and therefore my performances between the sticks - and not in a good way.

As you know, I changed from a living and performing 'in-the-moment' kid, with an unpolluted mind, into a self-conscious, nervous and underperforming player who no longer had a future in football. It was an odd situation really. I mean, we're meant to improve through time and effort, through training and coaching; not regress.

Well, you'd think so. But not if your mental game is undeveloped, and mine was clearly in terminal freefall at the time!

I was being besieged by a host of unsettling and seemingly uncontrollable thoughts and feelings that stuck to me like a leech.

Negative thoughts, images and troubling emotions pulsed through my psyche and body from the moment I woke up on a Saturday morning, right through to the final whistle later that day. In fact, by the time I was fifteen and playing for my club's senior team, my anticipatory anxiety was kicking-off from the Thursday evening training session, just after the team had been announced for the weekend's game!

The vice-like grip of bodily tension and queasiness would greet me in the changing room every Saturday and shadow me during the early part of each game.

As the match unfolded, my mind became peppered with thoughts and mental snapshots that either dragged me back to a mistake, or forward through the medium of 'what ifs?' to the mistake yet to happen.

This shuttling between the past and the future kept my focus away from the present – the very place where the match was happening!

The message from this briefest of personal vignettes is this: **It is impossible to perform at your peak and to meet your sporting goals, when your mental monster has its foot on your neck!**

Having studied and witnessed this mental menace for many years, I now realise I was let off relatively lightly.

I mean, just have a look at what the mental monster is capable of inducing in its victims.

IT'S AUTOPSY TIME!

# MONSTER AUTOPSY

Let's carry out a living autopsy on our mental monster. An examination of its key 'body parts' is always a revealing and fascinating exercise with my clients. Invariably, they concede to being familiar with several of the parts. By trawling through the 46 labelled body parts, below, you too can assess how large and influential your own mental monster is.

So fetch that pen and get ticking. Oh, by the way, when I first assessed myself several years back, I came out with 34 matches. Mine was a monster of many parts.

What's yours like?

**Table 1:** Forty-Six Ways Your Mental Monster Can Affect You

1.  Your self-esteem is low. You really don't value yourself at all
2.  Deep down you believe you'll never succeed
3.  You fear failure
4.  You fear success
5.  You fear being embarrassed and ridiculed
6.  You have difficulty asking for help
7.  When successful you often attribute it to good fortune
8.  You are perfectionistic. There are no shades of grey in your life
9.  You loathe and dwell on mistakes
10. You have difficulty living/performing in the present moment
11. You identify yourself through your achievements
12. You need to be top dog, no matter what the situation is
13. You protect your reputation and save face at all costs
14. You engage in self-pity
15. You get angry easily
16. You have a low threshold for frustration
17. You cannot cope with change and uncertainty
18. You are agitated by your past and worried about your future
19. You are easily distracted
20. You frequently engage in 'What if? thinking' and can always find something to worry about
21. You often feel ill-at-ease, insecure and self-conscious
22. You feel inferior/superior to others
23. You need to be liked; you are a people pleaser
24. You are quick to judge people

25. You feel envious and resentful of your friends' and rivals' successes
26. You have difficulty accepting *what is* and dwell on *what should have been*
27. You constantly worry what people are thinking about you
28. You worry that people will find out you're a fraud
29. You are always searching for something, never content in the moment
30. You are an expert fault-finder in yourself and other people
31. You have problems accepting compliments
32. You like to have people around you. Being on your own is uncomfortable
33. You don't fully trust yourself
34. You are often underhand
35. You keep doing the same old things expecting different results
36. You are conceited
37. You are over-sensitive
38. You are forever putting things off
39. You are very impatient
40. You are highly self-critical
41. You run defeatist memories and negative images through your mind
42. You feel that your emotions are running you; that you have no control over them
43. You are a slave to your mind, rather than its boss
44. You see life as separate to yourself
45. You're existing, not living
46. You're waiting for life to begin

---

Right, how did you get on? Did you identify with many of the descriptions? Indeed, do you feel you've just looked in the mirror? Well, if you have, welcome to the human race. You are suffering from a mental virus that's at pandemic level in the Western world – the Frankenstein Factor!

Incidentally, every single description you ticked represents something you have LEARNED.

That's right; in fact, all 46 descriptions are *learned* behaviours. You were born with *none* of these things!

## MONSTER-MUNCHED IN EVERYDAY LIFE

Okay, time to see our mental monster at its dirty work in daily life. The three scenarios below will be familiar to you. We've all been there; times when we found threat in apparently benign, everyday experiences.

## Scenario 1

While in town one afternoon, a fellow shopper walks past you and as he does he seems to snigger. You immediately assume it's a reflection of your physical imperfection, and your enthusiasm for a bit of retail therapy wanes. Little do you know that the guy had just, at that very moment, recalled an amusing incident from the previous night's party. He was so amused, that he just couldn't suppress the laugh. Yet *you* get the next bus home to Self-pity City.

## Scenario 2

You wave across the road at a good friend, but she doesn't return the salutation. You wonder what *you* have done to offend her. She, on the other hand, is looking for her 8-year old son who has gone missing. A wave from you was not on her radar. Yet you, with your precious ego hurt, traipse disconsolately on to work.

## Scenario 3

A pregnant pause occurs in a conversation with somebody important to you; say a team selector, your boss or college tutor, or that girl or fella you've fancied for ages. The urge to fill the silence is so overwhelming that you say any old thing and compound an already awkward moment. In fact, at some level, you believe the pause in conversation will reflect badly on *you*. Therefore you simply must fill it. Like criticism, you find silence very hard to handle.

You will have many examples of your own I'm sure; times when you misinterpreted situations and found threat where none existed.

You will notice too, that the perceived threats were seldom, if ever, physical, but rather were around affronts to your self-esteem and importance.

## MONSTER-MUNCHED IN SPORT

We're now going to look at how your mental monster can specifically affect you in sport, beginning with that bewildering and common phenomenon – performing much better in training than in competition.

# Practice and Competition:
# Two Versions of the Same Sport

One irregularity in my own sporting meltdown was that while my competitive performances deteriorated, I continued to train well, indeed quite impressively at times. It was the playing in goal at 3 o'clock on a Saturday afternoon that threw me! This anomalous scenario turns out to be a universal feature of sporting life, and though it baffles many an athlete, it is easily explained.

The reason why athletes don't perform as well in competition as in training, is because training is a relatively non-threatening experience. It doesn't intimidate the ego, as the potential for humiliation and insecurity is negligible or absent altogether. Consequently, the mental monster butts out allowing the athlete's true self to run the show. And what do you know, training becomes a more productive and enjoyable experience for him, with skills executed in a much less self-conscious and more fluid way than in competition.

### Competition is a Monster-Magnet

Competitive sport is results-driven. It involves judgement, scrutiny ("oh no, what will they think of me?") and the potential for humiliation. It is therefore something your mental monster would prefer you skipped altogether. Unlike training, competition threatens its love of certainty, control and the status quo.

Accordingly, the monster attempts to put you off competing by turning the dial up on mental interference. This in turn makes peak performance difficult to attain. The mental noise is just too loud. Through such sabotage, your monster hopes that you'll become so miserable that you'll pack it all in. That you'll simply accept you're not up to it, that you're useless.

# Competition is a poultice that draws out the mental pus of anxiety, self-consciousness and distraction

Training is rarely configured in a way that simulates competition. Indeed, golfers have remarked to me that there are in fact two games called golf: tournament golf *and* practice range golf.

This is why I urge athletes, from all sports, to devise training sessions that approximate the competitive context. In this way they can flush their monster out and defeat it in practice, clearing the way for peak performance in competition.

We will look at the technique of simulated practice in greater depth in Part Two of the book. But I can tell you now, it is absolutely vital that you train in this strategic way.

## Pro Teeth-Cleaning - *LIVE TONIGHT!*

All of life is a performance in that we use what have become everyday skills, to complete tasks to get us through our waking hours.

However, there is no real threat to our egos in all of this.

But I have no doubt that if we selected an ordinary daily task – cleaning our teeth for example - and made it a competitive sport (e.g. set standards for it; have a league system or an Order of Merit; have an audience for it; and media coverage) we would soon start to see competitors' monsters emerging from the cerebral shadows, interfering with what was once an unthinking, automatic activity.

The once simple act of cleaning one's teeth would become threatening to our inner saboteur. Not because the task is difficult, but because of the potential for failure and ridicule.

Competitive teeth-cleaners would, for the first time, find themselves analysing the activity: "Is it left-to-right first, or up-and-down? I just can't get this. Grrrr!!"

It would become a different task, now that people were watching and judging and comparing.

The teeth-cleaners would soon start to focus on results, try too hard and become obsessed with the mechanics of it all. Books would abound on each of the 'skills' involved; technology would promise new cutting edge equipment; and teeth-cleaning mind gurus would prowl around practice areas (bathrooms!) offering advice for money.

**COMMENTATOR** AT THE TEETH-CLEANING CHAMPIONSHIPS:

*"Oh no, Elliott's dropped the brush, the paste is everywhere. There's some paste on the mirror. I think it's all over it... It is now! He's down on his knees, can you believe it?!...Well that's it Dan, he'll not be in this year's final! The occasion got the better of him. Who would've thought it? The Colgate King is out."*

I've also no doubt that pro teeth-cleaners would also speak of their sport as being *psychologically demanding*, as if *it* caused their mental interference. This sport-centric mindset lets the mental monster off the hook big time. The athlete looks to the sport and not to himself for solutions to performance problems. Clever monster!

## YOUR MENTAL MONSTER AND THE *ZONE*

For your talent to shine through in the heat of competition, unhindered by mental interference, you need to:

- Possess a quiet and focused mind.
- Refrain from making judgements, such as good or bad, winning or losing, success or failure.
- Forgo thoughts about the past or future (even if the past is only a second or two ago).
- Become at one with the act of performing the task-at-hand, and *only* the task-at-hand.

Achieve these four prerequisites and you will perform in the magnificence of the zone. That magical land that time forgot; where time stands still; and where performances are excellent, effortless and enjoyable. Not only is time absent, but also in many respects you are too. You become absorbed in the act of performing and doing what you love with a quiet mind. You therefore merge with the experience. You're part of it; not separate and remote.

The reason why very few athletes perform in the zone on a consistent basis, is that the mental monster doesn't do quiet, non-judgemental and focused! Quite the opposite, actually. Due to your mental monster's despicable and underhand ways, it moves you further and further away from ever reaching and maintaining peak performance in sport. It assails your mind with interference and takes your focus to pointless places.

# TOP PERFORMERS ARE MYTH BUSTERS

When all is said and done, high-end, in-the-zone performances in sport are delivered by athletes who have not passively accepted the four illusions of: Separateness, Time, Fixed Ability and Specialness.

Unlike the vast majority of humanity, top athletes refuse to be slaves to their mental monster's instructions about the nature of reality. They refuse to accept that there isn't another way to think about themselves and the world around them.

By becoming mentally tough, they outfox these monstrous myths and begin to perform with excellence over and over again.

To do this, they learn to execute their skills *moment-by-moment* until the contest is over. In other words, they become aware of, understand and improve their ability to focus effectively.

The more effectively they concentrate on what is relevant to their performance, the more they become at one with the task-at-hand.

### ...And up in a puff of smoke goes
### the Myth of Separateness!

Remember this: we are part and parcel of our environment. We always have been. It's our natural state. Which is why when we perform in the zone, great things happen. If it wasn't natural then the opposite would occur.

While many of us comply with our mental monster's instruction to ruminate on the past and obsess over the future, elite sports performers do something different. They take back control of their language and interpretive ability. They learn to think in a productive way. By zapping their worry with logical challenges and interpreting situations constructively, these performers clear the path to excellence.

Top athletes grasp that the present is the only moment that exists and that dwelling on the past and future is a futile pursuit.

### ...And up in a puff of smoke goes
### the Myth of Time!

The only purpose the so-called past and future serve for these athletes are as gateways to learning and preparation. Learning from previous performances and preparing positively for competition.

The best performers in any field possess a flexible or growth mindset (Dweck, 2006). They view their genetics as merely the departure lounge, not the terminus. They know that the human brain is mutable and as a result is open to actual physical change. Elite talent is therefore not innate, but rather is the product of purposeful practice, commitment and perseverance.

### ...And up in a puff of smoke goes
### the Myth of Fixed Ability!

Now, I'm sure you've recognised that a major characteristic of the world's most successful sportspeople is *humility*. They think about themselves and their place in the world with a sense of perspective and appreciation. They have high self-esteem and integrity, and treat people with respect and parity. In this way, they obliterate the sham of specialness, which is the road to conceit, complacency and a *'me, me, me'* mentality.

**...And up in a puff of smoke goes**
**the Myth of Self-Importance!**

## *BEWARE!*
# Your Mental Monster exploits downtime
### — Just Ask Goalies!

I have worked with several ice hockey custodians over the years, including Great Britain and current Cardiff Devils netminder Stevie Lyle, as well as Chris McGimpsey, formerly of the Belfast Giants.

As I know to my cost, goalkeeping is an isolated position where you have to deal with pockets of inactivity and downtime. As a rule, humans are not particularly good at this. Why? Because our mental monster exploits downtime for its own despicable aims. This is why solitary confinement is employed as a method of punishment and torture throughout the world. And why it is only the mentally resilient who can cope with it.

Now, while ice hockey is much faster moving and more contained than soccer, there are still times when your team dominates and as the goalie, you are up the other end of the rink, with just your mind for company. This is fine and dandy if your mind is trained to deal with such moments, but for the mentally inexpert goalie, it can become a feeding ground for the monster within.

Former NHL goalie Ken Dryden doesn't hit the pipes when he implicates the netminder in his own psychological disintegration:

**"Because the demands on a goalie are mostly mental, it means that for a goalie, the biggest enemy is himself. Not a puck, not an opponent, not a quirk of size or style. Him. The stress and anxiety he feels when he plays, the fear of**

failing, the fear of being embarrassed, the fear of being physically hurt, all the symptoms of his position, in constant ebb and flow, but never disappearing. The successful goalie understands these neuroses, accepts them, and puts them under control. The unsuccessful goalie is distracted by them, his mind in knots, his body quickly following."

*mentalgoaltending.com*

According to Dryden, successful hockey goalies find a way to manage the critical moments in a match. To do this, they participate in mental skills training. And though their mental monster may still make the odd cameo appearance, it isn't centre stage, it doesn't dominate their performances.

As a young soccer goalkeeper in the 1970s, my inner saboteur was most definitely centre stage; and the name of the show was 'The Monster Monologues'!

# THE 8 KEY SIGNS
# YOU'RE BEING MONSTER-MUNCHED

The eight descriptions below summarise the foremost signs that you are, RIGHT NOW, living, training and performing under the heel of your mental monster:

1. **You have never been entirely sure why you play your sport.** You seldom have the type of inner spark that hauls you out of bed to train on a wet and windy winter's morning. When you search your conscience, you have to admit that you're much more driven by pleasing your coach and other people, than by the love of the sport and performing well for your own intrinsic satisfaction. In a nutshell, you just don't enjoy your sport as you should.

2. **Your goal-setting activity is half-hearted.** Good intentions soon give way to world-weariness as your goals are seldom your own, but rather represent a patchwork quilt of your coach's and parents' objectives for you. As the ownership of your goals is subcontracted out to other people you feel compromised, and have lost sight of what *you* actually want.

3. **You ooze self-doubt.** You have difficulty picturing yourself being successful. It doesn't sit easily with you. As far as you're concerned, success happens to other people. You seldom give yourself credit when you perform well, often attributing victory to good fortune or your opponent's "off day". Though you train hard, it does little to boost your confidence as you never feel you've done enough. As a result you often enter competition with little trust in your technique.

4. **You find it difficult to control the corrosive and anxiety-provoking mental chatter that goes on in your head, before, during and after games.** Much of your thinking is self-critical, and you have a strong tendency to make pessimistic predictions, finding threat where little or none exists. In anticipation of a forthcoming competition your 'what ifs?' and 'ah buts!' chase spools of unsettling mental imagery round and round your mind.

5. **You leave no wiggle room for making errors, chastising yourself greatly when performances are imperfect.** Fundamentally, you believe that you must meet your extravagant expectations. Mistakes can strike a devastating blow to your confidence, and it is anathema to your self-esteem to let yourself down in front of other people. Other people's opinions are important to you; far too important, if truth be told.

6. **You find that your focus seesaws between the past and the future, and that you have considerable difficulty attending to what matters in the 'here-and-now'.** For you, the precious present is an elusive place during performance. Once distracted, you have difficulty regaining composure and concentration. As a result, you seldom perform in what is ubiquitously called 'the zone', that awesome mental state where performance flows in an effortless blend of mind and body in harmony.

7. **You regularly feel uneasy before competition.** Nausea, dry mouth, an urge to use the toilet, palpitations, hurried breathing and muscle tension run on a spool system around your body. The agitation is unpleasant and the more you try to ignore the sensations the more you become aware of them. This vicious circle is fed by tangents of feral thoughts and images convincing you that catastrophe and humiliation lie ahead. That a nightmare performance is inescapable.

8. **Your sport-life balance is out of kilter.** Life is far too one-dimensional, in favour of sport. Consequently, you are missing out on your kids growing up, and your relationship with your partner is beginning to fray around the edges. You rarely visit your parents now, seldom see your friends, and that assignment for college is already two weeks late. The tectonic plates of your life are now starting to scrape off each other, with the resulting quake reverberating across all aspects of your life. The accumulated guilt, angst and frustration are, in turn, interfering with your training and performance. You are unhappy and feel lost.

So what do you think? Are you currently being monster-munched? Or are you in charge of your mind and therefore on top of your mental game 

performances?

Have a think and note down your respo

## Sneaky Monster

The mental monster is incredibly devious
reason why athletes need a mental game            , and
why many athletes don't do anything about it.

This most cunning of inner opponents has ensured that one
of our destructive behaviours is to AVOID ASKING FOR
HELP, particularly on issues to do with the mind. It is seen
as a weakness by many to seek out help in such matters.

Best to just soldier on and bottle it all up.

Here we see the mental monster trapping us in a double-
bind. It's not only behind our problems, but also ensures
that the means of addressing these problems is
stigmatised!

# TOP ATHLETES KNOW WHO THEIR TRUE OPPONENT REALLY IS

Having worked with some of the best performers across the
world, I can tell you that they know who their real
opponent in sport is. They know that their chief adversary
lies within. They realise too, that it is *only* by overcoming
this inner adversary that they can ever expect to compete
with excellence in their sport. Let's hear what five world
class performers have to say on the matter.

## Brian Magee

Interim WBA World and former European super
middleweight champion, Brian Magee, knows that to box at
his best he must firstly chin his inner opponent. Not with

...uthpaw action, but with a well-honed mental ...er strength allows Brian to release his outer ...ness and boxing guile.

> **"You're always fighting a mental battle in your head, wondering if you're good enough, did you train hard enough and in the right way. Your mind and self are always telling you why you shouldn't be able to do something, giving you reasons to doubt yourself and give up, especially in times of stress and lonely times. It seems to want the easy option when the going gets tough. But you gotta stay strong, keep your mind on your goal and tell your body and self that you deserve to be here and rehearse what you intend to do."**
> **Brian Magee** - *Personal communication, 28.03.10*

## Tommy Bowe

Ospreys', Ireland and Lions' wing magician, Tommy Bowe, knows that when there is technical equivalence on the rugby pitch, it is largely mental toughness that accounts for who wins. Tommy is equally convinced that mental toughness is about overcoming the inner saboteur.

> **"If a player is talented enough, then there is only one person who can beat them and that's themselves."**
> **Tommy Bowe** - *Personal communication, 01.04.10*

## Paul Brady

Paul Brady is a sporting legend. The world handball number one and multiple Irish, United States and world titleholder, is viewed by many as a Roger Federer figure, as he is so dominant in his sport.

Indeed, handball 'Hall Of Famer' Fred Lewis wrote in *The Magazine* that "Paul is the equivalent of an 8 foot high jumper, 30 foot broad jumper and 9.6 second 100meter sprinter" (*July, 2010*). Now that's what I call a compliment!

The key factor in Paul's amazing ability and record-breaking success is his psychological strength. I have been Paul's sport psychologist for the past five years and I have to say that he possesses the total package.

Nothing is left to chance; his preparation is complete.

When it comes to psychological preparation, Paul is clear that the mental game is played against that self-sabotaging part of the human condition.

In the same way that his outer game is executed shot-by-shot, his inner game involves him keeping on top of the negatives spewed-out by his mental monster.

> **"I find that the most difficult aspect of sport is dealing with my own internal thoughts and emotions. It is a constant process of dealing with negative thoughts as they arise and reframing them into positive ones."**
> **Paul Brady** - *Personal communication, 04.06.10*

Isn't it reassuring to know that one of the greatest performers in the world has to keep battling his own inner saboteur?

Paul is only too aware that the moment he thinks he's nailed the mental game, is the moment his monster smiles.

Okay, two more views from the top table of sport.

## Tim Henman

The former British number one and world number four tennis player, Tim Henman, cuts to the chase in a BBC interview, placing the demands of competitive sport fairly and squarely between the ears of players.

**"Pressure is all self-inflicted. It's only what your mind tells you.If you go into Wimbledon thinking about the 15,000 people watching you on centre court, the 10,000 people on Henman Hill and the 15,000,000 on TV, you're immediately painting a picture that adds a lot of pressure..."**

*- BBC SPORT, Raise Your Game*

Here we see Henman hinting at what reality actually is; that it's an inside job. That it's a product of athlete interpretation and therefore athlete choice. He can either choose to scare himself, or choose to be positive and excited:

**"...but if you go out there with the thought that it's your favourite court, it's your home tournament, you've had a lot of great results here, you're feeling good about the game, you've prepared well and you've practiced well, you've got a totally different picture. It's very important that you understand how the mind works."**

## Pete Sampras

While the watching public would see world tennis legend Pete Sampras playing the guy on the other side of the net, the truth of the situation was a little more subtle than that.

You see, Sampras was also competing against another and often more formidable opponent. And while this battle was hidden from the spectators and TV cameras, Sampras knew that when he won a match he had overcome two antagonists in the process.

**"In tennis, you always have two opponents out there–the other guy and yourself. You can't worry too much about the other guy, other than dealing with the shots he sends your way. The most important guy you have to beat is yourself–the**

**part of you that's prone to doubt, fear, hesitation, and the impulse to give up. If you're too busy struggling with yourself, like some players, you can hardly be expected to beat your opponents."**

*A Champion's Mind: Lessons from a Life in Tennis,*
*- **Sampras and Bodo**, 2008*

His phrase 'the part of you that's prone to doubt, fear, hesitation, and the impulse to give up' is an explicit reference to the mental monster.

### *PLEASE NOTE: Quick Name Change

For the purposes of semantic ease and symmetry, I will also be referring to your mental monster as '**YouMinus**' and to your true self as '**YouPlus**'. For me, the term *YouMinus* more fully conveys the cannibalistic trait of the inner monster. After all, it gorges on your true self. Or put another way, it subtracts from you everything you could become.

The two terms will be used throughout the rest of the book, along with the original nomenclature of *mental monster*, *inner saboteur*, *synthetic self*, *authentic/true self*, and the like.

## The Duel in Your Crown

When all is said and done, this is a book about two rivals, each competing for one prize. It is a challenge that all athletes encounter throughout their sporting careers and that champions meet head on.

It is a challenge for the control of the sporting mind - YOUR mind. This duel takes place within the head of each and every one of us, to differing degrees. The two adversaries are:

✓ Our true, goal-directed, authentic self, YOUPLUS; and,

✗ Our mental monster and inner saboteur, YOUMINUS.

We are born with the former, and create the latter.

# Chapter 2

## OVERCOMING THE FRANKENSTEIN FACTOR

### *Mental Toughness*

"A tough player is someone who can react well to the internal pressures rugby brings. Pressures increase as the level increases, so being able to 'up your game' and not get bogged down by expectation is essential. Also, being able to mentally recover from a mistake or defeat, is a further key element of mental toughness."

*TOMMY BOWE*
Rugby wing: Ospreys, Ireland, British and Irish Lions
- Personal communication

"As with any sport, I think the key characteristics of mental toughness include: confidence in your ability and belief in yourself, always. Also: commitment to the pursuit of training and competition goals; determination and perseverance - steady persistence in a course of action or purpose towards achieving these goals in spite of difficulties, obstacles, or discouragement; and a desire to achieve something unique in sport and in life."

*PAUL BRADY*
Handball player and World Number 1
- Personal communication

In this chapter you will:

- Learn that mental toughness is the *only* solution to the problems imposed by your mental monster.
- Discover the 6 key characteristics of a mentally tough athlete.
- Come to understand that mental toughness can be learned.
- Have access to real world examples of mental toughness in action.
- Meet athletes who are working on their mental games.

*"...thou didst seek my extinction, that I might not cause greater retched-ness."*

**- The Monster**, *Frankenstein*

Like a typical bully, your mental monster, YouMinus, is really a coward. It quakes at the notion of you working out all of the lies it has been spinning you. It trembles every time you lift a book on mental toughness, or receive a talk from a sport psychologist. And it will be really trembling right now, as no other sport psych. book has ever unmasked this brute the way this book has. Chapter 1 has laid bare the monster's illusory ways and now it's time for you to fight back, by becoming mentally tough.

## MENTAL TOUGHNESS is the weapon of choice in your battle AGAINST YOUMINUS.

YouMinus knows that by becoming mentally tough you will reconnect with your true self, the one replete with boundless potential. When this happens, its reign of inner terror is over and its arsenal of mental interference decommissioned.

## OVERCOMING YOUR MENTAL MONSTER

The reality is this: the mental monster can only be overcome by a robust mental game. There is no other way. The best athletes on the planet know this. Both Tommy Bowe and Paul Brady, cited above, are certain that mental toughness is a prerequisite to peak performance. At the elite level, it's what separates the wheat from the chaff when it comes to sporting success.

World-class athletes like Bowe and Brady were not born with mental strength. Rather, they developed a range of mental game skills to ensure they 'got out of their own way' and allowed their talent to do the talking. In doing this, they faced-up to the monster within, and won. The skills they use, which you will learn in Part Two of the book, fall into six distinct categories:

1. **Motivation**
2. **Self-Belief**
3. **Constructive Thinking**
4. **Focus**
5. **Imagery Control**
6. **Emotional Control**

It is no coincidence that these are the six areas that your mental monster influences to maximise its control over you, to keep you captive in a prison of fear, doubt, distraction and worry. But all of that is about to change! You're going to fight back; you're going to overcome the blaggard for good and to start making massive strides in your sport. It's time to say "Auf Wiedersehen Pest" to your mental monster. And here's how.

## THE SIX PATHWAYS TO MENTAL TOUGHNESS

The *Six Pathways* programme, in Part Two of the book, will help you to regain control over each of the six mental game areas listed above. By following the programme, you will develop an awesome range of strategies and techniques that, once acquired, will leave you mentally tough. You will eliminate the habitual self-sabotaging responses that have held you back, allowing you to perform with a silent mind, a firm focus and distinction. You will rewire your brain for 'in-zone' performances.

You will overcome your mental monster and in doing so you'll get in touch with your true self. The Table below sets out the key differences between an athlete who is under the malevolent influence of his mental monster and an athlete who is mentally tough.

**Table 2:** Being Monster-Munched Versus Being Mentally Tough

| Features of the Mental Monster (YouMinus) | Features of Mental Toughness (YouPlus) |
|---|---|
| **Externally-motivated** | **Internally-motivated** |
| • Attached to possessions and status; and to gaining validation and approval from other people.<br>• Controlled by external circumstances.<br>• Always comparing self to others.<br>• Intolerant of uncertainty/ change.<br>• Fearful of failure and ridicule. | • Driven to succeed from within. Wanting to develop as an individual and to feel satisfied at a job well done.<br>• Tolerant of discomfort.<br>• Trains and performs against self.<br>• Not one bit worried about what other people are thinking. |
| **Low Self-Belief** | **High Self-belief** |
| • Does not value self.<br>• Self-conscious.<br>• Feels oh so special and superior. | • Enduring sense of self-worth.<br>• Durable self-confidence.<br>• Unpretentious. |
| **Destructive Thinking Ability** | **Constructive Thinking Ability** |
| • Believes that reality is 'out | • Shapes own reality. |

| | |
|---|---|
| there'.<br>• Slave to left brain chatter.<br>• Thoughts are taken as facts.<br>• Unaware that emotional state is self-created.<br>• Overanalyses.<br>• Ruled by perfectionism. | • Knows that the gateway to emotional strength is through the absolute power of interpretation.<br>• Challenges and changes self-limiting beliefs and thoughts.<br>• Led by preferences, not demands |
| **Distractible**<br>• Lives and performs in the past and future.<br>• Fixated on the outcome of training and performance. | **Fully focused in the 'Now'**<br>• Lives and performs in the present.<br>• Focuses on the process of training and performance.<br>• Regularly performs in *The Zone*. |
| **Imagination runs riot**<br>• Imagination restricted.<br>• Imagination not under control.<br>• Negative imagery runs on a loop system around the mind. | **Imagination harnessed**<br>• Imagination limitless.<br>• Can control mental images.<br>• Uses imagery for a host of positive and constructive purposes. |
| **Trapped in fear, anxiety and worry**<br>• Forecasts poor performances, embarrassment and ridicule.<br>• Oblivious to own role in generating fear, anxiety and stress.<br>• Imprisoned by fear.<br>• Feels controlled by the mind. (i.e. the tail wags the dog). | **Mentally free**<br>• In control; free to choose relaxation, positive thoughts and in-the-moment focus.<br>• Skilled at identifying and adjusting unhelpful emotional states.<br>• Liberated, excited and determined to overcome the challenge ahead.<br>• Feelings of flow and control. |

# The End is in the Beginning

I recall a rugby player I worked with two or three years ago, who suddenly cut to the chase five minutes into our first session together. I was in the throes of explaining the structure to the sport psych intervention – our roles and so on – when this giant of a youngster sat forward in his chair, looked me straight in the eye, apologised for interrupting, and asked: "This mental toughness I hear talked about a lot, what is it really; I mean, how will I know I've got there Doc?" What a great question!

An intelligent inquiry from an ambitious athlete, who needed to know where he was heading and that the hard yards would be worth it.

Indeed, it's the type of question that our world leaders should face, particularly those engaged in the 'War on Terrorism'. Former US President Bush needed to be asked, "Hey, George Dubya, this war on terrorism, tell me, how will you know when you've won it?" Oh boy, can't you just imagine his answer? "What d'ya mean? There is no war...in fact *tourism* has never been better."

Right, let's whet your appetite. Let's have a glimpse into the future of *your* mental game, should you follow the advice in this book and journey along each mental training pathway, in Part Two, with purpose and action.

Let's see how mentally tough you can become, and look at the specific characteristics you will possess. Basically, how you'll know you've got there.

# CHARACTERISTICS OF THE MENTALLY TOUGH PERFORMER

As confirmed earlier in the chapter, the best athletes in world sport are mentally tough. They possess a range of mental game attributes that I have categorised into six areas. These will now be described and as you read them, consider the status of your own mental game by comparison.

## ☑ Motivation

You are highly motivated to succeed, motivated to do so out of an inner desire to be the best you can be. It is not a chore for you to pursue excellence in your sport, as you are working towards *personal* goals. They mean a lot to you and, as a result, your hunger to succeed is insatiable: nothing will stand in your way. You persist in the face of setbacks, remaining positive, confident and focused.

You possess a high tolerance for frustration and see change as a challenge, not as a threat.

Your motivational energy is not plugged-in to the external grid of money, public acclaim and fame. Instead, it's internally generated from the considerable satisfaction and enjoyment you get from making progress and performing well in your sport. You are therefore a self-contained human unit intent on shaping your own success.

However, you are pragmatic and seek out help when needed. You will not let a problem fester when there are experts on hand to help.

## ☑ Self-Belief

You possess a steadfast sense of self-worth. You are at peace with yourself, accepting who you are and valuing your place in the world. You are so comfortable in your own skin, that you do not obsess about what others think of you.

You are true to yourself and will settle for nothing less. You live *your* life, no-one else's. Born an original, you refuse to die a copy.

You also possess a high level of self-assurance. This is not a confidence born out of arrogance. Rather, it is a calm sense of knowing that you have the skills and ability to achieve your goals and to successfully progress in your sport. At the same time, you are a modest, down-to-earth person; the guy at the bus stop, the girl at the check-out.

## ☑ Constructive thinking

You have excellent thinking skills. Your interpretative ability enables you to shape your own reality and to regulate your emotions, boost your confidence and sharpen your focus.

Realising that perfectionism is the gateway to despondency, you approach life with preferences rather than demands. While you would prefer not to make mistakes, you know full well that demanding flawless performances is an absurdity, as well as an unnecessary burden.

## ☑ Focus

Your concentration no longer scuttles between the past and the future, like a frightened mouse. Instead, you have developed the ability to focus fully on what matters in the 'here-and-now'.

While performing in the precious present used to be an elusive experience, you now compete moment-by-moment with a calm, non-judgemental mind. You shift focus effortlessly during performance and consistently perform at your optimum.

Your ability to concentrate on what's relevant to your sporting role ensures that your talent is not lost within the mental landfill of external distraction, rumination, worry and regret.

## ☑ Imagery Control

You have control over your mental *iPlayer*. You access again and again, your unmissable collection of excellent performances, which are stored on mental tape.

These memories and images are yours, and ready at a moment's notice to replay in your mind.

You are skilled in using imagery, finding it to be the most versatile of mental game tools. Its utility across the performance cycle is amazing and you exploit this capacity to help you prepare for competition, manage critical moments during performance, and to review your performance after competition.

## ☑ Emotional Control

Your relationship with your sport is built on passion *and* coolness - the passion to pursue excellence and the coolness to attain it. You love the pressure of competition and expect it. However for you, pressure isn't something in your external environment ready to pounce on your preparation and performance, but rather is an 'in-house' matter. Recognising this is empowering, as it places you in the driving seat. As a result, you have become your own emotional thermostat, capable of adjusting your mental state to its ideal level. You are always ready to perform, motivated and up for the challenge. Your pre-comp mantra is "Bring it on!"

These six pillars of mental toughness will be expanded upon in Chapter 3. Here you will be profiling your mental game in preparation for *The Six Pathways to Mental Toughness* training programme in Part Two.

Right now though, I'd like to row back a little and define what we mean by the term *The Mental Game*.

## THE MENTAL GAME, DEFINED

In its purest sense, an *effective* mental game is a game of mental skill development. It's a game of repeatable mental habits that keep interference at bay when pressure mounts, thereby enabling an athlete to perform to his potential.

An *ineffective* mental game is therefore one full of mental habits that block an athlete's ability to perform at his peak. If we follow this definition through, we see that your mental monster, YouMinus, is the embodiment of an *ineffective mental game.*

## The Peak Performance Formula

Another way to view the mental game, is to see it as making the peak performance formula work for you. The formula is:

**Peak Performance = Capability** *minus* **Interference**

By *capability*, I am describing the aggregate of the physical, technical and tactical elements of your sport; elements that your natural self, YouPlus, wants to discharge with excellence on the pitch, court or course.

But it is these very elements that your inner opponent, YouMinus, attacks with such mental *interference* as self-doubt, nervousness, fear of failure and distraction.

If YouMinus didn't exist, then the peak performance formula would simply be: *Peak Performance = Capability.*

Top athletes in your sport have sussed out the Peak Performance Formula and make it work for them. They are what I call Total or 4D Athletes. They attend to all four dimensions of their sport – the physical, technical, tactical and psychological.

# Ignore mental skills training at your peril

Without a robust mental game, without becoming mentally tough, you are allowing your mental monster to run the show.

This places a ceiling on your ability to deliver high level performances, particularly at the elite level where performers are about equal in terms of how well they have prepared their bodies for competition. Scottish rugby international wing-wizard Simon Danielli couldn't agree more:

> **"I think if you look at all the top athletes in the world and those at the top of their sport, their fellow colleagues and competitors always single them out as being mentally tough. All things being equal you would back the athlete with the strong mental game to be able to cope with the pressures and to be able to rise to the top."**
> ***Simon Danielli*** *- Personal communication, 19.05.10*

For up-and-coming surfing star, Ronan Oertzen, there is simply no other pathway to sporting success than through the brain. As the brain governs everything, surfers, and all athletes for that matter, must treat their minds with the same degree of respect as they do their bodies.

> **"I always keep pushing myself to achieve the best that I can. My ultimate goal is to become one of Europe's best surfers. That is why I train my mind as much as I train my body. In my opinion, if you have a strong mind there are very few things you cannot do."**
> ***Ronan Oertzen -*** *Personal communication, 04.03.10*

Lisa Kearney, top judoka (at 48kg) and gold medallist at the 2010 World Cup in Samoa, is also a total athlete. A highly determined and ambitious individual, Lisa approaches her mental game development with the same energy she affords her fitness and technical training.

This London 2012 prospect knows, from experience, that mental control lies at the epicentre of peak performance.

Only by strengthening her mental muscle, has Lisa been able to unleash her rich talent on her fellow competitors.

**"A prepared body without a prepared mind is useless. The mind controls the body, so limitations on the mind are limitations on the body or performance. Often mentality is the most important aspect. Everyone faces adversity; the mind is what gets you through."**
*Lisa Kearney* - *Personal communication, 13.05.09*

## Becoming Mentally Tough is a Choice

Given that mental toughness can be achieved through psychological skills training – in other words, it can be LEARNED - you'd wonder why the mental side of sport is neglected, or approached half-heartedly, by many athletes and coaches. While I acknowledge that times are changing, it remains the case that mental game development often sits alone against the wall in the Ballroom of Preparation. Yet, if invited to dance, the mental game can turn a stale party into a celebration. But it must be asked.

Those athletes whom we deem mentally tough, the Tommy Bowes and Paul Bradys of this world, one day decided to set about increasing their mental strength. That is, they invited their mental games to the preparation dance and engaged fully in psychological skills training. As a result, their mental strength increased significantly. By following *The Six Pathways to Mental Toughness* programme, you too can acquire the type of skills that ensured Tommy and Paul became mental game artistes and giants in their sports.

Take note of the following plain and simple truths about mental toughness:

- **No-one is chosen for mental toughness. They self-select, and so can you.**

- **Mental toughness can be learned.**

# MENTAL TOUGHNESS IN ACTION

To bring mental toughness to life, I have set out below several cases that illustrate its application in the real world of sport.

## ☑ Carolina Kluft is true to herself

Unbeaten in the heptathlon for some six years, you'd think that the last thing Carolina Kluft would do would be to change event, particularly on the cusp of the 2008 Beijing Olympics. But this is exactly what she did.

And the reason for this surprising change?

Simple really - she was no longer enjoying the heptathlon. So she moved across to specialise in the long jump.

For me, this is one of the greatest demonstrations of mental strength; though the media coverage, at the time, failed to notice. Instead, their focus fell on the apparent absurdity of Kluft's decision.

But let's listen to what she said in a later interview:

> **"I cannot be what I am not...I was not enjoying it [the heptathlon], and I have to feel it, to be myself...I cannot just go with the flow of everyone else around me. Then I would lose myself, and that's my biggest fear."**
> **Tom Fordyce** - BBC SPORT, May 2010

Kluft knew herself completely and was not willing to compromise her well-being, simply because other people recoiled at her decision to change event. We all know how difficult it can be to stand out from the crowd and risk ridicule. Yet Kluft was fully at ease with her decision.

## ☑ Brian Magee deals with gut-wrenching disappointment to become a champion

I have had the pleasure to work with Brian Magee for several years now. Not only is Brian a world-class boxer, but he's also one of the most pleasant and grounded people I know. He possesses that combination of hardiness and humility, so common in the elite athlete. But these qualities were to be tested to the max. As you'll see, he has faced more than his fair share of setbacks and disappointments.

The 17 March, 2005 sticks firmly in my mind. At the famous venue, the King's Hall, Brian was to face super middleweight champion, Joe Calzaghe. He had trained with purpose, was fully focused on the job he had to do and was excited at the prospect of testing himself against Joe. But misfortune struck right at the eleventh hour - Brian's big fight was cancelled. The World Boxing Organisation had pulled the plug on the event. They refused to sanction it at the last minute, on a technicality.

Some 6,000 people had bought tickets for the fight. It was St Patrick's Day, and this Irish boxer was left shattered:

> **"I'm disappointed for myself, but also for the many fans who bought tickets. I have trained like a champion, so to have it taken away from me at this late stage is devastating."**
>
> *Daily Mirror, 18 March, 2005*

So, at 29, Brian had his dream stolen, not by Calzaghe, whom he felt he could beat, but by the authorities. But as devastated as he was, Brian did not lie down; he refused to capitulate to this sporting setback. Instead, he chose the mentally tough route – he persevered. He took advice from his manager and others and reset his goals. As Brian explains:

> **"To adapt to any situation you have to set yourself goals. You might have to take detours to get there, but you have to believe it's gonna be ok and just get on with things."**
> *Personal communication, 28.03.10*

Shortly afterwards, Brian was nominated to fight Ukrainian Vitali Tsypko for the vacant European super middleweight title. Game on! Career back on track. The fight took place in Nuremberg, Germany, on 16 July 2005. But after 12 rounds, and Brian having clearly won, the judges gave the most controversial of decisions. On a split vote, they gave the contest to Tsypko. Another setback and another challenge to Brian's mental and spiritual fabric. Even an apology from the governing body did little to assuage the gut-wrenching disappointment felt by Brian and his team.

But once again he bounced back. Once again, Brian looked at the big picture and reignited his motivation. He took a short break with his family and then it was back to the gym, while his manager investigated options. Controlling only what he could control, Brian persisted and never lost faith.

In December 2008, he landed the British title by beating Stevie McGuire, and though injury meant he had to vacate this title, he swept aside the irritation and moved on. Brian then readjusted his career compass, pointing it back towards Europe and to a massive fight against the then European super middleweight champion, Mads Larsen.

On the 30 January 2010, Brian Magee fought and beat Mads Larsen in Aarhus, Denmark. A seventh round stoppage of the home favourite was a remarkable achievement. Without mental fortitude, this would not have happened. By keeping going in the face of misfortune, and seeing beyond the setbacks in his career, things had clearly paid off for Brian:

> **"I can't describe it; it's been such a year. After that, I really deserve this and so does the team. It's for them as well as me... Desire and will got me that result."**
>
> *boxingscene.com, 31.01.10*

## ☑ Simon Danielli accepts what is

Scottish rugby international and Ulster wing, Simon Danielli, approaches his sport with what I call a 'matter-of-fact mentality'. This enables Simon to resist becoming 'sucked-in' by some setback or other and losing his focus.

While he would favour a trouble-free career in rugby, Simon accepts the inevitability of unmet goals and disappointment.

An acceptance of *what is* helps him sidestep the emotional middleman of dejection and self-criticism and instead to move to the solution:

> **"I think the main thing here is to recognise that this [disappointment] is part of sport. Depending on the disappointment in question, realise that it is inevitable and that there is almost always a solution; and that it is to this solution that my mind and energy focuses on."**
>
> *Personal communication, 19.05.10*

## ☑ Paul Brady keeps his focus & composure

Paul Brady, the world number one handball player, was preparing for the 2008 US Nationals in Kansas City,

Missouri, when out of left field came a wholly unexpected announcement. The legendary American handball player, David Chapman, was coming out of retirement.

At the time, Paul referred to the news that Chapman was returning as "a bolt from the blue". Would this upset his preparation? Could Chapman's return pull the carpet from under Paul Brady's feet?

Not a chance.

In a display of pure mental toughness, Paul quickly placed the news in context. It was just news, that's all it was. He would choose to dismiss it as irrelevant. Only if he was to play him, would Paul take note of Chapman's presence at the tournament.

Until then, he would continue to do what he always does - concentrate on his own preparation and performance:

> **"I was very taken aback at first, to be honest, but I'm focusing on myself now. Initially, Chapman is going to strike fear into anyone because he's such a great player, but at the end of the day, that is very temporary and then you start to focus on yourself."**
>
> *hoganstand.com*

Paul won the event, making it four US Nationals in succession, a record. He never met Chapman in the tournament, who went out in the quarter-finals. So any fuss would have been for nothing. He was right to focus on his own game. The mentally tough learn that this is always the wise option.

At the time of writing, Paul has beaten his own record twice. In June 2010, he won his *sixth* consecutive US National Singles title!

Incidentally, commentators have referred to Paul as 'the Roger Federer of handball', but for me, Roger Federer is 'the Paul Brady of tennis'! I am truly privileged to work with such an awesome athlete.

## ☑ Jason Smyth stays focused in spotlight

Twenty-three year-old sprinter, Jason Smyth, is the embodiment of mental strength. In July 2010, he became the first paralympic athlete to compete in the mainstream European Athletics Championships. Not only did he compete at Barcelona 2010, but he also qualified out of his 100m heat for a semi-final berth. In both races, heat and semi, Jason was up against French sprint star, Christophe Lemaitre.

As the result of Stargardt's Disease, Jason is partially-sighted and legally blind. He was diagnosed with the condition at age eight. Now while his sporting journey is fascinating, and is in itself the epitome of mental toughness in action, for the purposes of this section I am going to isolate just one particular aspect of the journey – the Barcelona experience.

Having qualified for Barcelona, Jason was going to be the centre of attention. He was big news right across the globe. Barcelona was therefore a minefield of potential distraction for Jason. But he was ready for it. The double gold medal winner at the Beijing Paralympics coped admirably with his newfound status. It was 'just' another day of sprinting.

Displaying a maturity way beyond his years, Jason responded to the occasion with a mix of modesty, composure and focus. Not for one minute did he become distracted from his singular purpose. He was in Barcelona to race in the 100metres, end of.

**'Yet the chilled sprinter, who took double Paralympic gold in 2008 in his partially sighted category, was totally unfazed by all the attention.'**

*Belfast Telegraph, 29 July, 2010*

After qualifying out of a very tough heat, the attention escalated. But again, Jason reacted with poise and self-possession. This is what he said at the time:

**"Obviously it's very nice, but generally I get on with it and let people say what they want to say...I train with Tyson Gay and it's really not that big a deal, where other people would get scared. I don't mind what way people remember me but I'm coming here and performing well as a mainstream senior international and I'm trying to move forward to qualify for London 2012."**

*Belfast Telegraph, 29 July, 2010*

Jason's grandfather underlines his grandson's mental toughness, in the most moving way:

**"Jason, you are a credit to all your family, but your best talent is your humility, not your running. For this reason you will succeed beyond your wildest dreams. You make us all so proud that you have never lost the common touch, and your feet are firmly on the ground."**

*Comments made to The European Athletics Association, and quoted in The Telegraph, 28 July, 2010*

## ☑ Rafael Nadal performs in the only moment that exists

Newly-crowned 2010 Wimbledon champion, Rafael Nadal, explained to the salivating press corps, that hard work and desire were the secrets to his success. But he said much more too, giving a more specific insight into the mentally tough athlete. On his commitment to the present moment, Nadal explained that:

> **"I expect to play my best on every point and fight for every point like it is the last one. I don't think if the match is going to be difficult. I just go on court and fight point by point."**

> *www.express.co.uk*

Note too, that Nadal doesn't become caught up in judging how the match is going to turn out, *if it is going to be difficult*. Rather, he sees what lies ahead of him on the tennis court as a succession of 'now moments'. And if he plays every point with passion, then many more times than not, he will win. It's a very simple philosophy. Yet, how many of us practice it? For Nadal, you create your own success by managing each aspect of performance as it unfolds: "But the important thing is to be there all the time."

## ☑ Chris McGimpsey swats away the swarm of distraction – and makes history in the process

During my time working for the Belfast Giants ice hockey team, several of the players would have consulted me for individual sport psychology sessions. Back in early 2005, one of these players was back-up netminder Chris McGimpsey.

This smart, talented young goalie, wanted to prepare his mind for the biggest game of his ice hockey career. He was to start for the Giants against Basingstoke Bison, in an Elite League game. And the game was to be played at the Odyssey Arena in Belfast, the Giants' home rink.

Chris knew he would be playing in front of his family, friends and the knowledgeable and passionate Giants' supporters. He knew that he needed to exert control over the occasion, as it could easily overwhelm him, such was the attention placed on his full debut.

Distraction was hovering around his head and it was essential that he parked all of the hype to one side on the lead up to the match.

He had to find the means to keep his focus on what he could control and to have a toolbox of techniques to assuage troubling emotions.

Prior to his full debut against the Bison, Chris would occasionally have come off the bench to play the last ten minutes or so of a game. This in itself was challenging, as he never knew when he was going to get on the ice, if at all. But for the Basingstoke match, Chris knew exactly what was happening. There was no ambiguity this time – he was playing the full sixty minutes.

Chris and I remain good friends and though he has since retired from pro hockey, he has come away with something very precious, something no-one can ever take away from him – the memory of the time he rocked the Odyssey.

I was at the game that night, in January 2005, and will always feel proud of Chris's courageous and outstanding performance, one that earned him a 'shutout', as well as the Man-of-the-Match award. In addition, he received a standing ovation, as the final hooter sounded.

Afterwards, Chris informed the media that his performance was down to his mental game makeover; that he had strengthened his mind and that this allowed his talent to come through, unimpeded by interference. It was a clear advertisement for the effectiveness of sport psychology. Chris has chronicled his mental game transformation, kindly allowing me to reproduce a substantial extract from it here, for you to read.

"At first, I had difficulty getting used to the idea that I was to make my full debut against the Bison. My mind started racing with thoughts of what was to come in this game and what had occurred in previous games. It even impacted on my night's sleep. My thoughts would inevitably be filled with negativity, which would be compounded by the tiredness brought by inadequate rest.

As the first Irish player to sign for the Belfast Giants, there was intense media interest on how I would fair in the upper echelons of British hockey. This speculation reached a crescendo when it was announced that I would make my first professional start against the Bison, our bogey team. It was all the more stressful, as our other goalie had been suspended and my backup for the match would be an untried youngster. I was, in reality, on my own. I decided to give the Giants' sport psychologist a ring. My mind needed to be on the game.

Through my sessions with Mark, I learned to train my mind to dismiss negative thoughts. The breathing techniques I implemented reduced my anxiety at the toughest times. All the techniques were to prove invaluable before and during what is probably the highlight of my time in the professional leagues, the game against Basingstoke - January 14, 2005.

I found, to my surprise, that nerves simply were not an issue, despite the volume of television, radio and newspaper interest there was, not only in the UK, but also as far away as North America.

My night's sleep was uninterrupted, my afternoon nap was restful and even in the locker room, up to and after warm-up, the old jitters were conspicuous by their absence. I really only had butterflies as we took to the ice before face-off. In fact, the dominant feelings were of nervous excitement/adulation.

During the game, I employed the 'guardian method' where I mentally placed my beloved Bearded Collie, Molly, behind me in the net. There was no way I'd let her come to harm!

The game proved to be a cagey affair, with long lulls followed by periods of wild goalmouth action. The worst type of game, in many ways, for a goalie. But we won 3-0 and I ground out a shutout and a MoM performance. I can say, with every certainty, that the pivotal factor in achieving this level of performance, in this game and in the remainder of my career, was the new mental training I undertook. The regimented thought techniques and processes reduced mistakes, eradicated 'what if' worries and allowed me to focus simply on putting into practice the physical aspects of my sport. Mentally, there were only recollections of good play and feelings of 'when would I get the chance to repeat these performances'; real self confidence."

*- Personal communication, 03.08.10*

## ☑ Elgin City recover their belief and focus to NOT break a record

'An Ulsterman has helped prevent Scots Third Division club Elgin City from claiming the most unwanted record in British football history.'

*- Stuart McKinley,*
*Belfast Telegraph, 21.10.06*

In October 2006, I had the opportunity to work with Elgin City FC, of the Scottish Third Division. Elgin, managed at that time by Scottish and Aberdeen legend Brian Irvine, were in dire straits, facing the prospect of holding one of the most unwelcome of records. Usually football teams would want to emulate Manchester United, but not on this occasion. Manchester United set the record of losing *twelve* successive games at the start of the 1930-31 season, and Elgin were now on the verge of equalling this record, or 'bettering' it.

| ELGIN CITY - 2006/2007 - Results and Fixtures | | | | | |
|---|---|---|---|---|---|
| Scottish Division 3 | East Stirling | 2-1 | Elgin City | | 05-08-2006 |
| Scottish Division 3 | Elgin City | 1-2 | Queen's Park | | 12-08-2006 |
| Scottish Division 3 | Montrose | 2-0 | Elgin City | | 19-08-2006 |
| Scottish Division 3 | Elgin City | 1-2 | East Fife | | 26-08-2006 |
| Scottish Division 3 | Stenh'semuir | 2-0 | Elgin City | | 03-09-2006 |
| Scottish Division 3 | Elgin City | 0-2 | Dumbarton | | 09-09-2006 |
| Scottish Division 3 | Albion | 3-1 | Elgin City | | 16-09-2006 |
| Scottish Division 3 | Elgin City | 1-2 | Berwick | | 23-09-2006 |
| Scottish Division 3 | Arbroath | 2-1 | Elgin City | | 30-09-2006 |
| Scottish Division 3 | Elgin City | 2-3 | East Fife | | 07-10-2006 |
| Scottish Division 3 | Elgin City | ?-? | East Stirling | | 14-10-2006 |

*soccerbase.com*

While my intervention was brief, the sport psychology equivalent of fire-fighting, it nevertheless helped the team to take back control of their minds and to start to believe in their individual and collective abilities.

You see, this was not a poor team; they were not that far away from turning the corner. Indeed, in the previous season, Brian Irvine had guided Elgin to a league position just outside a play-off place.

Accordingly, hopes were high of an even stronger league campaign in the 06-07 season. But these hopes were crushed early on, and with each successive defeat confidence decreased.

The problem was clearly mental in nature, rather than technical. So, with the unwelcome record looming on the horizon, it was time for the players to dig deep mentally. To facilitate this, I worked with the team on the week leading up to Elgin's eleventh league match. This would be against East Stirlingshire, on the Saturday.

Brian Irvine lead from the front in welcoming my input, and his players followed. As is often the case, there wasn't a dramatic absence of mental strength. Instead there was a blunting of it.

The players' focus was being drawn to extraneous matters surrounding their plight. As one player said to me: "The media vultures are waiting to swoop down on us if we keep losing. It's hard to keep our minds on playing football."

My work with the team was succinct and straightforward. I believed the players needed to go back to basics and re-engage with their jobs on the pitch. They needed to focus on what was relevant to their roles and, by doing this, to desist from worrying about public and media opinion.

We agreed that the 'so-called' record was a vaporous distraction and that it was vital to concentrate on what was under the players' control.

The team responded well to this logic. They acknowledged that Elgin City employed each of them to do a job and that *becoming distracted* was not part of the job description. So getting back to basics was paramount.

I instructed the team on the use of imagery and encouraged them to mentally rehearse four key elements of their roles. The players were also urged to challenge any thoughts that dragged them away from the process of preparation and performance. If they were to beat East Stirlingshire, it would be because they remained wedded to robust and focused mental preparation. To maintain focus on the pitch, the players adopted a "next ball" mentality, a verbal cue that ricocheted around their ground, Borough Briggs, on the Saturday afternoon. As a team, Elgin needed to perform in the present and not allow their minds to rock back and forth between the past and future. The *next ball* mantra helped in this respect.

On Saturday 14 October, 2006, Elgin ripped East Stirlingshire apart. To a man, they executed their roles with belief and passion. Three-nil up at half-time, Elgin went on to bag a super 5-0 victory. By concentrating on the process of performing, the outcome took care of itself.

> **"I found the services of Mark, the sport psychologist, invaluable to help me and, more importantly, to the players at Elgin, to get their heads right and get the result needed to avoid an unenviable record of having made the worst start to a league campaign. The transformation from losers to winners was dramatic. The difference was as comparable as night is to day. With the right mental tools the players delivered, and from losing 10 straight league matches we recorded a 5-0 victory in front of the BBC Football Focus cameras to prove Mark`s mental toughness methods work."**
>
> *Brian Irvine*

## Mental toughness in person

Before we move on to meet several athletes who have struggled due to a lack of mental toughness, I would like you to read a media commentary on one of my top clients, namely world number one handball player, Paul Brady.

You have met Paul already in this chapter and he appears several more times throughout the book, offering fantastic insight into his mental game and how it has helped him reach legendary status in his sport.

Now it's time to know him a little better. The following description of Paul confirms what I've known for some time - he is a total athlete.

Indeed, he's mental toughness personified.

> **"Brady's passion, commitment and will to win in handball are an inspiration to us all... matched with utter belief and conviction. The first thing you notice about this handball star are his boyish good looks, clear sparkling eyes, softly spoken demeanour, well mannered, polite, intelligent, good humoured, serious but, underneath it all, he has what sets him apart from all other handball players. His great self/inner belief, steely determination, his attitude to the sport and, above all, his will to win no matter what obstacles are placed in front of him."**
>
> *eircom.net*

## LACK OF MENTAL TOUGHNESS IN ACTION

In this section you will meet Steve, Hannah and Gary who all have had problems managing the mental side of their sport.

The fact that they have had difficulties in this regard is not one bit surprising, as none of them underwent any significant mental skills training during their development.

Nothing meaningful was ever offered to them.

All three are sure of one thing though - had they received mental game tuition from an early age, the following problems may not have arisen. And much angst could have been avoided.

## ☒ Steve focuses on things he cannot control

Twenty-two year old Steve was a golfer on the third level Europro Tour. A promising player, and highly feted in his early teens, he began to experience problems when he failed to equal the progress of his peers.

Steve was part of a golfing Brat Pack in the mid-2000s. But out of the four guys involved, all touted for great things, he was now lagging well behind. Of the three, one was on the main European Tour, one on the Asian Tour and one on the Challenge Tour. Steve felt very aggrieved, if not a little envious.

As a result of this unhealthy focus on other members of his peer group, Steve's performances in tournaments deteriorated. Fundamentally, he thought he didn't belong on the Europro Tour, arrogantly believing it was a bit beneath him.

Unsurprisingly, he just about remained on it.

Steve was desperately trying to recapture his ability, but was focusing on the wrong things. Nothing external to him was ever going to turn his game around. It had to come from inside. He had to waken up to the truth of his situation. He had to knock the chip off his shoulder, accept that he had to change and then formulate a plan. Conceit, jealousy and distraction were never going to work.

## ☒ Hannah keeps up appearances

Hannah, a 28 year old marathon runner had been making great progress in her sport. In fact, she had just come second in a big city marathon and at the time felt very positive. Commentators and marathon aficionados alike, described Hannah as a good prospect, one to keep an eye on. However, within months of this success, something appeared to go awry with Hannah. Her performances dipped and her coach, Bob, noticed that she was quieter in training and much less motivated than usual. When he asked her if she was troubled by anything, Hannah firmly said no.

But when Hannah pulled out of her own city's marathon and hinted at forgetting about Olympic qualification, Bob pushed for a reason - the real reason.

They met in Bob's house that day - he insisted upon it. In a heartfelt plea, he once again asked Hannah what was up, particularly as there was no injury. And at last the answer came.

Hannah's then fiancé was having an affair with a work colleague.

Hannah had spotted her fiancé and the young woman, walking hand-in-hand through a remote area of a local Forest Park. Hannah seldom ran through this particular park, but that day had gone there just to vary her training route. While she spotted them, they were oblivious to her presence. Returning home in shock, Hannah was at her wits' end. She was distraught. But instead of tackling her fiancé when he returned from 'work', Hannah acted as if nothing was wrong. She kept up this act for almost three months.

However, the effort involved in maintaining this façade began to catch up with Hannah and she found that her mood nose-dived. Lethargy set in, her self-esteem decreased and she withdrew from people around her. It was no surprise that her sport suffered too. Yet speaking to her coach and disclosing her problem in full, set Hannah off down the road to recovery. It was a road she couldn't and shouldn't have had to travel alone. She believed that if she ignored the problem, it would go away; that the affair would end and her relationship would pick up again. It was a high risk strategy and one that could have destroyed her sporting career, as well as triggering significant depression.

## ☒ Gary fears success

I met up with Gary, an 18 year-old elite amateur golfer, on what turned out to be the warmest June day for ten years. It was also four days after Gary had flunked at a big tournament, where he was the hottest of favourites to win.

It became clear from our conversation, that the weight of expectation was too heavy for Gary to bear. Instead of focusing on quality practice and feeling excited about the tournament, Gary began to ruminate on a whole host of stressful scenarios. His YouMinus was exerting considerable control over his mind and working overtime by urging him to maintain the status quo and not to better himself.

Remember 'bettering himself' would have involved change and discomfort and YouMinus doesn't do *change and discomfort*! As you listen-in to an extract from our conversation, you will see how insidious and twisted Gary's mental monster was:

**Gary:** "To tell you the truth Mark, I was concerned about all the reactions I'd get from people if I'd won this event."

**ME:** "If you _won_?"

**Gary:** "Well yes. It might sound odd, but yes, absolutely..."

**ME:** "Go on."

**Gary:** "You know more than most what it's been like for me over the past couple of years. There was all the fuss about those three big wins I had, how I was the next big thing. Then all the recent talk about me turning professional, especially if I won this tournament. It's like everyone else is planning my career for me. And I'm left without a say in the matter."

**ME:** "Okay - and 'everyone else', they are...?"

**Gary:** "Well, there's my coach, my parents, particularly my Dad. Then all the old geezers at the golf club. I'd be on the practice range and they'd drift over uninvited, and say, "It'll be great to have another club member turn pro". You know that sort of thing. Drives me mad, puts pressure on me..."

**ME:** "But you do still want to be a professional golfer, don't you?"

**Gary:** "Well, yes of course, ever since I was a kid that's what I've wanted, but..." [_Deep sigh_]

**ME:** "You're okay Gary, take your time."

**Gary:** "...But not if it's going to be like this Mark. Look, if this is what it's like when I'm _not_ a professional golfer, then what the heck will it be like when I am? I'll be swamped when I come back home and they'll all expect so much from me, just like last week. You know, I was actually relieved when I didn't make the cut."

**ME:** "Gary, forgive me if this sounds forward, but did playing below your potential and missing the cut actually serve a purpose? Did you get some kind of emotional payoff from your poor play?"

**Gary:** "I think I did Mark! For the first time in my golfing career I felt a release after a poor tournament. And if I was being really, really honest with you, I believe I was afraid of winning, which isn't healthy. You know, maybe I should pack it all in and go to college and do teacher training or something. I'm maybe just not cut out for the professional game."

**ME:** "And what precisely do you mean by 'professional game'?"

**Gary:** "Well, I do enjoy the actual golf side of it, but it's the people, all the fuss and expectancy that comes with being successful. I could just do without it. I'm a shy guy at heart and don't need it. But I'm also a b***dy great golfer Mark and I don't really want to waste my ability."

**ME:** "Right, so it's 'the people bit' and not the 'golfing bit' that trips you up. In actual fact then Gary, you possess the very 'bit' many people *don't* have – the talent!!"

**Gary:** "I know - I should be more grateful for my golfing skills. I'll just have to learn to cope better with people and all the attention."

**ME:** "Look, how about we book a session in for next week to cover this area of your game? I've several tips I can give you to knock this one on the head. What do you think?"

**Gary:** "Great Mark – what time suits you?"


Gary feared success because he predicted a torrid time coping with the public expectation and media attention.

How ironic, and what an insidious twist on the more common athlete experience – fearing failure and ridicule. But when all is said and done, fear is fear, whether of failure or success. The outcome is still the same. The person experiencing the fear, remains cocooned in the narrow confines of his comfort zone, preferring to settle for a life half-lived, than face the risks involved in big change. This was where Gary was heading, until he recognised that he was close to sacrificing his childhood dream on the altar of inflated fear.

As you see from our conversation, Gary left our session with an altered and more balanced perception of his situation. This formed the basis of some great mental game work over the ensuing months. As I pen these words, I'm pleased to report that Gary is currently in his second year of a golfing scholarship programme with a top university in the States. He will be turning professional when the programme ends.

An important point to remember is that Gary, as with all of my clients, had plotted his own course to mental toughness. He became his own SATNAV. Now, what do I mean by this? Well, he assessed his mental game at our initial meeting, and in doing so set a baseline against which his efforts to improve mentally could be continually evaluated. This helped him to set crystal-clear goals and to devise an action plan to achieve them. This process is called 'profiling' and my *Pathways Profiling System* is available to you in the following chapter.

# Chapter 3

## PROFILING YOUR PATHWAYS

*Distance already travelled,*
*Distance yet to go*

Like one, that on a lonesome road

Doth walk in fear and dread,

And having once turned round walks on,

And turns no more his head;

Because he knows, a frightful fiend

Doth close behind him tread.

**- Samuel Taylor Coleridge,**

The Rime of the Ancient Mariner

Quoted by Victor Frankenstein in Shelley's *Frankenstein*

In this chapter you will:

- Press the zoom-in facility on your mental game
- Discover how mentally tough you are
- Identify the mental game work you still need to do
- Set the coordinates for your journey to mental toughness
- Meet Rick, Aaron, Taylor, Iain, Natalie and Grant, real athletes with real mental game profiles.

Performance profiling is an excellent learning and development tool. It enables you to scan your current skill level and gain incredibly valuable knowledge. Your self-awareness soars as a result, and the information generated can be used by you and your coaching team, to design and develop specific training programmes.

Profiling allows you to pinpoint where you are right now, in terms of the range of skills you require to carry out your particular sporting role.

Let's call this the *Gold Standard Scan*, as it profiles the requisite skills across *all* four performance dimensions (i.e. the physical, technical, tactical and psychological).

However, in this chapter, we are going to focus on a subset of this scan, the *Mental Game Scan*.

## MENTAL GAME SCAN

In this chapter you will be guided through a Mental Game Scan. This will enable you to assess where your mental game is currently, when measured against the standards laid down by each of the six pathways, in Part Two's mental toughness training programme.

Three things will be achieved by scanning your mental game – each extremely positive:

- You will discover how mentally tough you are at this time.
- You will realise that you've already made progress along each pathway; perhaps to differing degrees, but progress nevertheless.
- You'll gain a sense of what you have to do and begin to think about setting big goals and ways to achieve them.

The knowledge gained will blossom into action as you move through the rest of the book.

And there's more. Carrying out the profiling process in partnership with your coach will help advance your relationship. It will promote discussion and any variance between views can be thrashed out, thereby starting your journey to mental toughness from a base of openness, clarity and agreement.

## It's Behind You!

As you travel along each of the pathways on the *Six Pathways to Mental Toughness* programme (in Part Two), you will be releasing yourself from the clutches of your mental monster, your inner saboteur, your YOUMINUS, whatever you wish to call it. But take note: never become complacent!

Keep practising and progressing, for the monster lurks a few strides behind, waiting for you to drop your guard.

# PATHWAY PROFILING

To ensure that you assess your mental game accurately against the six pathways listed below, it is essential for you know what each pathway actually means.

### The Six Pathways To Mental Toughness

**Pathway 1 - Pathway to Motivation and Momentum**

**Pathway 2 - Pathway to Total Self-belief**

**Pathway 3 - Pathway to World Class Thinking**

**Pathway 4 - Pathway to Effective Focus**

**Pathway 5 - Pathway to Imagery Control**

**Pathway 6 - Pathway to Emotional Control**

As the Pathway Profiling rating system runs from zero to ten, what I've set out in the following section, is a comprehensive description of what a '10' looks like for each of the six pathways.

And it is against these descriptions, that you will plot your position along each pathway on the Profile Chart provided.

Remember too, it's extremely unlikely that you're a 'zero' on any of the ratings. Whether you know it or not, you'll have travelled some of the way already.

Read the descriptions through a couple of times before then rating yourself/plotting your position from 0-10 along each pathway. It's a straightforward rating system; the most effective always are.

Your six ratings will represent your baseline assessment. Then as you progress through the training, in Part Two, you'll periodically return to update your progress along each pathway.

A fresh Profile Chart is available in Appendix 1 for photocopying.

# The Six Pathways Described

It's now time to find out what a rating of '10' means. In other words, you'll see the characteristics you need to possess to score yourself a ten for each of the six pathways to mental toughness.

## PATHWAY 1: MOTIVATION AND MOMENTUM

### A Peek down Pathway 1 – What a rating of 10 looks like

Your desire to do well in sport is an inside job. That is, your motivation to succeed is internally-driven - you're doing it for you. You are living *your* life and therefore the goals you set for sport are meaningful to *you*.

Long gone are the days when you worried about what other people thought, and how you could best meet *their* needs. Days whenever you sacrificed your true self and boundless potential on the altar of inferiority.

While you have people assisting you in your journey to success, and many others rooting for you, the hard work you put in is *not* for them. It's not for your coach, or your parents. It's not to prove your worth to your old college coach who said you'd never make it. Nor is it to settle a score with a certain childhood friend, who called you a "geek" and a "loser" many years ago. You realise that such external sources of motivation are fleeting.

Sure, you take pleasure from seeing your folks or coach happy at your success, and you gain some satisfaction from hearing the words "well done" pass the lips of a naysayer. You concede, too, that you welcome the public adulation, the sponsorship, the prize money, the media interest and so forth.

But, and this is a big BUT, you understand that these are merely agreeable by-products of your deliberate efforts to meet your own sporting objectives. You are so focused on the *process* of achievement that such outcomes are never really on your radar.

Your inner spark is kindled by the challenge of stretching your ability, shaping your skills and maximising your God-given potential. Accumulating a host of possessions does little to float your boat. You see the big picture of life, and material gain doesn't figure in it.

You understand how your motivation ticks, what works best for you to get the most out of your efforts. You don't feel you're making sacrifices. On the contrary, you enjoy working towards your goals. Goals which are laid down in such an effective way that you move gradually, but inexorably, beyond your current comfort zone.

Your achievement plan is designed to maximise the control you have over meeting your goals. This in itself is motivating, as little is left to chance.

You are pragmatic and solution-focused when goals are not met, and when setbacks occur. You review your programme of training and evaluate your performances with an eye to learning and not with the aim of beating yourself up. You learn from your errors and defeats and have developed the capacity to live and perform more fully in the present. You know that the present is the only moment that exists and that to build up momentum, you must exploit each moment. This is not to say that the past and future are ignored.

Rather, they are mental landscapes you visit for educational and planning purposes.

Put plainly, you learn from what has gone before and you prepare positively for what is yet to come.

When commitment and enjoyment waver (as you accept they will, from time-to-time) you are able to ratchet up your enthusiasm and to persevere.

Such is your inner drive that any phase of indifference generally passes swiftly.

**Do This ✓**

---

**In terms of Pathway 1, my rating out of 10 is ____**
(Now shade in your rating for Pathway 1 onto the PROFILE CHART, below).

---

## PATHWAY 2: TOTAL SELF-BELIEF

### A Peek down Pathway 2 - What a rating of 10 looks like

You have a solid self-belief and an inner acceptance of your value as a human being. Not only do you like what you have become, but you are at peace with yourself and don't need other people to validate your existence. You know your own worth and that's good enough for you.

But it's not conceit; far from it. It's an internal cosiness. You are a self-booster, not a self-boaster. You have no desire to tell people of your achievements, unless prompted to do so.

Even then, you do so with modesty. You have passed what I call, 'The Solo Hole-in-One Test'.

This is a test of self-belief and assuredness. It comprises of one question only:

> "Hand-on-heart, how would you think and feel, if you scored a hole-in-one in golf and no-one was there to witness it?"

An athlete with robust self-esteem will simply be happy that *he* was there to see it! He would feel no less satisfied due to the absence of onlookers.

You possess a confidence about your ability to successfully manage the various challenges of competitive sport. You trust yourself, you trust your training and you trust your technique.

When doubt creeps in, as it occasionally does, you quickly counter it with constructive, evidence-based self-talk and self-boosting imagery. You top-up your confidence account through your mental iplayer, and play past successes over and over again. You refuse to put doubt in the debit column of your confidence account. Negative equity is not for you!

You are a smart strategist. Realising that some of your 'What if?' worries could well happen, you devise effective contingency plans. This in itself fuels confidence, as it provides a sense of mastery. It's a 'win-win' strategy - if the situations occur, you know how to handle them; if they don't well at least you were prepared. You live by the maxim, 'A surprised athlete is an athlete in trouble'.

You possess a 'growth mindset' and are excited about the possibilities this affords you. Everything is possible. Realising that nothing succeeds like success, you set effective goals that move you incrementally towards your dream. As each goal is accomplished, your confidence account is boosted.

As you have also developed a 'preference-led attitude', you are seldom too upset by underperformance or unmet goals. This is in stark contrast to the approach you had prior to mental game training.

Back then, you reacted to things going wrong with temper tantrums, despondency and distraction. It was as if you'd demanded that bad stuff shouldn't happen; that you should be superhuman. But nowadays, your perfectionism has been replaced by preferences.

**Do This ✓**

---

**In terms of Pathway 2, my rating out of 10 is \_\_\_**
(Now shade in your rating for Pathway 2 onto the
PROFILE CHART, below).

---

## PATHWAY 3: WORLD CLASS THINKING

### A Peek down Pathway 3 - What a rating of 10 looks like

You have come to understand something incredible. And it is this: between every stimulus and response is your *interpretation*. The life-changing thing about this discovery is that it places you in the driving seat.

It means that what your experience in life and sport is a direct product of how you interpret each of these things. As a result, you have developed effective thinking skills.

This ability enables you to find positives, where you never thought to look before.

This does wonders for your mood, confidence and focus.

**Do This ✓**

---

### In terms of Pathway 3, my rating out of 10 is____
(Now shade in your rating for Pathway 3 onto the
PROFILE CHART, below).

---

## PATHWAY 4: Pathway to Effective Focus

### A Peek down Pathway 4 - What a rating of 10 looks like

You focus only on those things that actually matter. You switch your attention to only those thoughts, images, feelings and actions that advance your lot. You realise that it has to be this way, as concentration is a limited mental commodity. You are no spend-thrift when it comes to concentration. Gone are the days when you freely gave away your focus to any old stimulus. Remember?

- You made a mistake and dwelled on it.
- You felt a surge of anxiety and questioned your readiness for competition.
- You heard your coach yelling at you and couldn't shake off the embarrassment.
- You crumbled mentally after a spectator lambasted you.

Well those days are well and truly gone now, and the feeling of control is amazing.

You know that effective focus is about managing the swarm of stimuli that shower your sporting experience before, during and after performance. You know your role inside-out and have a clear sense of what is relevant to your performance and what is a distraction. You have learned to switch seamlessly between focusing styles and to remain in the present.

It is all about process these days, not outcome.

You control only those aspects of preparation and performance that you can. In this way, you conserve concentration for when it really matters. For you, your store of focus is a pot of gold dust. You will not waste it on things you can do nothing about.

Crucially, you've also learned to detach your sporting world from the multi-circled Venn diagram of 'the rest of your life'.

There is minimal, if no overlap. You have built a mental firewall around your sporting activity, so that problems emerging from your role as boy/girlfriend, brother or sister, best mate or student, do not interfere with training and performance.

On the odd occasion when your mind drifts to matters domestic, you are able to recognise it, regroup and refocus, as you do for all moments of distraction.

**Do This ✓**

| |
|---|
| **In terms of Pathway 4, my rating out of 10 is ____** |
| (Now shade in your rating for Pathway 4 onto the PROFILE CHART, below). |

## PATHWAY 5: IMAGERY CONTROL

### A Peek down Pathway 5 - What a rating of 10 looks like

You have recaptured your childhood appetite for placing your mind in exciting places. You regularly engage in effective imagery, using *all* of your senses to prepare for competition.

You have an enhanced understanding of the mind-body connection and realise that your internal *I-PoD* system (*Imagery-Pictures on Demand*) is a significant asset to your mental game repertoire.

You have become extremely adept at creating clear, vibrant and relevant images. It is an enjoyable activity and one that you continue to hone. You have cultivated several uses for imagery across the performance cycle. For example, you use imagery to: enhance the learning and acquisition of your technical skills; rehearse your performance; and revise your game plans, routine and strategies.

**Do This ✓**

> **In terms of Pathway 5, my rating out of 10 is ____**
> (Now shade in your rating for Pathway 5 onto the
> PROFILE CHART, below).

## PATHWAY 6: EMOTIONAL CONTROL

### A Peek down Pathway 6 - What a rating of 10 looks like

You know your way around your emotional landscape. You have the mental game equivalent of a London Cabbie's *Knowledge*. You are no longer lost in an emotional maze. *You* run your emotions now. You're the boss. You're in control.

While feelings of stress still emerge – you are human after all – the difference now is that you have a toolkit of cutting edge techniques to eliminate the discomfort.

You've become your own emotional watchdog. Having monitored your good and bad performances over time, and the associated mental states, you now know your *Personal*

*Ideal Performance State* (PIPS). This knowledge is vital as it prompts you to make adjustments when, prior to competition, you're either too flat and lethargic, or too hyper and psyched-up.

One of the most significant moments on your journey to emotional control, was when you were introduced to the profound influence your thoughts have on your mood, focus and energy levels.

You discovered that this thing called *stress*, isn't in the sporting environment waiting to ambush you, but instead, is invited in through your negative interpretations of the situations you face.

You therefore know that a missed penalty only torments the footballer when he interprets it as a catastrophe.

And that slicing a little white ball, only distresses and distracts the golfer, because he has labelled the miss as a harbinger of a poor round, or as a symptom of his uselessness.

As a result of this discovery, you have developed your interpretative ability, something you supplement with other emotion-management techniques.

Among these are relaxation strategies and positive imagery. You anticipate specific emotional challenges and prepare to meet them head-on.

You 'inoculate' yourself against stress by engaging in simulated training sessions and mental rehearsal.

In this way, you learn to fight off any challenges in your mind before they rear their ugly heads in competition. Such forethought is empowering, and your confidence keeps on growing as a result.

**Do This ✓**

## In terms of Pathway 6, my rating out of 10 is ____
(Now shade in your rating for Pathway 6 onto the
PROFILE CHART, below).

# Your Profile Chart

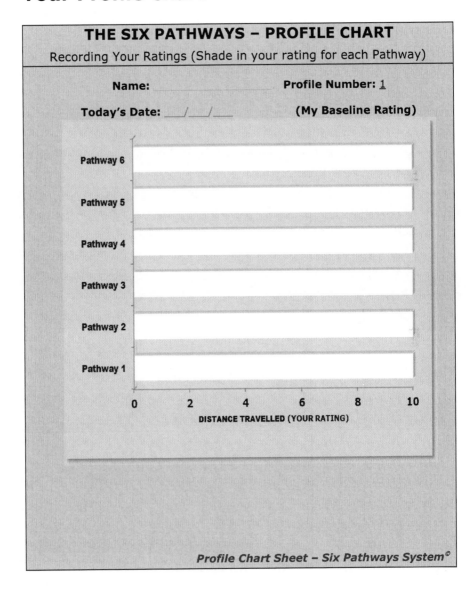

**THE SIX PATHWAYS – PROFILE CHART**

Recording Your Ratings (Shade in your rating for each Pathway)

Name: _____    Profile Number: 1

Today's Date: ___/___/___    (My Baseline Rating)

- Pathway 6
- Pathway 5
- Pathway 4
- Pathway 3
- Pathway 2
- Pathway 1

0    2    4    6    8    10

DISTANCE TRAVELLED (YOUR RATING)

*Profile Chart Sheet – Six Pathways System*°

## Congratulations!!

You've taken the most important step on your journey to mental toughness. And it is a frank and open step; one that sets the compass and organises the coordinates for your mental game development.

Now you know how far you have left to travel, and the direction of the journey. This is vital, for without a strong sense of where you are now, you have no chance of reaching where you'd like to be.

## THE PATHWAYS LESS-TRAVELLED

You now have a baseline of six ratings, a starting line if you will, for your journey to mental toughness. These ratings describe your mental game strengths and weaknesses across the six key areas of mental toughness. The next step in your journey is to prioritise those Pathways *less-travelled*. These are the mental skill areas you need to attend to right now and to set powerful goals for. As you know, each mental skill area has a Chapter/Pathway devoted to it in Part Two.

To help you prioritise, I suggest you mark out for attention those pathways along which you have travelled less than a rating of EIGHT. Do this now please, placing a tick beside those pathways rated as 7, or under.

Unless you have only one such pathway (and congrats if you do; your mental game is in pretty good shape), then a further act of prioritising is required. It is best to work on no more than two pathways at-a-time, otherwise you'll become cluttered and overwhelmed, and your best intentions to develop mental toughness are likely to become frustrated. It is important to remember that each pathway is a *set* of mental skills and not just one.

So, let's say you have four Pathways rated seven or under. Your next task would be to rank these in order against the following criteria.

You should give greater importance to:

- The Pathway that **will have the most significant and positive impact on your performance**. For instance, if you have a low rating for Pathway 5, *Imagery Control*, progressing well along it will spark positive changes in your confidence, concentration, and emotional control (i.e. Pathways 2, 4 and 6).

- **The obvious choice**. If you are besieged by unhelpful thoughts and limited self-belief and you have a national selection trial coming up in a month's time, or a massive game looming, then you should immediately engage with Pathway 2/Chapter 5 (Total Self-Belief).

Once you have shaded in your six ratings on the Profile Chart, I recommend you photocopy it. Use the enlarge facility to blow it up. Then fix it somewhere prominent - in your bedroom perhaps.

Don't worry about what others may think. Be your own person. Understand the process of developing mental toughness - that it's about overcoming your mental monster and that it takes dedicated work. Then sign up to the process and get working on it. Part Two provides you with the tools to do this.

## Pathways Profiling: Real World Examples

Now that you know what a rating of ten looks like for each pathway, it seems only right to balance this with some real world descriptions of athletes' *low* ratings. To this end, meet **R**ick, **A**aron, **T**aylor, **I**ain, **N**atalie and **G**rant, who have offered up their lowest scores.

As you meet these six athletes below, you will come to understand why they gave low ratings to their respective pathway. The six descriptions provide an intimate insight into the mental game difficulties and barriers to peak performance, suffered by this group of elite performers.

As you absorb the vignettes, you will notice that while each athlete speaks of *one* pathway, there are many overlapping and interconnected issues.

Above all else, if you are at all serious about your sport, you will identify the absolute need for mental toughness.

Before we meet Rick, please note that names and other identifying features have been changed and some of the cases are composites of several sportspeople I have worked with.

## RICK, 21, Professional Golfer
### Pathway to Motivation and Momentum.
### Rick's Rating, 2/10

Having read what a score of ten looked like, **Rick** scored himself a two on this pathway.

A very talented, but woefully inconsistent golfer, Rick realised that his problem lay with his mental game; specifically with his motivation. The issue was that Rick's motivational umbilical cord was attached to the outside world. He gorged on such psychological nutrients as adulation, recognition and status to inspire him to great golf. With appetite sated, Rick was a golfer who could blitz the course and the field, with apparent ease. When up for it, his talent lit up tournaments.

But when Rick's motivational umbilical cord to the outside world was clamped, his golfing ability deteriorated rapidly. He had no Plan B. In other words, he had no means of igniting an inner spark when he wasn't receiving attention, winning tournaments or playing well. It was a rather sad state of affairs really. He was, in effect, an empty shell of a golfer. His internal drive was a blunt instrument.

When all was going swimmingly, Rick purred like a well-oiled golfing machine. He loved nothing more than the gallery cheering his play. If one of his drives was met with a yelled, "Way to go Rick", or "You're the man", he would visibly bloom. With shoulders lifted and back straightened, you could be sure Rick would nail his next shot too.

When he was in contention to win a tournament he was very difficult to fend-off, as he was so stimulated by the situation. Being an attention junkie and a 'hey-look-at-me' sort of guy, Rick was in self-esteem heaven at such moments. He felt like a 'somebody'. He felt appreciated, approved and admired.

But the feelings never lasted. By the time Rick returned to his hotel room after the tournament ended, his mood would have dropped and an intense sense of anticlimax would have infused his entire being.

You can understand why Rick's performances vacillated so wildly. When the external rewards dried-up, he had no camel's hump of inner sustenance to get him through the drought and make things happen.

Although the tide of being in contention could carry Rick towards the winning line, he was regularly unable to lift his game when well down the leader board. At these times, the spotlight of media and public attention would be elsewhere on the course, shining on his golfing rivals. Rick resented this; he wanted to be top dog. His bitterness acted like a mental black hole at these times, sucking in his energy and focus and obliterating his technique.

Given his desire to impress other people, making a mistake was seen by Rick as the worst thing ever. It would put a dent in his fragile ego and very soon he would become sheep-dipped in the dye of self-pity and frustration. Then, in his eagerness to make amends, Rick would deviate from his game plan and take on a risky shot to impress the spectators. However, time and again this tactic would backfire and a further mistake would ensue. Rick would then become despondent and beat himself up for "being so stupid".

With focus compromised, it was often the case that several big numbers would be posted.

To illustrate the chalk and cheese flavour of Rick's golf game, I recall a round he played not so long ago. Having made three birdies and an eagle over the first four holes, he then proceeded to drop eight shots by the time he reached the turn.

The pivotal moment was on the Par 3 fifth, when Rick sent his drive into the water hazard. He was so appalled by his mistake that he lost focus and found the lake again, with his third shot.

The gallery that was following his match faded away and with it, went Rick's motivation.

Further examples of Rick's need for external stimulation included his:

- Inability to feel sufficiently motivated for those early tee-off times, when only the clichéd man and his dog would be present.

- Finding practice boring, unless a knot of spectators gathered round to watch.

- Garnering praise from others, by buying them presents, wining and dining them and lending them money.

- Purchasing one-third of a racehorse to impress his ever-growing circle of 'friends'!

- Experiencing a lift in his mood when his rivals were playing poorly.

- Boasting to all and sundry, when given half a chance.

Rick's conceit was off-putting for those who didn't know him well. However, beneath his swagger, Rick was a good guy with a big heart... and a colossal golfing capability. His true self was lost beneath layers and layers of mental interference.

He had been severely monster-munched!

## The Role of YouMinus in Rick's Mental Game

This is a textbook example of an athlete's mental monster at play. Rick's YouMinus had created an egofest and partied at his expense. It urged him to hanker after external rewards, fooling him that success and contentment lay outside of himself.

His YouMinus also insisted that he should avoid embarrassing himself and letting people down at all costs. Ultimately, Rick's drive and self-esteem were controlled by factors in his environment, rather than by himself.

Undoubtedly, Rick had a great distance yet to travel along Pathway 1. But we worked together for several weeks and considerable progress was made. You can find the solution to Rick's motivational problem **at the end of Chapter 4**, which covers this particular pathway.

## AARON, 24, Rugby Player (Fly Half/No. 10)
### Pathway to Total Self-belief.
### Aaron's Rating, 1/10

Once **Aaron** had understood and digested the characteristics of high self-esteem and confidence, he took his pen in hand and with a despondent, "This'll not take long" shaded to a '1' along Pathway Two. He confirmed his rating, emphasising that a 1 out of 10 did indeed represent where his self-belief lay along this Pathway.

Let's start at the beginning. Aaron, a 24 year-old professional rugby player, was eaten up and spat out by his mental monster during his debut game for his new team, a club in the English Championship. With his team five points up, Aaron, as his team's fly half and goal-kicker, had a seemingly straightforward opportunity to put a bit more daylight between the sides. The opposition had infringed and his team had been awarded a penalty. If he put the ball between the posts, they would be eight points ahead and, with just seven minutes remaining, their opponents would require at least two big scores to win. It was therefore a crucial kick and Aaron needed to nail it. But he didn't. Instead, he scuffed the effort and the ball didn't even reach the posts, falling short into the grateful hands of the opposition's full back.

With several minutes yet to go, Aaron knew, at an intellectual level, that he should put this error out of his mind and keep plugging away. But he didn't know how to. Emotionally he was gone and his focus was everywhere but in the present; and as a result his performance deteriorated. His handling was poor and defensively he was weak.

That his team went on to lose to a late converted try, merely rubbed salt into Aaron's already weeping mental wound. He recalls the devastation he felt in the changing room, after the game.

This was new territory for Aaron and, as it turned out, was the beginning of his mental monster's reign of inner terror; a campaign that intensified with each poor performance and one that very nearly led to him quitting rugby for good.

Aaron came to my sport psychology practice, a broken spirit. This strapping, handsome lad was a lost soul, having eventually been dropped from the starting fifteen and having no inkling as to how, or why, this had all come about.

He knew he had played poorly for four out of the last five matches and that his kicking ability, once his USP, had become very inconsistent. Yes, he knew all of this, but he was at a complete loss to explain it. "Why now Mark?", he pleaded. "And how can I have gotten so useless so quickly?"

Aaron and I spoke for about two hours at our first meeting. And what a productive session it was. This articulate young rugby footballer opened up to such an extent, that we were able to trace the slime of his mental monster back to the close season, when he first signed for his new team.

Aaron had been excited by moving to a bigger club and was eager to meet the challenge laid down by his new coach. Moreover, he and his fiancée Vicky loved their new apartment and had settled-in well.

However, as Aaron put it, "I underestimated the expectations the club and supporters had of me". He described an evening in mid-August, when he was the guest at a dinner run by the club's largest supporters' group. In particular, he remembered returning home that night, thinking new and unsettling thoughts and experiencing a sense of panic:

> **"For the first time Mark, I questioned my ability to play at this level, to perform at the level expected of me. The supporters had real high hopes that I would deliver big time. I remember driving home thinking differently about my ability. That's what happened. Well I can see that now, but at the time it didn't really register. I just thought the thoughts you know. Vicky'll tell you, I didn't sleep well that night. Tossed and turned a lot"**

Here we see the first heartbeat of Aaron's mental monster. Life had been breathed into it by Aaron's feelings of doubt and anxiety.

Of course, had he noticed this at the time and recalibrated his thoughts and focus, then his mental monster could have been snuffed out there and then. But he didn't, and it grew!

For the first time in his young life, Aaron became caught up in other people's expectations and opinions of him. His focus wandered away from the process of training and performing and onto results. Aaron also spoke about a "hurry sickness" that had been gripping him on a daily basis:

**"I've become obsessed about remedying my last poor performance; by making the coach happy, by hearing the supporters chant my name, y'know? I'm irritable and impatient for Saturday or Sunday to come round, which isn't good for home life, I can tell you. I'm edgy and as irritable as sin."**

The fixation with making people happy sucked out Aaron's inner drive, something that had served him well since he was a kid. For the first time, he was almost solely playing rugby to get the outcomes he desperately wanted – a top performance and approval. The fun had gone.

The pressure Aaron placed on himself grew by the week. The more he failed to deliver a high level performance, the more he berated himself for letting people down; and, the more he doubted he would ever make the grade at the club. His self-belief sunk like a stone in water and the ripple effect spread out to contaminate his motivation, concentration, and composure.

Aaron's anxiety escalated with the arrival of each match day. By the time he reached the changing rooms, the butterflies in his stomach were being out-fluttered by his heart palpitations. Images of failure would pop into Aaron's mind, cranked up by self-talk that predicted another poor performance. Yet he used to feel so excited at these crucial times.

But that was before his mental monster came on the scene and took control.

Where playing rugby once thrilled Aaron, it now threatened him:

**"Last Saturday was the most nervous I've ever been. No, not nervous, AFRAID. I was afraid of playing. Imagine that, after all these years...I was**

**afraid of playing badly again, not making my kicks again, making bad decisions again ..."**

From speaking with Aaron, it seemed that he had erased from his memory bank all of his achievements. While one shouldn't rest on one's laurels, Aaron was thinking and behaving like a man bereft of any merit whatsoever. This was ridiculous, considering everything that he had accomplished thus far in his young life, and not just in rugby football. He was a loved son, brother and fiancé, was popular with his friends and teammates and was a young man lauded for his kindness and charity work. In other words, he was a valuable human being. But Aaron didn't agree, and his was the *only* opinion that really mattered.

He had begun to define himself by his performances on the pitch and not as a human with considerable value and potential to put things right. He was, in his words, "hopeless", "pathetic" and "worthless".

He explained that his confidence had become so low, that he was shaking before taking penalty kicks at goal. His usual composure and sense of mastery had all but evaporated. What was left was a hollow man.

I was worried that Aaron's perceptions of himself, as a person and rugby player, were beginning to morph together.

He was also showing signs of mild depression; an unsurprising consequence of seeing oneself and one's plight as beyond hope.

The key expression of Aaron's low self-belief was a mix of despondency and fear. He feared failure, particularly as his new club had placed such faith in him. This fear crept up on him prior to games and all but strangled him when the spotlight fell on his goal-kicking. If he missed a kickable penalty, or made any error for that matter, then his confidence caved-in and his performance deteriorated. At this point, despondency and a vicious self-loathing would set in. "You're pathetic Aaron", "You prat", "You LOSER".

Aaron constantly compared himself to other people; specifically, the other new signings in the team who seemed to be progressing nicely. Unknowingly, he had become proficient at finding evidence to support his "uselessness". By the time Aaron consulted me, he had been 'rested' from the starting fifteen - the first time in his sporting life that this had ever happened to him. This for Aaron was the ultimate piece of evidence: it was 'proof' of his inability to ever make it at the elite level.

## The Role of YouMinus in Aaron's Mental Game

To observers and commentators alike, it appeared that as Aaron was struggling on the *rugby* pitch all his problems were therefore *rugby*-based. But of course they weren't. The source of Aaron's poor performances was not down to a lack of technique or physicality, but rather was due to a surplus of mental interference, which suppressed his ability to express himself freely on the pitch.

For the first time in Aaron's short life, he had begun to experience difficulty with his game.

For almost fifteen years, from being a mini-rugby player through to gaining provincial and international recognition at Under-18 and Under-20 levels, Aaron had played the game with relative ease and made progress as a matter of course.

In other words, he never really had to struggle to make it. But now things had changed and he couldn't cope.

He was now playing at a higher level from the club he left and was struggling to put together a performance that remotely met his potential. Unsurprisingly, this hiatus in his sporting development was 'manna from heaven' for his inner saboteur, YouMinus. It saw the fault line of self-doubt opening up, and exploited it rapidly:

> **"Mark, it just sort of happened out of the blue. All of a sudden, I was thinking I wasn't up to it after all. Maybe the move had been way too big a jump and that I was out of my depth. I had never thought these things before. I'm normally a confident sort of person, who just loves playing rugby. I mean, people would remark on how I played for fun, you know, with a bit of a twinkle in my eye."**

As Aaron described how his thoughts, feelings and behaviour had changed, I could see the nefarious shenanigans of his mental monster at play.

Aaron's motivation had become external-facing. That is, he was now playing rugby less for the enjoyment it gave him, and more to garner approval from his new management team and to feel accepted.

He had become very self-conscious. He was hardly able to walk around the rugby-loving town he'd moved to, without thinking that people were looking at him puzzled as to why their local club had signed such a jerk.

This was all YouMinus' spin of course, a heap of lies to keep Aaron trapped in fear and out of harm's way. But it is incredibly important to remember that, in reality, not one person had ever been disparaging towards Aaron. Even his team coach was compassionate, realising that it takes time for new signings to bed in. It was ironic, then, that while those around him were nothing but confident in him, Aaron had an entirely different view of himself and the situation he faced.

His self-talk was doom-laden. No shades of grey, let alone white, could permeate Aaron's rigid thoughts. It was an all-encompassing blackness, the ultimate manifestation of which was his urge to quit the game because "I am now a hopeless player".

Aaron's performances were being dismantled from the inside-out. His mental game, in which he had never been sufficiently trained, had been hijacked by his mental monster and it was striking out at his self-belief. By doing so YouMinus was, in effect, taking the batteries out of Aaron's ability to perform at his optimum. Devious monster!

As Aaron talked, I took down some notes. I then introduced him to the Frankenstein Factor and the mental monster; it was a condensed version of the information shared with you in Chapter 1. Aaron's 'light bulb moment' occurred there and then. He conceded that he had inadvertently created his own difficulties, before he then forgave himself for doing so. Clean slate! Then he vowed to fight back against his mental monster right away. Soon it was Aaron's turn to take notes.

As he left the office that day, Aaron experienced a spring in his step for the first time in quite a while. He was armed with new information and insight and above all, he had hope and a plan. With motivation rekindled, Aaron went on to make startling progress, developing powerful self-belief and a calm mind.

To discover how he achieved this, you need to turn **to Chapter 5** where Aaron's case is concluded.

## TAYLOR, 17, Elite Tennis Player
### Pathway to World Class Thinking.
### Taylor's Rating, 2/10

Having read what a score of ten looked like, **Taylor** rated herself as a two on this pathway. She didn't think highly of herself, worried far too much about other people and was constantly beating herself up.

Taylor was raised in a high-flying family. Her father was an ophthalmologist, her mother a school teacher and her older brother, Charles, a general practitioner with a busy city practice. So no pressure there then! Expectations were that Taylor would also reach great heights in life, be that through the professions or sport.

Taylor was just six years old whenever her father noted her ability to play tennis. He observed his daughter's keen eye-hand coordination, her ability to hit shots other kids simply couldn't and was bowled-over by her love of the game.

She was eons ahead of her peer group at Saturday morning coaching sessions, held at her father's Country Club. A good tennis player himself in his college days, Taylor's father started to dream. His daughter could be the next Martina - Hingis or Navratilova, he didn't care.

Two days past her seventh birthday, Taylor started receiving personal sessions from a professional tennis coach.

The next few years passed in a blur of triumph. Taylor was highly successful, winning many juvenile events. She was also selected to join her national Academy, where she would train and compete against the best young players in her country. So far, so good or so it seemed. However, this is where Taylor started to experience problems.

Moving to the Academy meant that Taylor was no longer a big fish in a small pond. She was up against the best in her age group now and knowing this unsettled her. She started to experience periods of intense anxiety and worry. All of a sudden, everything seemed so serious and Taylor began to place herself under considerable pressure.

She believed that she simply HAD to succeed, or else her tennis dream would melt away in the springtime of her career. And so it began - a shift in Taylor's approach to tennis. She no longer trained with enthusiasm, nor did she look forward to tournaments. And she certainly didn't see herself as "a star in the making".

In fact, she began to feel she didn't belong amongst her new cohort of peers. She was sure they were much better than her. After all, they appeared to be much more at ease with themselves and sure of their position at the Academy.

This change in Taylor's mentality was mirrored by her performances. She lost matches she should have won and was becoming angry on court, something that had never been seen before. One could almost feel her frustration.

It transpired that Taylor had developed a very influential inner critic that was interfering greatly with her training and performance. There was simply no room for mistakes in Taylor's inflexible world. Indeed, when she made errors during matches, her self-criticism could be extremely scathing:

> **"I'm useless!! I'm going to lose this now!!"**

> **"They [the spectators] are going to think I'm pathetic and can't even hold my game together"**

> **"What sort of stupid shot was that Taylor - you brainless moron!!"**

Taylor's self-esteem plummeted and she held little hope of meeting her goals. She was dispirited and anxious and feeding this was a mind that never shut up. It just seemed to automatically spew out all sorts of defeatist commentaries and forecasts, particularly on the lead-up to tournaments.

Like many athletes with poor mental games, there was a sense with Taylor that her mind was not her own. It was run by something else, which she called a "bullying freak".

And the more she struggled with her game, the more her inner bully stuck its oar it. And the more it interfered, the more she struggled with her game. It was the most brutal of vicious circles, one that Taylor desperately needed to break. Her confidence was tumbling at an inordinate rate.

She also became excessively concerned about her reputation and standing amongst her tennis-playing peer group and the tennis moms.

She would lie in bed at night unable to sleep, as a carousel of thoughts and images ran around her mind:

**"What if I never recover my best game again?"**

**"I bet Becky and her mom are having a good laugh at my performances right now"**

**"I'll never get on the [tennis] circuit at this rate. I'll have to get a job!"**

**"Why have I ended up like this? I'm such a loser"**

Then there were her parents. Taylor was petrified of letting them down, particularly her father. He had sacrificed so much, in time and money. He drove Taylor to the Academy every day, had paid for her private coaching and brought in tutors to help with her schooling. She simply couldn't disappoint him. It wasn't an option for her to fail.

As far as she was concerned, the leitmotif of her family was 'Achievement Is Everything. Failure Is For Wimps'.

## The Role of YouMinus in Taylor's Mental Game

Tellingly, Taylor remembers the criticism that was often rained on her during the 50 minute trip home from the tennis Academy.

Her father's manner was often cruel. He would call her names when she had played poorly and he would frequently compare her to others in the Academy who were progressing at a much greater rate.

All too often, Taylor would arrive home with tear-stained eyes.

Given this grounding in fault-finding, it was of little surprise that Taylor absorbed the method and applied it to herself. To all intents and purposes, she took over from her father and bullied herself relentlessly.

As such, she had unknowingly created a powerful YouMinus that attacked her sporting soul with venom and ripped her tennis technique to shreds!

Taylor's inner critic ruled her mind, keeping her shackled at the start of Pathway 3. She had to find a way to free herself from its grip and begin to make significant strides towards inner assuredness, self-compassion and confidence in her tennis.

I am pleased to say she achieved this with a lot of hard work and determination. Discover how she did it **at the end of Chapter 6**.

## IAIN, 25, Pro Footballer (Centre Forward)
### Pathway to Effective Focus.
### Iain's Rating, 3/10

Having understood what effective focus actually was, **Iain** rated his own capacity to concentrate as a three out of ten. As with many of us, Iain had never been instructed on *how* to concentrate, but had nevertheless received frequent criticism for his distractibility.

When we discussed his low rating, Iain explained that he had great difficulty keeping his mind on the game and in refocusing after becoming distracted.

The most significant distraction was when he made an error on the pitch, particularly when the consequences of the error appeared crucial to the outcome of the match.

Now, when playing well, Iain's skill-sets were executed with an unthinking smoothness and grace. His touch was sublime at these times, his reading of the game acute and his goal-scoring stats at their best. But make a mistake and - BOOM! - Iain's mind would stop in its tracks and his game flatline.

When this happened, he found it extremely difficult to breathe life back into his performance. His mind appeared to freeze in time and space and stay with the error.

He would dwell on the mistake, excessively criticise himself and feel the heat of (perceived) public scrutiny and derision. His most alarming sensation was feeling detached from everything around him, often followed by an overwhelming sense of self-consciousness.

Aside from making a mistake, Iain also reacted disproportionately to several other ego-threatening triggers in his sporting environment. A spectator's insult, a referee's unfavourable decision or his manager shouting at him, would all turn his focus inwards and away from the task-at-hand. Underpinning these reactions was Iain's low tolerance for frustration. If something didn't go the way he wanted, or if people acted contrary to his expectations, he would become highly impatient and irritated.

He was like this on the pitch with his teammates as well as around his family and friends. During these moments of immaturity, his focus would again go inwards as he dwelt on the distraction itself.

As is often the case, Iain had the added irritation in his sporting life of concentrating and performing much better in training, than in competitive matches. This bewildered him to the point of anger. It was clear that unless he took purposeful strides along Pathway 4 and learned how to focus effectively, Iain was going to fall short of his potential and drift out of the sport he once loved; or be unceremoniously cast out by a fed up manager!

## The Role of YouMinus in Iain's Mental Game

Iain's YouMinus was primarily about two things: avoidance and demand.

— Avoiding losing face.
— Avoiding making mistakes.
— Avoiding embarrassment.
— Demanding that life goes his way.
— Demanding that he never makes errors.
— Demanding that people meet his needs.

With a mindset established on these *rules*, Iain had no chance of focusing effectively. The rules were far too rigid and set him up for much angst, frustration and distraction. He seemed to forget that life, let alone sport, is fluid.

You need to be able to handle change, deal with setbacks and manage conflict. And you need to be able to manage yourself. Iain's beliefs made this impossible to achieve.

I challenge you to apply Iain's rules to your life for a couple of weeks and see how you end up feeling. I can guarantee that your performance will suffer, your relationships will fracture, and your stress levels will soar.

You will reach the conclusion, as Iain eventually did, that these beliefs/rules are one big distraction factory spewing out focus-spoilers by the minute.

Iain and I worked together for several months to improve his mental game, in particular his ability to concentrate effectively. It was really tough going at times, but positive results came in the end. You can find out how successful we were, **at the close of Chapter 7**.

> ## NATALIE, 20, Athlete (Pole Vault)
> ## Pathway to Imagery Control.
> ## Natalie's Rating, 3/10

**Natalie** scored herself a three on this pathway. She realised that all too often she used her imagination to set herself up for failure.

In essence, Natalie scripted, edited and produced her own video nasties - movies of the mind in which she saw, felt and heard herself suffer sporting defeat and humiliation.

Her 'Inner Tarantino' would splatter these images through her mind in the run up to competition. Not surprisingly, her subsequent performances were poor. Then, as if to torture herself further, Natalie would replay these performances through her mind *after* competition. All-in-all, her imagination had became a potent tool of self-sabotage.

These video nasties didn't appear in isolation. They were frequently triggered by Natalie's fear of failure, ridicule and loneliness. She would regularly engage in *what if* thinking and became highly skilled at finding threat in benign situations.

Natalie clearly had a network of core beliefs which fed her negative self-talk, defeatist imagery and anxiety. By the time I met her, she was consumed by all of these things.

In terms of sporting performances, Natalie's personal best on the pole vault had remained static for over a year. She felt embarrassed, believing that everyone was talking about her downfall. When her main rival began making significant progress, Natalie felt she could no longer endure the psychological pain.  It was at this point, that she contacted me for help with her mental game.

## The Role of YouMinus in Natalie's Mental Game

As with Iain before her, Natalie had also developed unhelpful beliefs and rules about life. One, in particular, gave birth to her mental monster.

From an early age, Natalie's overprotective but well-meaning mother, had insisted the world was a dangerous place. Although this opinion was verbalised in various ways, the central message was not lost on Natalie. Through time, a sense of vulnerability engulfed her.

By the age of ten, Natalie had turned into a highly anxious kid and prolific worrier; traits that she would 'colour in' with vivid imagery. And behold, her YouMinus was born!

Although Natalie's YouMinus urged her to avoid risk and discomfort, to her credit, she would frequently push on regardless. In fact, had it not been for this mindset, she wouldn't have attended the pole vault trials at school and discovered her untapped potential for the sport.

For a while, all seemed well in Natalie's sporting world - until the stakes were raised. Having moved up the rankings sufficiently, she began to compete at intervarsity and national levels.

The perceived magnitude of this contextual shift brought her YouMinus out of the shadows. It was darn sure she wasn't going to make a fool of herself at this higher level. Consequently, it alerted Natalie to the potential for disgrace and failure by commandeering her interpretive and imagery systems.

Suddenly, or so it seemed, the belief laid down by her mother in her early years re-surfaced, and her sense of vulnerability was laid bare. Competition had now become Natalie's 'dangerous place' and before she knew it, she'd incarcerated herself in the prison without walls called FEAR.

Her fear of failure and public scorn escalated quickly, and was soon affecting her preparation for competition. She fixated on making mistakes and bombing-out and regularly ran mental movies that upheld her worst fears. These images were so vivid that Natalie felt it inevitable that she would fail and let everyone down.

She was seldom ready to compete as her arousal levels were simply too high. Though she would carry on, her anxiety and tension undermined her focusing ability and led to a spate of underperformances. At the end of her tether, Natalie believed her only option was to give up the sport. The mental ache was too much.

She felt cornered and was starting to obsess, more and more, about what other people must be thinking.

Natalie's mental monster was doing what it does best. It was forcing her to retreat from the threat of public derision and personal failure by persuading her to abandon her sport NOW! It was selling her the option of a life devoid of fulfilment. Natalie, however, was having none of it and decided to fight back.

As you'll find out **in Chapter 8**, she overcame her mental game difficulties by becoming much more positive in the way she prepared for competition. Central to this, was her newfound ability to control her imagination for a competitive advantage, rather than employing it as a method of self-sabotage.

> **GRANT, 28, Professional Ice hockey player**
> **Pathway to Emotional Control.**
> **Grant's Rating, 2/10**

**Grant** settled on a rating of two to represent his ability to control his emotions. He had stumbled around in the dark for far too long with this one and was beset by physical and cognitive anxiety in the locker room.

This 28 year old ice hockey forward felt as if his emotions were calling all the shots.

His anxiety suddenly grew in anticipation of face-off. Yet it hadn't always been that way - far from it, in fact. In his late teens, Grant had been a rising star in his native Canada with several big North American clubs watching his progress. Although he was eventually signed up by a top team, he struggled to break through.

After a few bit-part appearances in the NHL, he moved to a lower league.

While disappointed at not making it in the NHL, Grant still enjoyed his hockey and was a popular player with all the clubs he played for over the years.

By the early 2000s, Grant had got married and was a father to three children under five. He was considering his career options and a possible return to third level education when, out-of-the-blue, he received an enquiry from a team in the UK Superleague (today's Elite League).

Both the team's manager and coach believed he'd be a perfect replacement for one of their players, who had shocked them by returning home to Finland. It was thought that Grant with his skill, experience and personality would be a big hit for the franchise as well as with the team's demanding fans.

To cut a long story short, Grant uprooted his family and moved to the United Kingdom. While his host club treated him well and smoothed the transition, he never fully settled.   He also thought that his wife and kids were unhappy.

Yet there was hockey to be played and Grant had to put his 'game-face' on and become the next big thing at the club. Expectations were high and soon he began to experience bouts of acute anxiety, especially on game day. His nervousness was too pronounced to be of any use to him and as a result his performances on the ice suffered. After four successive below par games, his confidence took a tumble. He began to doubt his ability to play and found family life hard to deal with. Soon he became moody and withdrawn.

The alarming thing for Grant was that over the years, he had always felt ready to play and in more demanding leagues to the one he was currently competing in. He would have felt excited on game day and was always set to hit the ice.

But that was in the past. Things were patently different now and he didn't know what to do. And neither did his coach. They had placed a lot of faith in their acquisition, and he simply wasn't living up to the expectation. At the end of the day, it was all about money, bums on seats and results. Grant realised this of course, which did little to assuage his anxiety or improve his performances.

As is frequently the case, the club contacted me when the situation had hit crisis point. By the time I met him, Grant was getting less and less ice time and his displays were below average. His inability to control symptoms of over-arousal before games was showing up with insipid first period performances.

Too much energy had been expended in the locker room, eaten up by rampant anxiety. By face-off he was often drained. Grant was right, the tail *was* wagging the dog and something had to be done.

## The Role of YouMinus in Grant's Mental Game

So how was Grant's mental monster ripping up the form book and turning him into a shadow of his former self? Well, for one of those rare times in his life, Grant began to attach his self-worth to external things. He hung his self-esteem hat on the hook of public acclaim (like Aaron, above) and was keen to meet the expectations of his new paymasters. But this weighed heavily on his ego and as a result his YouMinus urged him to escape all the hassle his situation was bringing.

Over-arousal and doubt are two key YouMinus weapons, in this regard. The mental discomfort created can be so pronounced that avoiding a situation can seem the healthier option. And this is exactly how Grant felt. His YouMinus was in such control that he was willing to return home to Canada after only three-and-a-half months of a two year contact. This was a lot to give up - but the urge was there. When it was all whittled down, Grant would have been heading home simply because his ego couldn't cope with the perceived opinions of other people. He told me:

> **"I was worried about what they [the supporters] thought of me – this so-called big name coming over to fill the gap left by last season's hero"**

> **"I'd be in the locker room Doc and my mind would be racing through all this negative stuff - *I better play well tonight. Must score early. Mustn't lie back. Must get stuck-in...* Then, as I sat there, I'd hear the crowd and the music. With 10 minutes to face-off I'd be shaking, f\*\*kin' shaking. And I'd think to myself - if I have a bad game again, it's all over!"**

Ironically, by focusing too heavily on other people's expectations, Grant allowed his attention to stray from the only means of meeting those expectations - **knowing his role and preparing his mind and body to execute it**.

You'll discover **at the end of Chapter 9**, that this irony wasn't lost on Grant, as he set about regaining control over his mental and emotional states. Okay, are you ready? You're on the cusp of something big here. You are now about to enter the *Six Pathways to Mental Toughness*. It represents a journey and an incomparable opportunity to build an exceptional mental game!

# Part Two

## Mental Game Action

*As a single footstep will not make a path on the earth, so a single thought will not make a pathway in the mind. To make a deep physical path, we walk again and again. To make a deep mental path, we must think over and over the kind of thoughts we wish to dominate our lives.*

**- Henry David Thoreau**

# The Six Pathways to Mental Toughness Programme©

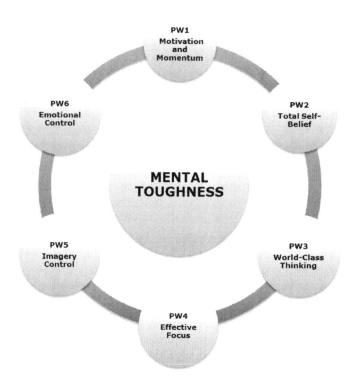

# Introduction to **Part Two**

So often times it happens

That we live our lives in chains

And we never even know we have the key

- **The Eagles**, *Already Gone*, 1974

## It's Time to Unlock Your Potential

In Part Two, you will find solutions to the problems imposed by the Frankenstein Factor. *The Six Pathways to Mental Toughness*© programme offers you six highly effective training modules that will move your mental game further and further away from the grip of your inner monster.

As mental toughness is a fusion of *learned* skills, you must treat the programme in Part Two as you would your physical and technical training. It takes planning, persistence and patience. In the same way as your fitness and technique only prosper under purposeful practice, so too with your mental game development. While each of the following six chapters is a standalone training system in its own right, it is the combined effect of the Pathways that will take your mental game to an entirely new level.

Having profiled your mental game in the last chapter, you now know the starting point for your journey to mental toughness and the distance you've yet to travel.

Remember, as with studying for an exam, you shouldn't just keep revising the stuff you already know. Yes, consolidate it, but get on with strengthening the weaker areas. After all, you are going to be tested on these too. So, for instance, if you prioritised 'Effective Focus' for immediate attention, then you should head straight to Pathway 3. Once there, you should begin by reading the chapter through in its entirety to gain an overall feel for the training involved, what's expected of you and the benefits to be had.

Approach the set exercises (i.e. the Pathway Pit Stops) with openness, honesty and enthusiasm. Also, have a notebook to-hand to jot down key insights as you travel along each pathway.

You'll notice at the top of each chapter there is a section headed 'Monster Watch'. The purpose here is to hit you straight away with how YouMinus sabotages your motivation, self-belief, thoughts, focus, imagination and emotions.

By reminding you of your true opponent at the outset, I hope to inspire you to work hard to defeat it. (Just as Rick, Aaron, Taylor, Iain, Natalie and Grant have all done). You met these guys, just now, in Chapter 3, where they detailed their specific mental game difficulties.

In Part Two, you will find out how they resolved them.

With its numerous skills, strategies and practical tasks, the Pathways programme is like no other. By targeting the brain's most influential systems, it offers you the chance for real and enduring mental game change. It is quite frankly, a rewiring system for mental toughness. You'll be taking YouMinus out by the roots! The six chapters in Part Two are:

- **Pathway to Motivation and Momentum** (Chapter 4)

- **Pathway to Total Self-Belief** (Chapter 5)

- **Pathway to World Class Thinking** (Chapter 6)

- **Pathway to Effective Focus** (Chapter 7)

- **Pathway to Imagery Control** (Chapter 8)

- **Pathway to Emotional Control** (Chapter 9)

Each pathway chapter concludes with a summary of the main issues and learning points.

# Chapter 4

## PATHWAY 1

# PATHWAY TO

# MOTIVATION & MOMENTUM

Believe that a further shore

is reachable from here

**- Seamus Heaney**, *The Cure at Troy*

By the end of Pathway 1, you will have:

- Understood the decisive role motivation plays in mental toughness, peak performance and meeting your sporting goals.

- Discovered how your mental monster twists your motivation for its own ends.

- Found out the difference between internal and external motivation.

- Learned how to remain motivated in the face of adversity.

- Learned how to attain your optimal level of motivation at will.

- Discovered how to set highly effective goals using the cutting edge PUMAA system.

- Been introduced to a method of training that will maximise your efforts to meet your sporting goals. That will transform you from an also-ran into a world-beater!

- Caught up with Rick, a case study from Chapter 3.

The cornerstone of mental toughness is motivation. Without an intense desire to succeed and the capacity to persist in the face of setbacks, it is almost impossible to turn sporting dreams into reality.

Select any one of the world's top athletes and you find a performer driven from within. He trains and competes for intrinsic reasons. He is his own person, a single-minded artisan of his sport, who pursues greatness in an orderly fashion.

Major goals are broken down into manageable chunks and he pushes the boundaries of his ability through focused training.

Always keen to improve his all-round ability and to build-up momentum, this self-driven athlete seeks out regular feedback from the best coaches and trainers available to him. No stone is left unturned in his pursuit of excellence.

He is, however, under no illusion - the pathway to world-class ability is paved with hard work and adversity.

As a result, he prepares for these moments, ensuring that he responds to misfortune by redoubling his efforts to succeed. His strong support team and family act as invaluable stress-absorbers during these times.

This athlete is not conceited. He knows that the best athletes on the planet surround themselves with genuine and capable people.

Follow Pathway 1 and you, too, will have an inner drive - the kind enjoyed by the world's best athletes.

# MONSTER WATCH

## How YouMinus Attacks Your Motivation

YouMinus would prefer you didn't try to better yourself. Actually, it demands it. Its mantra is "stay as you are". Positive change threatens YouMinus' very existence. It exposes it to uncertainty - and boy does it hate that! It also realises that if you do make great strides, it'll be seen for the malevolent 'spin doctor' it is. Its lies will be laid bare. In fact, the moment you realise you're capable of massive success and fulfilment, is the moment YouMinus starts to die.

Given the threat to its survival, YouMinus uses all sorts of tricks to dissuade you from making progress in your sport. It will attack your inner drive, as this is the power pack for your transformation. Its goal is to extract the batteries that make change possible. It wants your heart, your soul and your spirit.

At times of change, YouMinus takes over your language, imagery and interpretive systems, in an all out con trick to convince you that you're incapable of attaining success. It'll do all it can to persuade you that good things don't happen to people like you. That you're no superstar; that you're a loser - that people like you shouldn't dream big dreams. It will urge you to play it safe; reminding you that being risk-averse has served you well up to now: "You mightn't be a super athlete, but hey, you're still alive, aren't you?" That's the deal YouMinus serves up – the status quo.

Let's look more closely at the five key ways your mental monster tries to control you.

## 5-PRONGED ATTACK

### Thoughts

You'll know YouMinus is asserting itself, whenever you catch yourself engaging in such self-sabotaging activity as negative self talk: "I'll never be able to do it, it's too difficult"; "I'm simply not good enough"; "What will people think if I fail?"; "I'll let people down, if I don't make it"; "I'll never be able to change"; "Greatness doesn't happen to people like me. I'm a 'no-hoper'".

### Images

You'll know YouMinus has hijacked your imagery system, when you find you're spending time 'seeing' and 'feeling' yourself fail and facing ridicule.

## Emotions

YouMinus will also try to discourage you by playing with your emotions. It knows that high anxiety and bodily tension can lead to avoidance. It's equally aware that lethargy can also worry an athlete into just not bothering or giving up.

## Behaviour

With such a build-up of negative thinking, defeatist imagery and the subsequent agitation or dulling of emotions, YouMinus has got you pretty well tied-up. It'll take huge delight in such behavioural signs, as you missing training sessions to avoid being selected for the team, or feigning injury or illness to get your excuses in early. And it will do cartwheels of delight when you party the night before a big game.

Why?

Because it knows you're moving towards failure. It knows that it's on the cusp of taking your motivation out at its core.

And it whispers, *Gotcha!!*

## Tactic of Last Resort

If YouMinus cannot sufficiently dampen your motivation, it will, as a last resort, ensure you're motivated by pleasing other people and by other forms of external reward.

In this way, it knows that during barren periods, you will become frustrated and despondent. You will be unable to sustain momentum.

*Gotcha* - again!

# FROM PROFILING TO PROGRESS

## Raising the Pulse of Purpose

In the last chapter, you profiled your mental skills and, possibly for the first time, gained an insight into the strengths and weaknesses of your mental game.

You now know the distance you've yet to travel along the six pathways to mental toughness. You have, in effect, drawn a big red arrow on your mental game map saying, *I AM HERE!*

Profiling has helped you prioritise the key areas to work on. You now have a clearer vision of what you need to do to improve your performance in training and competition. The platform for mental skill training has been laid down. The next stage then, is to translate your profiling information into goal-setting activity. Why goal-setting activity?

Well, as the Chinese proverb goes, 'talk doesn't cook the rice'. In other words, intention alone isn't enough – you need to TAKE ACTION!

Your motivation to improve mentally should now be starting to rev up. The first seeds of momentum should be growing and you should be starting to experience a rise in your *pulse of purpose*. Good, because you need to.

Without purpose and direction you have nothing. Life becomes flat and meaningless. However, having something to aim for, something your heart truly desires, ignites the inbuilt human spark to get the job done.

This spark is a human given - a gift ready to catch fire. It put the first man on the moon, broke the four minute mile, and brought Jenner and the vaccination for smallpox together.

Indeed, it brought you to sport and I trust it will continue to flame your desire to improve and reach the top.

Motivation is the basis of success in sport, as well as in life. It moves you from where you are now to where you want to be. And as this journey will have troughs to it as well as peaks, then only the highly-driven will keep going when setbacks occur. But a high level of motivation is not enough on its own. The source of that drive needs to be *internal*, as opposed to external.

## INTERNAL DRIVE

It is more important to be motivated to succeed, for the pleasure and satisfaction it provides you, than for a host of externally-sourced incentives. It should be about self-growth, mastery and satisfaction for a job well done. It should be about *wanting* to do the hard yards, not *having* to do them. And it should be about the love of competing, rather than the fear of failure.

All of this could be said of world number one handball player, Paul Brady. This modest genius is one of the most driven and focused athletes I have ever worked with. It's not surprising that many consider Paul to be one of the greatest athletes in world sport today.

Just read what he has to say about his motivation.

His considered yet passionate approach to his game is impressive:

> **"My primary motivations for playing handball are definitely intrinsic. I am motivated by a deep-rooted desire to achieve something unique in life and if I'm honest, an underlying need to achieve great things. I constantly remind myself that you only live once so I want to make the most of life.**

**I want to leave a sporting legacy long after I am finished and to raise the standard of the sport to where it has never been before. Records are meant to be broken; limits are there to be pushed and I love the challenge of trying to do just that"**

**Paul Brady** - *Personal communication, 04.06.10*

## Taking pleasure in the little things that make up a performance

The mentally tough athlete is process-focused. This means he attends to what he is doing right now and aims to do it well. This is the wellspring of his motivation; gaining satisfaction from executing each element of a performance, as best he can.

Instead of pinning his motivation on the outcome of his display on the pitch, course or court, he realises that the final result is merely the accumulation of all the little things done well during a performance.

This is the approach taken by England World Cup winning cricketer, Claire Taylor:

**"I concentrate on the smaller things. The motivation comes through striking the ball well, being able to control an innings and being able to bat. So rather than being motivated by the benefits that come from being known in cricket, I am motivated more by playing well and that's what keeps me going."**

**Claire Taylor -** *Raise Your Game*

Incidentally, Taylor's motivational compass was once 180 degrees away from this process-mentality. She used to base her worth as a person, on what she had achieved in cricket. As a result, her self-esteem and motivation would rise and fall, depending on how well she was doing. Attaching your self-esteem to outcomes is dangerous territory; which is why this cricketing star consulted a sport psychologist:

> **"We [Taylor and her psychologist] talked about my dependence on cricket for self-esteem. When the cricket was going really well, I was really happy and everything would be great, but when the cricket was going really badly, I became unhappy and I found it really difficult to motivate myself."**

## Enjoyment – it is allowed you know!

Have you been brought up with the *sacrifice culture*? That to do well in your sport you "must make sacrifices"? Well if you have, the implicit message is one of deferring enjoyment - make your sacrifices, do the work, accomplish your goals and *then* you can start to live and enjoy life.

It goes against all logic to believe that by *not enjoying* something you'll get better at it! Yet this appears to be the motivational lever used by many coaches on their protégés. It is my strong belief that enjoyment, happiness and success can coexist.

While an ambitious athlete must trim around the edges of their social life and diet, such manicuring is a positive thing, *not* a sacrifice. It is hyperbole to use such a term as sacrifice.

> **"'Sacrifice' seems like such a strong word to me because I wouldn't say I've sacrificed anything. If I didn't enjoy what I do, I wouldn't do it. I feel I've made the right choices in the way I've lived my life."**
>
> ***Liam Tancock** - BBC SPORT*

As with Olympic swimming ace Tancock, top Welsh European Tour player, Rhys Davis, is yet another elite performer who doesn't view the hours of practice as some sort of life forfeit. Rather, this young golfer asserts that "I'm happy to put in hard work and graft."

You have already heard from Carolina Kluft in Chapter 2, when we examined mental toughness in detail. You'll recall that this Olympic champion changed discipline from the heptathlon to the long jump, doing so to rekindle her motivation and enjoyment. This demonstration of mental strength was built on two things.

Firstly, Kluft was being true to herself. While the sporting public and media were shocked by her decision, especially as it occurred on the eve of the Beijing Games, Kluft knew herself well and trusted her instinct.

Secondly, Kluft was only too aware that for athletes to be successful, they must enjoy training and competing, not for the adulation or rewards to be had afterwards, but for the intrinsic glow that is fired up during the process.

> **"For me, medals have never been the main motivation. I train all year round and do every practice because I am competitive and I enjoy it, not because of the medals."**
> **Carolina Kluft** - *Tom Fordyce Blog, 19.05.10*

I find that, like Kluft, many of my top performers also speak of enjoying the cut and thrust of competition. They tell me that mental training has reignited their love for their sport. Being released from the grip of YouMinus interference has freed up their minds, and they begin to experience the levels of excitement and joy they used to feel, when starting out in their sport.

I think you'd agree, that of all the top rugby players in the world, Tommy Bowe performs with the freedom of a man who loves life, who appreciates the moment he's in and who revels in playing the sport he loves on the big stage. The pleasure in Tommy's eyes and his beaming smile upon scoring one of his trademark tries, is testament to this.

> **"I play rugby because growing up I had a strong love for the game. I still have that love and am more passionate about it than ever."**
>
> **Tommy Bowe -** *Personal communication, 01.04.10*

And Tommy is not alone, of course. Just listen to athletics legend Lord Coe, Scottish international rugby star Simon Danielli and skeleton bobsleigh Olympic gold medallist, Amy Williams. To a man and a woman, they each passionately emphasise the need for inner motivation.

- *Lord Sebastian Coe* ... and enjoyment

**"Motivation isn't something that you can shout into somebody by standing at the side of the track. It is internally driven. "My motivation was simply that I really enjoyed what I did. I enjoyed racing, I enjoyed training and I enjoyed the environment that I was in. If I hadn't enjoyed it, I would have probably gone on to do something entirely different"**

*Raise Your Game, BBC Website*

- *Simon Danielli*... and enjoyment

> **"I think there are many reasons why I play sport, but first and foremost is enjoyment. I experience intrinsic enjoyment in the sport itself, but also the enjoyment of competing and trying to beat an opponent"**
>
> *Personal communication, 19.05.10*

- **_Amy Williams_** ...and enjoyment

> **"You have ups and downs in sport and unless you really enjoy what you're doing, you won't ever get through those times"**
>
> _Raise Your Game, BBC Website_

Up and coming surfer, Ronan Oertzen, is equally sure that a love for his sport is a key ingredient in his rapid progress. This young athlete is literally making waves on the surfing scene.

> **"I always keep pushing myself to achieve the best that I can. I just love to surf and compete. I entered my first event after only six months and came 2$^{nd}$"**
>
> _Quiksilver.com_

I think these guys are trying to tell you something here... wonder what it is? - Oh yeah - ENJOY YOURSELF OUT THERE!

## This time next year...

You know even Del Boy, of _Only Fools and Horses_ fame, came to realise that the process was the enjoyable, motivating and truly important part of the journey; not the outcome.

Even if that outcome was to become super-rich: "I always wanted to be a millionaire. Always wanted a Rolls Royce, big house in the country, jet off to the Caribbean and all that...But it's not like I thought it would be.

All the dreaming and the scheming and the trying... that was the fun part... I want to feel like I used to feel; all eager and alive." (Del Boy, _Time On Our Hands_, 1996).

## Self-driven and sensible

Although captaining his own ship, the internally-motivated athlete is a pragmatist. He seeks out guidance and support when appropriate, and accepts errors and hardship as an expected part of the deal, rather than as insults to his ego. Jenson Button, the 2009 world F1 champion, is such a performer.

Button is a realist who knows that life's experiences are not a linear affair. Each day isn't always better than the one before. Similarly, each qualifying session or race isn't going to outdo the previous qualifying session or race. For Button, 'the slings and arrows of outrageous fortune' are only ever a chicane or two away. The solution though, is to persist in the face of adversity and not to kid yourself that misfortune will always pass you by.

> **"You have to realise that not every day is going to be a good day, sometimes you have bad days, and you've just got to fight through them, if you really love it that much. You have to be dedicated and always think of yourself as learning. You're always learning. I'm learning and I'm in F1."**
> **Jenson Button**, *Raise Your Game, BBC Website*

As with our athletes above, Button also testifies to the importance of loving what he does and viewing the totality of his sporting experience as teaching him something precious. This F1 superstar realises that if we only learn from the good times, then we limit what we learn.

Clearly, the athlete who runs his sporting experience from the inside has a motivation that is self-perpetuating. He doesn't have to wait for a particular outcome to occur before feeling worthy and driven. Now while this is the ideal motivational state, you'll be only too aware that there are many performers out there, maybe even yourself, who compete primarily to attain external admiration and fiscal rewards. These are the athletes who love to bathe in the afterglow of their success. Who flash their cash and buy eight cars, when one would do.

In today's ego-soaked society, realising your fifteen minutes of fame has never been easier. And for many, sport is a gateway to such celebrity.

# EXTERNAL DRIVE

As emphasised at the beginning of the chapter, your motivation can be heavily influenced by your YouMinus and its need for control and acclaim. You may discover that, far from being motivated from within, much of what you do in life, is to meet the expectations and goals of *other* people: parents, peer group and coaches, to name but a few. If you recognise yourself as being *externally* driven, then be assured, your YouMinus is calling the shots. Just ask Danny. He knows this only too well!

## Danny

'Danny' met me in the restaurant of Belfast's grandest hotel, the Europa - a citadel of toughness itself, having been bombed on a regular basis throughout 'The Troubles'.

As with many footballers labelled as aggressive or hostile, Danny, a six-foot-two bruiser, came across all sweetness and light.

Softly spoken, mannerly and gracious, he met me with a firm handshake, let me select a suitably private table, and ordered up two hot teas to melt away the cold of a bitter November's night. At heart, Danny was clearly a gentleman – he was intelligent, pleasant and affable. I was curious as to how this presentation could sit, cheek-by-jowl, with the stories I'd read about him, and his fall from grace. He was currently stagnating in his team's reserves, and 'The Sword of Damocles' hung over his career - an inch or so from it, it seemed.

Once we settled-down at our table and began chatting, Danny's demeanour changed significantly. The lustre of his early interaction had given way to darkness. I soon realised that he was in big trouble, that his life was spiralling downwards, out-of-control.

A centre-forward with a top British club, Danny was in meltdown. Now 23, he was but an echo of his younger footballing self. Signed by his club at 18, he displayed the smooth, unruffled prowess of a footballer in control of his mind and body. He joined the club highly motivated, worked hard and earned a starting place in the first team. He never looked back over the next three years.

Leading scorer for his team, Danny's stock rose exponentially. He was acclaimed at the top table of celebrity culture and his life, on paper, seemed better than ever. He ticked all the celeb boxes: the money, the looks, the car, the apartment, the model girlfriends and the media coverage.

By age 21, Danny had the world at his feet.

However, over the next couple of years, he unwittingly crossed the line of complacency and conceit, to a life of no meaning, failure and regret. Performances on the pitch deteriorated as off the pitch he lived the life of an in-demand VIP. When it comes to ego-enhancing monikers, 'Very Important Person' is right up there with 'Your Majesty'! Caught up in himself and his perceived importance and indispensability, he felt it unnecessary to train as he used to.

He was Danny after all and that was good enough. In fact on entering the changing rooms on match day, he could be heard shouting out, "Danny's here. All will be well lads".

He had never really been this sort of conceited lad, but all the attention had clearly gone to his head: clearly something malevolent was stirring inside.

The young mannerly guy I met in the foyer of the Europa that night was the real, authentic Danny. But something had taken over. The genuine Danny was under the thumb of a mental force that was now running his performances and life.

At that first meeting, I introduced him to his mental monster, the malevolent puppeteer that now ran his world.

I explained that it was behind his vanity and self-righteousness. That it was distracting him from the very mindset that made him an attractive prospect at eighteen, and turned him into an awesome footballer, who performed with grit, flair and fun at the highest level.

Danny's star had faded rapidly.

He was in and out of the team the season before our meeting and was close to being put up for sale. Managers from the lower leagues were sniffing around, but tentatively so, as they were wary of his increasing aggression and bad behaviour both on and off the pitch.

Sent off on three occasions and with only one goal in eight matches, he placed his manager in a difficult position.

But credit to his gaffer, he didn't make a hasty decision. He still saw what I saw, the real Danny. But clearly help was needed.

At the time of our meeting in early November, he was back in the reserves. He had started on the bench for the first team at the beginning of that season, but he couldn't even maintain that spot.

There was a certain inevitability about it all. He was on his way down and out, unless...

The 'unless' for Danny was to "get his bloody head sorted out or be put out". His manager's words, not mine. This plea-cum-threat, eventually led to our meeting up.

I'm pleased to tell you that within five weeks of us meeting, Danny was back in his first team doing what he did best. Playing well and scoring goals.

He got rid of the sycophants and fair-weather friends, became disciplined again, and touched base with his roots by returning home for a week with his family.

I also asked him to speak to the kids at his old school. Again, this was to bring him back to ground level and lift his head out of the noxious clouds of celebrity life.

In sport, external motivation can certainly kick-start your efforts, but it has a short half-life as Danny's case bears out. If your motivation for performing and competing is primarily to attain external rewards (public adulation, media coverage, money, status and so on), then it will become increasingly difficult for you to bounce back from adversity and to sustain your drive and momentum.

After all, your motivation is dependent on events outside of you, which places the control of your emotional and mental state, in the hands of other people. This is why many of us can feel a deep sense of anticlimax after attaining a major goal. Once the praise and recognition die down, we are left with ourselves and what ensues, is often a distinct blunting of mood and a strong sense of "now what?" All of a sudden, life seems rudderless.

## FROM THE EXTERNAL TO THE INTERNAL

Camilo Villegas is a superb golfer. The 28 year old Colombian hit the ground running in his rookie year on the American PGA Tour. In 2006, Villegas amassed $1.7 million; not bad for a first year's return. And there was more to come the following season, when he won almost $1.9 million. He achieved eight top ten finishes that year.

Villegas' first win in the United States came a year later in 2008 - the BMW Championship - followed shortly by his second tournament victory, The Tour Championship. Life was good for the young South American.

Not only was Villegas attracting attention for his phenomenal talent as a golfer, but he was also receiving rave reviews in *People* magazine about his good looks and his eligibility as a single guy or, as the media put it, one of sport's "hottest bachelors (with) more screaming female fans than Justin Timberlake".

## "Where did it all go wrong Camilo?"

It's hard to believe that this question is necessary at all. It seems as tongue-in-cheek as the legendary question aimed at George Best in his heyday.

If you aren't aware of this story, it goes something like this.

A hotel bellboy delivers vintage champagne to George's room. As the waiter opens the door, he is met with the sight of the soccer superstar in bed with a naked Miss World; Mary Stavin, I believe. And strewn across the duvet, are tens of thousands of pounds, won in the hotel's casino earlier in the evening.

Upon seeing all of this, the bellboy enquires, "Mr Best, where did it all go wrong?"

We know that George loved the high life, the glamour and the range of other external rewards that came with being the best footballer on the planet. Unfortunately, we also know that this shy Belfast boy succumbed to his alcoholism at the relatively young age of 59.

When you are handsome, as George Best undoubtedly was, young and the most talented footballer in the world, then it is almost inevitable that your motivational compass turns towards the external. We saw this with Danny above, and it seems that it beset Camilo Villegas to some degree too. 'The Lure of the External,' as I call it, started to interfere with his golf.

However, Villegas had the foresight to seek assistance to address the issue, before it took legs and ran away with his career. He teamed up with Florida-based golf psychologist Dr Gio Valiante and together they turned things around, resetting Villegas' motivational dial to INTRINSIC.

## 'Attitude of Gratitude'

Villegas took a step back and noted his privileged position. He realised that he had become too caught-up in results, rather than focusing on the process of great play. He had been seduced by outcomes and began to beat himself up for failing to reproduce his 2008 form.

In an interview with Mark Williams, of pgatour.com, Villegas described his new 'attitude of gratitude' as a mindset that shifted his focus back to enjoying his golf again:

'Villegas coined the phrase 'Attitude of Gratitude' with his mental coach Gio Valiante. "...this is, I believe, my fifth year on TOUR. When you're a rookie, you've got nothing to lose. You come out here, you're trying to have fun, trying to play good golf, and you're a little more free. Five years later, I mean, won a couple times, got to seven in the world, obviously a lot of distractions, media, World Rankings, all the stuff that starts coming around, and it just distracts you. I was getting a little too concerned with my World Ranking position and the Money List and this and that, and I just got a little tight on the golf course. So I needed to put all those things aside and remember that I'm playing golf for a living, and there's a million people out there that would love to be in my shoes and have fun with it."'

*Mark Williams*, pgatour.com, Feb. 25, 2010

In a profound demonstration of our need to be grateful for what we have, Villegas went on to win the 2010 Honda Classic within a month of his attitudinal adjustment.

It seems that an 'attitude of gratitude' is a weapon against YouMinus interference. The moment you appreciate the opportunity you have in front of you, is the moment you kick mental interference to the kerb. While we're on the subject, what are you grateful for in your life? Do you appreciate that life is a gift? Or do you tend to take it for granted? In a similar vein, do you see training and competing in your sport as a privilege or as a right?

## MEASURE YOUR MOTIVATION

In light of what we have covered so far, I would now like you to assess your own motivation, in terms of its *force* and *source*.

Remember, the strength and source of your motivation is key and that only the highly motivated, internally-driven athlete, is set up for success.

## Look, Use The Force

So, how highly motivated are you to attain success in your sport? What is the *force* or strength of your desire; your degree of commitment to do all that needs to be done to meet your sporting goals?

Not sure?

Then carry out the following assessment exercise, which will guide your analysis.

### Pathway Pitstop 1.1

**Force**

Rate your *Motivation to Succeed* on a simple zero to ten scale, with a '10' indicating that you're *very highly motivated*, and a '0' signifying you're *very poorly motivated*.

Make a note of your assessment score, before then examining your response to a deeper level. Let's say you rate the strength of your motivation as a '6'. You would then take some time out to consider what needs to change, in order for the rating to increase.

For instance, how would you know that your motivation had reached an '8' on this scale? Consider changes to your thoughts, attitude, feelings and behaviour. It may be also be useful to have a chat with your coach about this.

## Location, Location, Location –
## The source of your motivation

Jones and Moorhouse, in their 2008 book, *Developing Mental Toughness,* depict motivation on a spectrum that ranges from, *total internal motivation* to *total external motivation*; and that for every task we do, we approach it from some point on this scale. So depending on the assignment at-hand, we might be highly self-motivated to succeed, doing it for the enjoyment, sense of mastery and intrinsic buzz; or we may instead feel we must do it solely for the external rewards to be had. Indeed, how many of us go to work simply for the cheque at the end of the month, and not for personal growth, enjoyment and the love of the job? Probably millions of us. This would explain why many employees retire with no real improvement in their skill level, even after decades in a particular job.

**Table 3:** Characteristics of External and Internal Motivation

| TOTAL EXTERNAL MOTIVATION: Key Characteristics | TOTAL INTERNAL MOTIVATION: Key Characteristics |
|---|---|
| HERE THE ATHLETE is motivated by external enticements, such as fame, status, recognition, one-upmanship, approval, praise, trophies, money and gifts. The tangible and ego rewards are *everything* to this athlete. **Advantages** Being motivated by outside factors can generate some initial progress. **Disadvantages** External motivation is unsustainable, as its control lies outside of the athlete himself. When external rewards are absent, then the athlete has nothing to fall back on. Accordingly, his enthusiasm diminishes and his efforts to reach his goals stagnate. | HERE THE ATHLETE is motivated from the inside. His satisfaction comes from the activities he engages in. His goals are personal to him. He owns them, is accountable for their realisation, and he enjoys the work involved. He trains in a systematic and purposeful way. **Advantages** Internal motivation generates self-sufficiency, persistence, and a get-up-and-go approach to training and development. There is a sense of freedom as the athlete is not shackled by a needy ego. He is his own person, connected to all that he does. **Disadvantages** None! |

You have assessed the force of your motivation; now take a few minutes to assess its SOURCE (Pathway Pitstop 1.2).

The location of your motivation will have a profound effect on your capacity to meet big goals, to persist during training and to attain powerful performances in competition.

## Pathway Pitstop 1.2

### Source

Read the synopses of the two extremes of motivation provided in Table 3 above and, as you do so, consider your own motivation. Then place an **X** along the continuum, below, where the source of your motivation lies.

**Total External Internal Motivation**                    **Total Motivation**

Okay, so where does your supply of motivation come from? Somewhere around the centre of the continuum, maybe? Or do you know darn rightly, that you crave rewards from the outside world (from people and things), and therefore you placed your **X** firmly towards the far left?

Perhaps you're a self-sufficient and assured individual who, though enjoying the fruits of your success, gains most from the intrinsic rewards to be had. If you are, then I guess you placed the source of your motivation much further to the right.

Jones and Moorhouse explain that the further to the left side of this continuum you are "the more pressure and stress there is to perform, and the harder it is to recover from setbacks...Mental toughness, therefore, is not associated with the left hand side...It is about ensuring continuous learning, persistence, interest, creativity, energy, well-being, sense of competence, autonomy and belonging that grow as you move towards the right hand end of the continuum" (2008, p128).

While the ideal is to be 100 percent motivated from within, it's best to concede that as we're human this is an unrealistic goal.

So it's about maximising the internal and keeping to a minimum the influence of the external.

## Bit of both

Be reassured, even those at the top of their sport can be seduced by the lure of the external. Interviewed by BBC SPORT, European Tour golfer and Ryder Cup star, Paul McGinley, courageously concedes that while the force and source of his motivation is strongly internal, there is a part of him that's enticed by the glitz, glamour and glory that can come with playing golf at the highest level:

> **"The big motivation for me was to see how good I could get. Ego was probably part of it too, as you want to play in those big occasions and you want to win big events."**
>
> *Lessons from the Legends, BBC SPORT*

Simon Danielli is similarly motivated. Like McGinley, he plays his sport for largely intrinsic reasons, but at the professional level there are external rewards that are understandably attractive and important to him.

> **"I think any professional player would be lying if they did not acknowledge the individual element to team sport...**
> **Your talents and achievements will be recognized financially, which is a motivation when it is your source of employment."**
>
> *Personal communication, 19.05.10*

## Motivation Relocated

If you are too heavily focused on the external rewards to be had from your sport, and not on a journey of self-discovery, learning and advancement, you need to begin to relocate your motivation to your internal drive.

---

### Pathway Pitstop 1.3

#### Enjoying The Process Of Development

How could you more fully enjoy the process of achievement? Consider this question now, and note down your thoughts.

You should also have a chat with your coach about making training more fun. Remember, **top athletes** tend to view each training session as an end in itself. They look forward to it, engage in it and praise themselves for putting in a good shift. When they go home they bolster the intrinsic reward by recalling satisfying moments from their training session.

As hackneyed as it sounds, elite performers love their sport and delight in the process of improvement. They have learned that a fixation with the prize is a soulless pursuit and, ironically, takes their focus off the very process designed to get them there!

---

## GOAL-SETTING – WHY BOTHER?

'I have a method, a plan, a target. This
is why I'm a success'
**Jose Mourinho,** *Daily Mirror, 24.08.10*

Up to this point in the book, you have gained mind-changing information and insight in Chapters 1 and 2, profiled your mental game in Chapter 3, and prioritised those areas warranting immediate attention.

You are also aware that you need a high level of inner drive to translate your mental game assessment into tangible mental game gains. Not only this, but you also need an achievement plan to help you plot the course from where your mental ability is now, to where you want it to be.

The first step in bridging this gap is to set goals, effective goals. The simple fact is this: athletes who set effective goals are more successful than those who don't bother. Why? Because goals provide:

— Motivation, perseverance and momentum.
— A focus for your mind.
— A road map for action.
— The opportunity for powerful learning and self-growth.
— A gateway to tangible performance gains.
— An opportunity for enhancing your self-belief and zeal as progress is made.
— A route out of a rut.

World handball champion, Paul Brady, has no doubt that without goals athletes are left grabbing smoke. Effective goal-setting has provided Paul with the coordinates for his journey to sporting greatness:

> **"Goal setting forms the focal point of all my training, so obviously its importance cannot be underestimated. Without clear, specific goals I feel athletes are more or less 'feeling their way through the dark'. If I don't know where I am going or what it is I am trying to achieve, then I cannot possibly get there!"**
> ***Paul Brady*** *– Personal communication, 04.06.10*

In the following section you will be introduced to the PUMAA goal-setting system. The PUMAA method will enable you to develop the types of meaningful goals that will rally your resources to enhance your mental, technical, tactical and physical abilities.

The primary function of goal-setting is to make concrete your purpose; to give wings to your action. Without setting goals and taking action, your attention will be directionless. Your commitment and resolve will diminish and your chances of acquiring the necessary skills to reach the top will be negligible.

# Goals give wings to your action.

European flyweight boxing champion, Cathy Brown, draws a parallel between academic and athletic development. She says that structure is vital to making progress in both fields: "When I was at school, I'd have a timetable so I'd know that I'm revising such and such in the morning and such and such in the night. It's the same with boxing, it's so important to plan. I like to know what I'm doing for the week and what I need to achieve".

Brown contends that goals direct her focus, ensuring that she doesn't waste time prevaricating. If you've got a plan, you know exactly what you've got to do and you get on and you do it".

## Principles of Effective Goal-Setting

Goal-setting has made its way from the boardroom to the changing room. Born in the world of business, hence the propensity for nifty acronyms, goal-setting as a strategy, has filtered through into all areas where improvement is required and desired. Sport is an obvious place to find it, where performance and results are everything. Let's now examine the five keys to effective goal development. These five principles are set out below, in the guise of the PUMAA system, a more useful alternative to the ubiquitous and lightweight SMART procedure.

# THE **PUMAA** SYSTEM

If you use this system correctly, you will be able to declare that:

**"My goals are...**

**P**recise, **U**nderstood, **M**ine, **A**chievable and **A**djustable"

Now, let's take each of these five principles in turn and get to know them.

## ☑ **PRECISE**

For goals to be effective, you should describe in exact detail:

- What it is you want to achieve (use positive language).
- The benefit you'll gain from achieving the particular goal.
- The precise action you're going to take to develop the targeted skill or skill-set.
- How the goal is to be measured (after all, you need to know when you've attained it).
- The timeframe for achievement.
- The schedule of review and evaluation.

## Bowe and Brady apply the stepping stone approach

It is important too, that you set different types of goals to help the journey along. Long-term goals should be splintered into precisely described immediate and short-term goals.

This stepping stone approach to attaining big goals, is less-daunting and you can achieve quick wins. The resultant sense of mastery will boost your confidence and increase self-efficacy. Motivation will increase and momentum will start to build. Let's listen in to what Tommy Bowe and Paul Brady have to say on the subject:

> **"Goal setting is very important; personally it is always important to have something to aim for. I set myself short term goals, for things like training and matches and then medium term goals, and eventually long term goals of where I would like to be and how I want to be playing in the rugby world cup next summer. Professional sports persons are all competitive people and react well to setting goals and setting targets for what they want to achieve."**
>
> **Tommy Bowe-** *Personal communication, 01.04.10*

> **"As a starting point, I set longer term goals which take the form of career goals or yearly goals. Then I break down the yearly goals into more manageable, medium-term goals. An example would be a six week physical training phase which focuses on speed-endurance. As a peak period of training or competition approaches I set more specific, short-term or daily goals... I take each day and each session as it comes during this period and focus clearly on what I am trying to achieve. Mental goals take precedence during this period as I taper down my physical training."**
>
> **Paul Brady –** *Personal communication, 04.06.10*

Here you can see how these two giants of their sports, DESIGN their way to success.

Nothing within their control is ever left to chance.

# Young Jaguar approaches his goals inch-by-inch

Twenty year old David Leathem is on a golf scholarship at the University of South Alabama. He is an integral part of the *Jaguars*, the college's golfing team. I have been working with this young Jaguar for three years and he is making steady progress.

Dave's mental game development has been built on a foundation of effective goal-setting and a process-focused mindset.

He knows that his dream of making it onto the professional tour is down to doing the small things well and being patient.

> **"Goal setting is very important. Without goals you're chasing your tail. You can have a big goal, for example mine is to make it on the PGA Tour. However, that goal is very wide-angled. It's the little goals I set myself that will help me achieve this. Like making sure I do my routine on every shot, committing to my well thought out practice plan. I can say my goal is to win a college tournament. That's fine, well and good, but it's all of the little goals added together that'll make it happen."**
> **Dave Leathem** - *Personal communication, 07.10.10*

# Mental Game Goals

In terms of developing mental toughness, you will be setting goals that are not easily measured, in the conventional way. They are not quantifiable. As you will be improving such skill areas as self-belief, confidence, concentration, imagery and emotional control, your goals will set out the precise thoughts, feelings and behaviours you want to attain; and by how and when.

Being precise in your goal-setting activity also means identifying potential barriers to progress. This is important, as life is fluid and can serve up the inconvenient and the badly-timed. To offset this, you should devise contingency plans - the goal-setting equivalent of the reassuring headache tablet in the pocket of a migraine sufferer; it's always there, just in case.

Such attention to detail at the beginning of your journey, smoothes the path and hastens your progress. As with any journey, it's always best to plan for it.

Precise, well-defined, uncomplicated, broken down goals are much more likely to be attained than those described in a vague, ambiguous or open-ended way.

Our minds work best with strict, verifiable and visible goals. As the actress and comedian Lilly Tomlin once remarked, "I always wanted to be somebody, but now I realise I should have been more specific."

## Evolutionary Echoes

As an interesting aside, evolutionary theory suggests that our cave-dwelling ancestors were rewarded for precision, and that this became hardwired into the human brain as it was linked to survival.

The hunter who could pierce the heart of the Smilodon not only lived to tell the tale, but also brought food home for his family.

As a result, his family thrived and his bloodline continued. Conversely, the hunter who only wounded the big cat was open to retaliation and possibly injury or death.

## ☑ UNDERSTOOD

Make certain you are at one with your goals and achievement plans. Go over them, ensuring that they make sense to you. Try to envision the audit trail of progress and how each step advances your lot until the goal is realised.

Be sure to understand the methods you will employ to attain each goal. To ease any confusion or doubt, or to gain reassurance, consult your coach or sport psychologist.

Now change isn't easy; even positive change. But surely the alternative of standing still isn't a viable alternative for the ambitious athlete? Understanding the process of change is therefore reassuring and motivating.

## Don't Think It, Ink It!

To reinforce your commitment to the process of change, it is recommended that you record your goals and associated achievement plans. You could set them out on a whiteboard in your bedroom, as some of my clients have done – a sort of mission control – or you could record them in your training log.

## ☑ MINE

Well *yours* actually. Your goals should be just that - *yours* and yours alone. They have to be - your goals, whether for your technical, physical or mental games, need to motivate and inspire *you*. Otherwise your commitment and perseverance will be stymied with the inevitable negative implications for goal-attainment and performance enhancement.

If goals are thrust upon you by your coach or someone else, then your commitment to them will be compromised. Unless of course, you are one of life's pleasers who live to harvest approval from others by following everything they say. Here again, this externally-dependent motivation will not be sustainable in the long run.

So by all means, set goals with advice and guidance from your coach and others, but make sure that you own them and that the buck stops with you. In this way, your goals will not only be fit for purpose technically, but also fit for you personally.

Goals that are *yours* should be attainable by *you*. As far as is humanly practicable, the goals set should be within your control to achieve. You need to feel that if you do the work, you *will* progress and meet your goals.

Your progress should not rely on other people behaving in a certain way (e.g. your rival failing to turn up at the meet), or on the presence of other factors (e.g. dry weather for your 6am run). Liam Tancock again:

> **"I set goals, but they're mostly very personal goals. I never try and set a goal where 'I want to win this,' or 'I want to do this,' where other people can affect what I do. If I want to swim a new best time, I sit down and work out the best way of doing that. Whether I can shave a few tenths of a second off a turn or the start, my goal is putting them all together in a race. That's the way I set my goals."**
>
> **Liam Tancock,**
> *World record holder and World champion swimmer.*

## ☑ ACHIEVABLE

You should set challenging, but realistic goals. Realistic goals are pragmatic and sensible, not simple and undemanding. Goals should stretch you to the edge of your abilities, but not so much that failure is inevitable.

Goals that are achievable in this way will excite, ignite and delight. You will be keyed up and stimulated by the challenge laid down and delighted when the goal is attained. You can see how this principle of effective goal-setting can create a self-perpetuating cycle of motivation and momentum.

## ☑ ADJUSTABLE

Now, while your goal-setting needs to be time-framed, and your progress towards the goals regularly reviewed, there needs to be sufficient wiggle-room to allow for the unexpected. You may become ill or injured and therefore need to adjust your goal and time-limit. Also, on the more positive front, you may realise that you are making sterling progress towards a particular target, and now need to amend the goal and timing to take account of the rapid improvement.

## Evaluation

Central to this, is the need to evaluate your progress against the achievement plan. This means that you should have a method of evaluation built-in from the beginning of the process. After all, how else can you discover whether or not you have reached your individual goals, and if any adjustments need to be made?

> **"Goals are very helpful and motivational, but for me they are best used if constantly evaluated and modified. I think most sportsmen would have a long term goal, perhaps a certain team selection or trophy success, but it is the short-term goals that get you there that are most important, and they should be re-evaluated regularly."**
> **Simon Danielli -** *Personal communication, 19.05.10*

To help you get a handle on how to evaluate your goals, ask yourself this deceptively simple question: **When I achieve Goal X, what precisely will I be able to do *then*, that I can't do *now*?**

In terms of evaluating your mental game goals, you have already been introduced to the Pathways Profiling system, in Chapter 3. This comprehensive and effective mental game evaluation tool enables you to assess your progress towards mental toughness.

Effective goals are therefore embedded in reality and observe the maxim that, 'self-development is a *human journey*'. In other words, stuff happens – good and bad - and you must modify your goals accordingly.

By the way, the need to adjust goals reminds me of the following witticism from actor Walter Matthau:

> *"My doctor gave me six months to live, but when I couldn't pay the bill, he gave me six months more"*

## Go lie on your Death Bed and have a good last think

If you become stuck on what you really want to achieve, carry out what admittedly sounds like a rather morbid activity. Go lie on your death bed and have a good last think. Honestly, go there now. You're on the bed and have time to think and reflect on your life, especially your sporting career, or lack of it.

With the push of perfect hindsight on your side, and the pull of the Grim Reaper behind you, there is a great clarity of thought. Be right there right now and answer this question:

### What do you wish you *had* achieved?

Note down your responses to this question, as these will inform your goal-setting. You can then tidy them up by following the PUMAA principles.

On the 19 July, 2009, my mother Dorothy died. She had been suffering from Alzheimer's disease for many years. I was with her when she died and the experience hit me deeply.

One lasting memory was the overwhelming sense of my own mortality. It *does* end; life *is* short. What were once casual clichés became very real. The scales fell from my eyes and I 'woke up' and thought: "Oh s**t! You do die!"

A heartbreaking time subsequently became peppered with a strong sense of urgency. I had so much to do, so much yet to achieve and time was short. How did I not know this before? Goals that had lain dormant surfaced. This book is one of the goals and has been ticked off the 'to do list'.

My mother's mortality reflected my own, and it reflects yours too. So, let me ask you this:

### If not now, when?

When are you going to eradicate all of the nonsense that worries you and sit down with a blank page and start again?

What is it you want to be? What is it you want to achieve, feel and experience?

## Nicole

Nicole, a 25 year-old triathlete, responded with renewed energy to this part of our work together. She had been having significant difficulty plotting her course in life, let alone in setting any sports goals. She lacked direction and asked me to help. We met for an hour-and-a-half one evening in late November, 2009 and as I related the story about my mother's passing, I could see Nicole's body language changing. Pennies were dropping at a rapid rate.

Then she sat bolt upright and, with tears in her eyes, picked up a marker pen and started to write on my flip chart. I sat quietly and watched her ideas come to life.

Out of nowhere, Nicole was able to jot down several thoughts, dreams and desires. Visibly bemused by her sudden bout of clarity, Nicole turned round to me and said, "Mark, it's time for me now. I'm going to do things for myself, before it's all too late".

She then tore the sheets of paper off the easel, folded them gently and placed them on her coffee table. She stated with absolute certainty that she would convert these ramblings into a coherent set of goals. So I left her a handout covering the PUMAA principles. We then shook hands and agreed to meet in a week's time.

It was a rather abrupt, but very encouraging end to a session.

First thing the next morning, I checked my email and there it was; a message from Nicole sent at 01.14! Headed-up NICOLE'S TIME TO SHINE was a word document setting out her goals, sub-goals, timings and rationale.

No doubt about it - she had experienced the same sense of urgency that I had felt at the time of my mother's passing. At last she was striking out for the life she wanted to lead.

**From:** Nicole ███████████
**Sent:** 22 November, 2009 01.14
**To:** Mark ██████████
**Subject:** NICOLE'S TIME TO SHINE

Hi Mark,

Thank u for coming to see me this evening. I don't think u'll ever truly know how much u helped me. Sometimes u just need to see the truth, a look at what life really is. You triggered this off in me. I've spent way too long waiting for things to happen.

It's my time now to <u>make</u> them happen. I'm clear now. After what you told me about your Mum, something clicked in my head. It was as if a fog had lifted from my mind and I could see things clearly again.

Thanx so much!!

You'll see that I've attached my goals. I worked on this from the moment u left. I also phoned my mum to thank her for everything and tell her how much I loved her!!

See u next week.

Nic :-)))

# THE CULT OF RESULTS

## Focus on the process of achievement

It's easy to fall prey to the cult of results. After all, we have been socialised to focus on outcomes and 'brainwashed' into attaching our worth to our achievements. Throughout our lives, we are faced with an avalanche of questions about our accomplishments. Here's a tongue-in-cheek selection of such queries:

"How did you do in your spelling test? How did your friends do? What do you want to be when you grow up? How did your Carl do in his 11 plus? Grammar or Secondary school? How many GCSEs are you sitting? What grades did you get? Are you doing A-Levels? What grades did you get? Going to University? Which one? What degree did you get? First, Upper Second, or *just* a Third? Driving test passed yet?

Bought a car yet? What type? Got a girlfriend? Has she got a good job? Boyfriend yet? Has *he* got a good job? What do his parents do? Are you getting engaged? Can I see your sparkler? When's the wedding then? Where's the reception? Big Hotel? How many are going? How much did your dress/reception/honeymoon cost? Any kids yet? Oh two girls, how lovely. But wouldn't you have liked a son?"

*Ahhhh!!* And so it goes, on and on...until we end up saying to the newly-bereaved, "Those natural oak coffins are brilliant - great result for old Bob there, eh? He'd have been so pleased with it – erm - if he was still alive"

For goodness sake, what sort of superficial people are we? From birth to death, it's product and one-upmanship. What about self-fulfilment, happiness and enjoying the *journey* of achieving big goals?

## It's not about the pursuit of success, but the **success of your pursuit!**

Don't you see? You have to look beyond all this nonsense and sustain your inner spark by staying with the process of achieving goals. Feel the cosy reassurance that comes from knowing you have a plan to follow: have confidence in it and the drive to achieve it.

As long as *you* know you're on the right track, then other people can think whatever they wish. Remember, your sporting goals are personal to you, understood by you and it's you who'll be putting the hours in.

Right, let's move on now to the three kinds of goals available to you for goal-setting purposes. These goals will drive your training, fuel your perseverance and provide meaning and structure to your efforts.

## Three Types of Goals

### Russian Dolls

The journey from where you are now, to where you want to be, is guided by three kinds of goals - *outcome*, *performance* and *process* goals. All three are important and linked and all three interweave to create momentum.

Briefly, outcome goals focus on results; performance goals on achieving particular standards of performance; and, process goals on improving technique and strategy.

You will be familiar with the Matryoshka or Russian doll. These are nested or stacked dolls of decreasing sizes, one placed inside the other. Think of the large doll as characterising your outcome goals, with each doll inside representing your performance and process objectives. This simple symbol of interdependence could be depicted on your training diary, to remind you of the purpose of each step you take.

## OUTCOME GOALS

Outcome goals fork into two main categories:

- Short-term goals, and

- Long-term goals.

In either guise, outcome goals focus on the RESULT of your efforts and could be as simple as 'winning', or beating a specific team or individual opponent.

While obviously important (as they convey your ultimate objective) outcome goals are really not that useful to you in the long run. Because they focus on outshining your rivals and beating them, they amount to ego-inspired goals and as such play straight into the hands of your YouMinus.

If these are the only types of goals you set, you'll become far too focused on other people and *their* plans and not on what is relevant to *you* and *your* performance.

In goal-setting you need to focus on the process of attainment. Defining success solely in terms of an outcome is foolhardy. Ultimately, outcome goals are deceptive.

And here are two reasons why.

## Deceptive Scenario 1

Take Taylor for instance, the 17 year old tennis player you first met in Chapter 3. During our work together she recalled a match for which she set one goal and one goal only – *winning*.

Although Taylor performed well in the match - in fact it was one of her best displays for weeks - her opponent was simply having one of those 'golden' days. In the end she lost 7-5, 7-5. Now because the result was everything to Taylor and she lost, she ended up deriving nothing useful from her display. Indeed, she berated herself and was depressed for several days. No learning occurred and her motivation nose-dived.

## Deceptive Scenario 2

Now take the situation when you *do* win, having set winning as your sole goal. However, you only gained the victory because your opponent underperformed to a greater degree than you did. But without having attached goals around *your own* performance, you end up learning very little from the experience and instead live in a 'fool's paradise' for the following few days, where you soak up the rays of social adulation. But then what?

### Achievement Plan

Clearly then, outcome goals are very limited. They do not express what you are actually *going to do* to increase your chances of winning, or of making the national team, or of qualifying for the next round and so on. To attain your outcome goals on a consistent basis, you need to design and then act upon an Achievement Plan.

The Achievement Plan should decode your ambition into performance goals and process goals. See your outcome goals as destinations, the achievement plan as the map and your performance and process goals as your journey.

And view your coach, your sport psych., your physical trainers as individual SAT NAVs that provide expert direction and reassurance when you've lost your way.

## PERFORMANCE GOALS

It is vital to set goals that are attached to your performance as it is largely under your control. Whilst outcome goals are about you compared to your competitors, performance goals are about self-comparison. They relate to attaining a specific standard of performance, which is set relative to your previous performances.

So a 100 metre sprinter, who sets a goal of running his next race in 10.30 seconds, has just set a performance goal. If he attains this goal and it is an improvement on his best-to-date, then he will have set a new personal best, or PB. This means that the athlete, while maybe not winning the race, can still draw intrinsic satisfaction and confidence from his efforts and attainment.

Essentially, this sprinter is competing against himself. This keeps his focus where it belongs - on himself and his *own* performance.

> **"I was raised on a small farm in southern Indiana and dad tried to teach me and my brothers that you should never try to be better than someone else. Always learn from others and never cease trying to be the best you could be. That's under your control."**
>
> ***John Wooden*** - *Distinguished basketball coach*

Performance goals serve as an important and accessible source of feedback and therefore act as fuel to your motivation and impetus.

## PROCESS GOALS

### No Blocks, No Apex!

An analogy I often use with performers is to imagine an outcome goal as sitting at the apex of a pyramid. I then ask the athlete or team this question: "Where is the power located in the pyramid?" More often than not I hear, "It's at the top Doc". But of course it isn't. It's in each and every one of the blocks underneath it. I then tell the players that these blocks represent their process goals. Only by sculpting the blocks in a deliberate and precise way, and guiding them into place, can the pyramid take shape and the apex reached.

So, once you have set an outcome goal (e.g. to win; to make the national squad) you need to ask yourself this: "What do I need to do to realise this goal?

When you have answered this question, translate your responses into specific actions. For example, the precise process goals for a sprinter could be:

- To be relaxed and focused for the race ahead
- To leave the blocks with greater speed
- To concentrate on a point ahead of me
- To get into the acceleration position smoothly
- To maintain tall posture
- To dip head at the line

Now if the sprinter fulfils these process goals, it's likely he'll race at his optimum and so maximise his chances of winning. In other words, sufficient blocks will have been put in place to make reaching the apex a real possibility.

Talking of sprinters, Paralympic superstar and European Championship semi-finalist Jason Smyth, provides an insight into his process-orientated mentality.

Speaking about his debut at Barcelona 2010, Jason emphasised that while he wanted to win, what was more important was "to give a strong performance in a good running time." He added that "Even if I didn't win a medal, I could then say I gave it my all and that is an achievement in itself".

Undoubtedly with wisdom like this and with his excellent coach Stephen Maguire helping to sculpt his technique, this young man is going to keep breaking records.

In fact, don't be surprised if Jason enters the history books next year, by making the London 2012 Olympics!

## Set goals for training

"Knowing what you want from a training program is important, because you need to know what you are chasing; then you are more likely to get it. It gives you a reason for all the hard work."

*Lisa Kearney*

In the same way that dogs aren't just for Christmas, goals aren't just for competition. From my own work, I have found that athletes and coaches often place greater emphasis on setting goals for the forthcoming match or competition, than for practice.

But this imbalance in goal-setting is yet a further example of YouMinus sticking its oar in. Remember, it wants you to obsess about your performance in competition, for that's where *its* attention lies. It's sees competition in two ways:

— As a *boost to the ego* should you win (thereby attaining adulation, approval and status); and,

— As a *threat to the ego* because you could fail in front of other people (thereby leading to embarrassment and ridicule).

YouMinus, therefore, takes your focus away from the process of achievement. By doing this, it leaves you underprepared for competition and worn out by worry and tension. To overcome this YouMinus trait, you must develop a process mindset. You must go back to basics and get your training right.

In the early to mid-2000s, I had the pleasure and privilege to work as a sport psychology mentor to top Canadian ice hockey coach, Dave Whistle. During this time, he took the Belfast Giants to the summit of British hockey.

Dave now shares his considerable expertise with the next generation of hockey stars at the Pursuit of Excellence Hockey Academy, based in Kelowna, British Columbia. This world-renowned talent factory recognises that attention must be paid to the process of achievement, otherwise big outcome goals can never be realised. The Academy's motto says it all:

# Our Games Are Won In Practice

*pursuitofexcellence.ca*

It is quality practice that leads to quality performance. Therefore, goals must be set for training as well as for competition. It is in practice that learning takes place; and it is in competition that this learning pays off. As Lord Sebastian Coe told the BBC SPORT Website: "Winning medals was confirmation for what I had got right in training."

## Pathway Pitstop 1.4

### Your Approach To Training

This is a good time for you to reflect on how you currently train or practice. I have set out below, and in no particular order, a number of questions to prompt your thinking. As you consider the quality of your training regimen, note down your impression of where you're at now, and what needs to improve.

*Prompts:*

Do you prepare for and plan out your training sessions? Do you know your ideal emotional state for training? Do you set performance and process goals? Are training and practice sessions evaluated against set goals? Or is training a bit directionless and stale? Are your training sessions generally enjoyable? Or are you merely going through the motions?

Do you find yourself practising the easier skill-sets and drills to the detriment of the more difficult elements of performance? Do you know your role intimately? That is, do you *specifically* know what you need to master, in order to reach peak performance consistently?

Do you reproduce or simulate competition conditions in practice? Or does practice and competition almost amount to two versions of your sport?

# Commit to your goals today: Leave Procrastination 'til Tomorrow

**"Nothing so perilous as procrastination"**
**John Lyly**, *1579, Eupheus*

Procrastination is not only the thief of time, but a stealer of dreams. It is a symptom of your YouMinus at work. YouMinus, your mental monster, is all about ego and so, at the beginning of a journey of self-development, it is inclined to steer you away from possible failure and ridicule. This is especially the case for those of us high on perfectionism. If we believe we must always succeed, then engaging in a training programme (that has built-in evaluation) can seem very threatening indeed. And what's the foolproof way for us to avoid any kind of failure here? Exactly, avoid the programme altogether!

*Defer no time,*

*delays have dangerous ends.*

**- Shakespeare**

## Excuses, Excuses

I want you to be candid with yourself and note down the excuses you make for not training as thoroughly as you should. (Now if you are a total athlete, fully committed to your sport, you can skip this exercise).

Maybe you miss practice sessions under the cloak of tiredness, but really it's a lack of conviction and commitment, or a dislike for the coaching methods employed, or fear of letting yourself down in training. You may convince yourself that tonight's training session isn't really that vital and instead of consolidating your skills, you stay at home.

Perhaps you keep telling yourself that you'll engage in mental skills training someday soon, but somehow you just never get round to it. You search your soul, and concede that you're wary of all things 'psychology'. Yet your mental game continues to let you down. Maybe your latest hollow promise, is to make big changes to your physical conditioning regime, "starting from tomorrow" – but tomorrow comes and goes. And so does your fitness.

Whatever the excuses for your insufficient commitment to training, please list them in the left-hand column below in Pathway Pitstop 1.5. I have left room for up to three, but feel free to record more on a separate page. Once listed, I want you to then engage in some strong challenging.

## Pathway Pitstop 1.5

### Challenge Your Excuses

Take each of your excuses, one-at-a-time, and come up with logical alternatives, recording these down the right-hand column. Where possible, rebut each of your excuses by finding a positive reason for committing to training. I say 'where possible', as some excuses will be valid.

What you want is to weed out and eliminate those excuses that are a pretext for avoidance, be that out of anxiety, a deflated mood, or simply not being bothered. It's time to overcome procrastination. Many athletes I've worked with have had great results from challenging their unhelpful thoughts, not only with great logic, but also with a slightly sarcastic and mocking tone.

Treating the excuse, the disproportionate self-criticism, or the unjustifiable worry with disdain, weakens the grip each has on an athlete's emotional state, confidence and focus. Try it out. You'll be surprised. I have offered, below, two examples from real athletes, with real excuses.

| Excuses For Your Insufficient Commitment To Training | Counter Statements *(Talking back to yourself in a productive way)* |
|---|---|
| "I really can't be bothered with training today. Got a bit of a cold" (RICK) | "Come on now Rick. Be honest. Your cold hardly raises a sniffle. You're a big boy now! Get up, pack your kit, splash your face and once you're at the club you'll feel differently." |
| "Sport psychology's not for me. I'll be alright without it" (THEO) | "Right, so the best performers in the world praise mental training, engage in mental training, and state that mental training has been central to their rise to the top. Yet you say it's not for you...Look you'll *not* be alright without a strong mental game. Deep down you know this, so get off your butt and go ring the club's psychologist, NOW!!" |
| 1. | |
| 2. | |
| 3. | |

# When to Begin Goal-Setting

To maximise its value, it is best to start profiling your performance and setting goals during the pre-season period. This is the neat, ideal way to proceed.

You will have drawn a line under the previous season, digested it and reviewed it. You will have an impression of where you're at, and already been forming ideas of the areas you need to work on.

## Achieving Your Goals through Deliberate Practice

As the longest journey begins with the very first step, the road to excellence begins with the very first minute, of the very first hour, of training.

But it's not the number of minutes or hours you put in that counts, but rather what *you put into* those minutes and hours.

'Deliberate practice' is an advanced learning and training system that encourages you to maximise your ability, by maximising every segment of training you engage in.

Deliberate practice is a term coined by researcher Dr. Anders Ericsson, of Florida State University, to explain how people develop true greatness in a field – including sport. From his extensive research into talent development and expertise, Ericsson identified that the elite train in a qualitatively and quantitatively different way to those who fall short of greatness. The bottom-line good news from Ericsson's work, is that the best aren't born; they're made, self-made! And here's how!

## ELEMENTS OF DELIBERATE PRACTICE

From reading and absorbing the growing amount of information out there, I have come up with the following distillation of what deliberate practice (DP) is. Remember, if you adhere to the following principles, applying them to your mental, physical and technical training, you *will* attain a massive improvement in your sporting ability.

Indeed, I strongly advise you to apply the principles of DP to this current programme – *The Six Pathways to Mental Toughness*.

## ● DP is a highly planned approach to performance enhancement

Deliberate practice is a calculated strategy of performance improvement that involves an athlete repeatedly stretching his abilities to just beyond the existing level. He shapes his skills through a rigorous cycle of planning, doing and assessing.

## ● DP exploits the brain's elasticity

Deliberate practice accepts the brain's invitation to expand its neurological 'muscle' and to make it into the greatest piece of sporting equipment available to any athlete anywhere in the world.

### Circuit Training: 'A Story of Talent and Myelin'

In his fascinating book, *The Talent Code* (2009), Daniel Coyle describes how deliberate practice (or *deep practice*, as he names it) translates into actual changes in the brain. He explains that quality practice and coaching creates neural circuits that are broadband-like in their proficiency. At the physiological level, this proficiency is brought about by a brain tissue called myelin.

Briefly, myelin is lagging that wraps itself around nerve fibres in the brain, in response to targeted, repetitious and focused rehearsal of a skill, action or thought. This seemingly magical insulation, improves neural pathway strength, speed and accuracy.

Coyle explains in his book that, "The more we fire a particular circuit, the more myelin optimizes that circuit, and the stronger, faster, and more fluent our movements and thoughts become." (2009, p32).

## Magee 'Broadbands' His Brain for Boxing Excellence

Top boxing coach, Bernardo Checa, works with one of my clients, Brian Magee. Checa has already trained several world champions and Brian is next on his list.

Speaking before Brian's first defence of his European super-middleweight title, against Roman Aramian in Dublin, Checa provides a valuable insight into deep practice in action:

> **"Brian is improving every day. His hand speed is better, the footwork has really come on. He's doing things he didn't do before – he's rolling better and the movement is better. We repeat and repeat them; it's like going to school. You learn by repetition and already he is starting to do things in a more natural way. He gives me his full attention every time, focuses very hard in training."**
>
> *Belfast Telegraph, 13.09.10*

Brian fought tremendously well against Aramian. From the first bell, he was up and about his work. He was so well drilled, that his skills were executed automatically and unerringly. The eight rounds (Aramian didn't come out for the ninth) were facsimiles of each other.

Brian had a game plan and a set of skills to carry it out. He didn't waver once. It was a joy to watch and you can't say that about many boxing matches these days!

Brian's brain had been trained to deliver a high level performance. But it wasn't any old training of course – it was deep training. Brian approaches his mental game development in the same way. From our work together over the past few years, Brian has learned that mental skills are not abstract things, but rather can be wired into his brain in much the same way as an awesome right hook or some other technical skill.

## Mental Game Myelin

When put in the language of the neurologist, the ultimate purpose of this book, is to help you myelinate your brain circuits for mental toughness.

You can achieve this, by applying the principles of deliberate practice to the *Six Pathways to Mental Toughness* programme.

When my clients do this, they end up laying down neural circuits for such mental skills as confidence, self-belief, premium thinking, imagery control, emotion-management and concentration.

This is real, tangible and enduring change in the brain!

# That's right, you can GROW
# mental toughness!

## • DP is an honest pursuit

An athlete who engages in deliberate practice, will begin with a frank and open appraisal of his ability to play his sport.

Aside from honest self-reflection, he will also seek candid advice and feedback from elite master coaches and instructors on where his ability is right now.

## • DP is about targeting skills with laser-like precision

Once an honest and accurate baseline is set across the physical, technical, tactical and psychological dimensions, the athlete will set about isolating those critical elements of performance that require immediate remedial attention.

By *isolating*, we're talking about an extraordinarily precise, meticulous analysis of the targeted skill. Here the athlete will identify and segregate precisely defined elements of performance that need improved. Each element is subjected to analysis and he will appreciate and describe the targeted skill. He will have an intimate understanding of the discrete skill area he needs to enhance, and will know exactly what progress will look like. In Chapter 3, I described what the specifics of mental toughness looked like. You were also invited to profile your mental game and prioritise those areas you need to work on right away.

Bill Muckalt of the *Ottawa Senators* speaks of isolating a specific technical skill within his skating routine, one that needed to be refined. To help him develop this skill, Muckalt sought out the best and subsequently hired the legendary hockey coach David Roy, who is also the Director of The Pursuit of Excellence Hockey Academy.

> **"One of the many ways Dave [Roy] has helped me with my skating over the past three summers was correcting my wide tracking. He showed me how to bring my leg recovery across my centre of gravity, giving me a longer stride and more speed using less energy....Without Dave's help I wouldn't be playing in the NHL."**
>
> *pursuitofexcellence.ca*

Such absorption in the targeted skill and the means of improving it is highly motivating for the athlete involved. There is clarity, precision and a sense of control over what needs to be done, and by when. Commitment to hard work is nailed down. At a psychological level, there is a strong buy-in to the process.

## • DP is hard work from the get-go

Immediate goals are set for the targeted skill, to stretch the athlete's ability just beyond his current competency: one size too big, as it were, so the goals can be grown into. 'Just beyond' should be challenging, but not unrealistic. And out of an accumulation of numerous 'just beyonds' comes superior ability. However it takes tremendous perseverance. The effort required is big, bold and enduring.

Joe Calzaghe, the former light heavyweight and super middleweight World Champion, highlighted this in an interview for the BBC's *Raise Your Game*:

> **"It takes a lot of dedication and commitment to be a champion. I've been putting in the hours since I was nine years-old."**

For World handball champion, Paul Brady, purposeful practice is now part of him. It's as if Paul's continuous application of deliberate training has changed his DNA:

> **"I study games, other players, sometimes video can be useful. From I get up in the morning, until I go to sleep at night, I'm thinking about it all the time. It's every waking moment almost, where I can improve, where other players are strong and how I can counteract it...Thinking about the bigger picture and what I want to achieve."**
>
> *Highball, September 2006*

Paul adds, "I love training, the slog is always worth it..."

## Repetition of the Correct Version

Deliberate practice encourages the athlete to engage in repeated quality rehearsal of *the best way* of executing the targeted skill. He should continuously stretch his ability, until sufficient progress is achieved. Only then, should he move on to the next specific skill area in need of improvement.

> **"A hockey game is just a series of reactions and instinctual reflexes that have been trained and taught day after day, year after year."**
> **Bobby Robins** - *belfastgiants.com*

This sounds like commonsense, doesn't it? But, you'll also know that common sense isn't commonly applied by us humans.

Although the essence of deliberate practice has been known for millennia – *habitually repeat the correct version of a skill* - many of us just don't get it, let alone act on it.

But it's simple really. Just ask Aristotle; well, when you next see him!

> **"Excellence is an art won by training and habituation... We are what we repeatedly do. Excellence, then, is not an act, but a habit."**
> **Aristotle**

So it's how you train, not just the time you spend training. How many golfers spend their practice time, hitting hundreds of golf balls on the range, with only the final shot having any sense of purpose and quality to it?

Many, I would say. And, why the last shot, you ask? Because the golfer wants to feel good before he returns to the locker room! If he hits the shot well, he may skip back to the clubhouse, deluding himself that "practice went well today".

Now, while quality trumps time, the hours you give to training are nevertheless important; so says the research into deliberate practice.

# ● DP requires patience

The 'rule of thumb' across the literature, is that attaining expertise takes around 10,000 hours of deliberate practice (Ericsson et al., 2006).

This is also referred to as *The Ten Year Rule*.

### Now We Know Why There Are So Few At The Top!

Given the industriousness required to attain expert athlete status, together with the need for massive motivation, self-belief and faith, we can see how deliberate practice alone, could separate out the world's best from the 'also-rans'. After all, if deliberate practice was easy, then we'd all be at the top of our fields, wouldn't we?

And I would have become the goalkeeper of my dreams, and have appeared on *Celebrity Big Brother* by now!

> **"The reality that deliberate practice is hard, can even be seen as good news. It means that most people won't do it. So your willingness to do it, will distinguish you all the more."**
> **Geoff Colvin,** *Talent is Overrated*

### Deliberate practice and 5 Star Premier League Academies

Call me old fashioned, but it's only common sense to learn from the good practices and systems run by other people and organisations. We simply must learn from those who achieve great things; be it from one other person, or from an entire sport.

I have often wondered why our footballing nations, here in the British Isles, have feverishly marvelled at Brazilian soccer, yet appear to have done little to understand how such technical ability can spawn in abundance from this South American country.

It seems that our soccer authorities assume that there is some sort of genetic difference between the *Samba Kings* and the rest of the footballing world. And, if they don't think it's a genetic thing, then they believe it must be because Brazilian boys grow up playing football barefooted on Copacabana Beach.

All nonsense, of course. It has little to do with these things and much more to do with a positive mental attitude, and an activity called *futsal*. Futsal is a corruption of traditional football and sharpens a player's technique in a very specific and deliberate way. If you wish to learn more about how the Brazilian Football Federation approaches technical development, you should read Daniel Coyle's book *The Talent Code*.

So, it was with some relief that I learned that the Premier League in England was taking on board the principles of deliberate practice.

It seems that they are no longer content to sit back and be in awe of other soccer nations and other sports. Instead, they're taking the bull by the horns and are intent on developing their soccer academies, much in the same way as the Pursuit of Excellence Academy (referred to earlier) has been doing for years. At last, there is the belief that excellence is learnable.

'**...the Premier League is planning a revolution in the academy system in an attempt to bring (success) to the England football team. The strategy is based around grading academies with stars depending on various factors, including how long young players spent with qualified coaches. The golden figure is considered to be 10,000 hours of training, widely accepted as the key to producing an elite athlete...A young English footballer only receives an average of 2,500. Young Dutch footballers are closer to 6,000...'**

**Daily Mail,** 05 August, 2010

## • DP encourages bespoke feedback from top-class mentors

As Bill Muckalt did above, the athlete following the deliberate practice protocol, will continuously reflect on his progress and seek out frequent, frank and tailored feedback from an expert mentor.

He will learn from errors and when necessary, fine-tune his goals and achievement plan. As purpose and effort are fused, his progress on each identified skill is inevitable.

It was management specialist, Ken Blanchard, who coined the adage 'feedback is the breakfast of champions'. I would go further with this metaphor and view feedback as the *staple diet* of champions.

It's their breakfast, *lunch and dinner*! It nourishes the ambitious athlete, at all times.

### YouMinus Alert!!

Adverse criticism is anathema to the mental monster. Therefore, expect your YouMinus to steer you away from garnering frank opinion from other people. You will know the mental monster is stirring, when you have such self-deluding thoughts as, "I don't need to ask for feedback. If I can't do it all myself, then what's the point?" or, "I know myself better than they do". So be ready to fend off the meddling monster, and do what is right to take you and your ability to world class level.

Take advice from the best.

## • DP welcomes errors

**"If you want to succeed, double your failure rate."**
***Thomas Watson** – Founder, IBM*

As deliberate practice is about training at the edge of one's abilities, the ambitious athlete expects to make mistakes. In addition, he views them as central to his learning and not as portents of permanent failure and embarrassment.

Making mistakes is seen as a 'rites of passage' to superior performance.

Viewing an error as a learning landmark along the pathway to excellence, allows the athlete to continually extend his skills outside his comfort zone and into the improvement zone.

### YouMinus Alert!!

I think you saw this one coming - YouMinus feeds on your mistakes. It spews out criticism and blame when you make mistakes, and pumps anxiety and dread into you, as you try hard not to make another one!

Put simply, YouMinus controls you in much the same way a dictatorship keeps its population in check – through FEAR!

So be mindful - YouMinus is the Fault-Finder General; an inner critic that skulks in the shadows of errors. Therefore, you must learn to welcome mistakes as sources of valuable information, before erasing them from your mind and moving on.

The more you meet, greet and delete your errors in this way, the fewer you will make.

## • DP and the performance cycle

The world's top sports performers maximise the *before, during* and *after* phases of training. Neither time, nor energy, is ever wasted.

### – Before Training

Top athletes plan thoroughly for their training sessions, by setting precise performance and process goals. Minds are primed in readiness for the forthcoming exertions, even if the session is only 15 minutes of targeted, quality practice.

### – During Training

During practice, elite athletes work on the targeted skill with full concentration, motivation and persistence. Their mindset is one of a desire to learn and improve, rather than to avoid failure and escape ridicule.

They monitor their efforts as they engage in training, and make adjustments, when necessary.

### – After Training

Once the session is finished, top performers evaluate their performance against set standards, and confer with their coach for further precise feedback.

For the elite athlete, practice is a seamless act of three parts.

# Case Study Update – Rick

## Rick Makes Progress Along Pathway 1

### Solution to Rick's Pathway Problem

You'll remember Rick's case from Chapter 3, and that he rated himself as **two out of ten**, along Pathway 1. You'll recall that this **21 year-old professional golfer** possessed little inner 'oomph' and instead was driven by external inducements.

By feeding off such motivational foodstuffs as public acclaim, prize money and media veneration, Rick was no longer in charge of his drive.

Instead, his motivation lay with factors he had little or no control over. In effect, he had unknowingly created the motivational equivalent of 'meals-on-wheels'.

Unless these external incentives came knocking on his door, his motivation was starved. It was not surprising then, that Rick's golf game became very erratic.

Clearly, he had to find ways to be motivationally self-sufficient. He had to identify ways to ignite his inner spark, without needing outside events to occur first.

By gaining control over the source and force of his motivation, Rick would be turning an important corner in his golfing career.

By revving up his motivational engine, he would start to practice with greater enjoyment and purpose, and to perform with more confidence, composure and consistency on the golf course.

He would start to play for himself and perform on the course with the unshakable confidence that comes from an inner will.

What follows now, is a summary of Rick's mental game journey from people-pleaser, attention-seeker and inconsistent golfer, to a self-assured, focused and steadfast performer.

**If you wish, flick back to Chapter 3 right away to bring yourself up to speed with Rick's case.**

## Sport Psychology Intervention

Rick and I worked intensively together for approximately four months.

As always with my work, there was a strong psycho-educational strand to the intervention. Central to this, was explaining to Rick how his mental monster stirred up and maintained his mental game difficulties; in particular, how it was twisting his motivational compass to the external.

Stepping back from his game enabled Rick to see things much more clearly. Soon he realised that he was in fact a patchwork quilt of other people's expectations, needs and opinions.

He identified that he was a people-pleaser, tracing its genesis back to his early years.

As a kid, Rick would often seek out his parents' approval, only feeling content with his own efforts when they endorsed them.

He also recalled being the 'class clown' at secondary school, seeing the role as a gateway to acceptance, acclaim and appreciation.

Eventually this need for outside admiration seeped into his golfing career. This insight liberated Rick. It was his 'Oh, I get it!' moment.

Having assessed his motivation in terms of its force and source, Rick started to look inside himself and tease out why he first took up golf as a kid. He recalled loving the game unconditionally, and that he practised and played from the inside-out.

In an effort to reawaken this mentality, Rick noted down the following nuggets of *intrinsic* drive:

**"I love the golf environment, the sense of freedom"**

**"I love bettering my ability to play golf"**

**"I love practising my shots"**

**"I love beating my previous score"**

**"I love the fact that it's an individual sport: it's all down to me"**

**"I love beating the course designer"**

Rick recorded these onto crib cards, laminated them, and kept them close-to-hand. He constantly referred to them to help him re-engage with his lost inner drive.

At the same time, with the help of his coach, he redesigned his practice sessions to increase the enjoyment, while still maintaining the quality. Goal-setting was central to all of this.

It was equally important for Rick to look deeply into his belief system and challenge those thoughts that fuelled his need for approval and praise. These needed to be weeded out and replaced with self-supporting alternatives.

By using several techniques from Pathway 2, Rick was able to raise his self-esteem to a new high. It was no longer controlled by any external factors.

Rick realised that it was a risky and immature strategy to garner his inspiration from the praise of others. Accordingly, he did a 180 degree turn on his motivational compass.

How did he achieve this?

Quite simply, Rick learned to refocus his mind on the process of playing great golf. Goals were set around his adherence to his game plan, his commitment to his pre-shot routine and his capacity for managing mistakes and staying in the present.

This structured approach to goal-setting was a massive step-up for Rick. After all, he'd typically been entering tournaments with the sole goal of 'attaining approval'.

It was a major turning point whenever errors on the course no longer stabbed his psyche. Using techniques from Pathways 2, 3 and 5, he learned to park errors, to maintain focus despite them and to accept that perfection was a futile aspiration.

Rick now enjoys golf - both practising and competing. His focus is on the process of performing and his motivation is from within. He wants to do well for himself and his goals are now clearly defined. He knows what he wants and how to get there. His practice is purposeful and he is much better placed, psychologically, to overcome setbacks.

He prepares for each session on the range, asks for precise feedback from his coach and refines his training when necessary.

Now that Rick's in charge of his game, people are commenting on his more mellow approach, especially off the course. The conceit has all but gone and he has developed into a more mature and likeable young man.

At this time, he is also in a steady relationship with a beautiful girl who loves him very much.

In terms of his golf, Rick is progressing well. He was always talented, but because he wasn't in control, it only came out occasionally during any given season.

Now he is much more consistent and has only missed one cut in the past ten events. He has had four top ten finishes, one top five and one win!

His goal of playing on the main tour is likely to be realised.

## Distance travelled

At the end of the sport psych intervention, Rick re-rated his position along Pathway 1, as a **nine**.

He had moved a distance of seven units, due to the work he'd put into his mental game.

This was remarkable progress.

What's more, he acknowledged that working on his motivation, led to him developing additional psychological skills:

> **"I'm certainly more motivated, truly motivated. When I practice and play, it's for me and my goals. But my confidence and concentration have also improved. I'm not focusing anymore on things I can't do anything about. I believe I've grown up a lot. I now see people for what they are and refuse to give my power away to them. I**

**appreciate my life and my place in it. I can control it now."**

This was a huge step forward for Rick and set him up for a fulfilling golf career.

# Key Points from **Pathway 1**

- Mentally tough performers are motivated from within. They love the challenge of improving themselves, and enjoy the process of achievement. They are self-contained, self-assured and resilient individuals, who train in a deliberate way and keep going.

- Your mental monster fears change and therefore sabotages the mechanism that drives it - your internal motivation and enthusiasm for bettering yourself. By assaulting your thoughts, images, feelings and behaviour, your YouMinus can dissuade you from taking risks, and persuade you to 'make-do'.

- Externally-driven athletes become heavily reliant on factors in their outside world for their inspiration. But when their supplies dry up, they go into motivational 'cold turkey'. Their performances deteriorate and they have great difficulty picking themselves up again.

- Effective goal-setting is central to developing mental toughness and attaining sporting success. The PUMMA system shows you how to plot your course to performance excellence.

- By applying the principles of deliberate practice, ambitious athletes can become world-class in their sport.

▪ Carry out the various tasks, techniques and strategies on this Pathway and you will develop a strong, and durable, inner engine that will take you from 'also-ran' to successful athlete.

# Chapter 5

## PATHWAY 2

# PATHWAY TO TOTAL SELF-BELIEF

Believe in yourself. Believe that whatever you want to achieve in your life is attainable. I had so much self-belief, and I knew what I wanted to do. If you have that conviction, and you have that deep belief, then anything is possible.

**- Rory McIlroy**

But my dear man, reality is only a Rorschach ink-blot, you know.

**- Alan Watts**, Philosopher

By the end of Pathway 2, you will have:

- Understood the crucial role self-belief plays in mental toughness, peak performance and meeting your sporting goals.
- Learned how your mental monster sabotages your self-belief.
- Discovered the difference between self-esteem and self-confidence.
- Learned how to develop steadfast belief in yourself and your ability to master situations through a range of powerful techniques and strategies.
- Understood the strong relationship that exists between your thoughts, emotions and behaviour.
- Caught up with Aaron, a case study from Chapter 3.

Strong self-belief and mental toughness are inextricably linked. The athlete with high self-belief has an inner assuredness that encourages him to take risks, to seek out new challenges and above all to grow as a person. He possesses a steadfast conviction that he can cope with whatever is thrown at him during performance. He approaches sport and life from the inside-out, ensuring that he is not a victim to external circumstances.

By absorbing the information within this chapter and through carrying out the set exercises, you too will start to appreciate your worth as a person; experience confidence like never before; and begin to make significant strides towards mental toughness and sporting success.

# MONSTER WATCH

## How YouMinus Attacks Your Self-Belief

High self-esteem and an inner conviction that the challenges ahead can be mastered, lie beneath massive progress in any walk of life. And YouMinus knows it.

Consequently, the mental monster sets about sabotaging your efforts to succeed, by infiltrating your belief system. It digs deep, down into your very soul. It wants to wipe out any semblance of self-assuredness. It wants you to drop those silly little thoughts, in your silly little head, that you can achieve great things. Just stay in your 'comfort zone' and leave greatness to the select few.

To do this, the monster takes charge of the way you think about yourself, about others and the world around you.

By placing a negative lens over your belief system, it ensures you find evidence to support your inability to prosper, as an athlete and human.

YouMinus moulds your mind to see the world as a type of Big Brother that scrutinises and judges your every effort. It wants you to feel so claustrophobic and overburdened by the push of expectation and the pull of low self-esteem that you simply opt out.

The way you see reality is driven by your inner saboteur. It promotes threat, self-blame, self-criticism and a sense of not belonging.

If YouMinus has difficulty reducing your confidence, it'll take an alternative tack and encourage you to overinflate it. It knows that overconfidence leads to complacency and that complacency leads to failure.

And Bang! Once again your monster creeps up and whispers, *Duh! Hello – Anybody In There?*

So it's vital that you understand what self-belief is and take the proper steps to strengthen it.

## THE ANATOMY OF SELF-BELIEF

Self-belief is a blend of two factors: *self-esteem* and *self-confidence*. Often these terms are used interchangeably, and though they are interrelated in powerful ways, there are important distinctions to be made between the two.

Self-esteem is your view of yourself, whilst self-confidence is how you view your ability to handle a task or cope with a specific situation.

- **Self-esteem is the 'global you', self-confidence the 'situational you'**

- **Self-esteem is enduring; self-confidence less so**

We will now take a closer look at these two facets of self-belief, before turning to some powerful techniques for building up your esteem and confidence. This is the pathway to total self-belief and world-class thinking.

## Self-Esteem

Self-esteem is the degree to which you value and like yourself, warts and all. It is made up of thoughts, feelings and behaviour around how you rate, accept and trust yourself.

It is about the extent to which you hold yourself in high regard and respect yourself.

It's about believing you have a right to be happy, successful and fulfilled. Indeed, if self-esteem was a famous make-up advertisement it would ask each of us, *Are you worth it?*

Self-esteem is the stable, inner opinion you have of yourself and the really good news is that you can control it fully. So no matter what you think of yourself right now, you can improve it.

You can develop high self-esteem.

Set out below, are the characteristics of high and low self-esteem.

An individual with **high self-esteem**:

- Accepts and values himself as a human being.
- Is at peace with himself, trusts and likes himself.
- Makes big decisions and takes risks without worrying about the consequences.
- Does not need external confirmation of his worth.
- Isn't hooked on pleasing other people.
- Is 'down-to-earth'.
- Welcomes change.

Someone with **low self-esteem**:

- Struggles to accept his worth as a person.
- Dislikes himself.
- Fails to give himself credit for his achievements.
- Is frustrated by life and feels unsettled most of the time.
- Needs outside approval to fuel his self-worth.
- Constantly compares himself to other people.
- Treats himself badly, yet elevates the worth of other people.
- Is a people-pleaser.
- Is often conceited.

- Engages in constant negativity, self-criticism and self-blame.
- Fears change; reluctant to take risks.
- Aims to avoid ridicule and embarrassment.

> *Low self-esteem is like driving through life*
> *with your hand-break on.*
>
> **- Maxwell Maltz**

Having digested what self-esteem is and what the ingredients of high and low self-esteem look like, I would like you to now assess your own feelings of worth. Pathway Pitstop 2.1 will take you through this self-examination.

## Pathway Pitstop 2.1

### Where's Your Self-Esteem Right Now?

Consider these questions, reflect on your answers and record your responses in a notebook.

- Do you believe you deserve to be loved and to have success in life?
- Do you need other people to tell you that you're great or have done well, or are lovable, before you can feel at ease with yourself?
- Do you respect yourself? Accept yourself as you?
- Do you think you can reach big goals?
- Do you judge yourself fairly? Or are you often unkind to yourself?
- Do you frequently treat strangers better than you treat yourself?
- Can you make a list of your accomplishments and feel good about them? If so, list them now.
- Are you able to list your personal qualities as a human? If so, list them now.
- Are you jealous of other people's success and happiness?

- Do you feel you belong amongst the best in your sport?
- Are you your own person, not taken off course by other people's opinions?
- Are you at peace with yourself, accepting who you are and valuing your place in the world?
- Can you make decisions unencumbered by doubt and worrying about what others will think of you?
- Are you able to accept critical feedback as a useful learning experience?
- Do you feel threatened by physically attractive rivals?
- Can you accept your mistakes as part of the package of life and making progress?
- Do you regularly feel hopeless? Or that you're a failure? That you'll never amount to anything in life?
- Or do you feel positive towards yourself? Do you believe that you are as good and as valuable as anyone else?

Your answers to these questions will give you a heads-up on where your self-esteem lies right now. If your self-opinion is low, you have some hard work to do, but you have come to the right place to do so.

This Pathway will help you to develop high and enduring self-esteem.

Okay, now let's turn to the related area of self-confidence, the second strand of self-belief.

## Self-Confidence

Self-confidence is the degree to which you back yourself to successfully manage a particular situation.

Sport is full of critical moments. To perform well, it's important to be sure that you have the ability to meet them head-on.

And above all that you can master any situation thrown at you.

Critical situations in sport include:

- that tricky five foot putt to make the cut in golf
- a potentially match-winning penalty kick in the last minute of a football match
- being eaten up with massive anxiety and self-doubt before a big game.

Now, in an attempt to draw a distinction between self-esteem and self-confidence some sport psych. books have used an analogy similar to the following:

'If self-belief was a house, self-esteem would be the foundation and self-confidence the bricks and mortar. Self-esteem with its more solid base is durable, while self-confidence is exposed to the vagaries of the prevailing weather or, God forbid, a demolition team.'

This type of illustration depicts an individual's self-confidence as in the hands of his external environment. It's as if the person is inert and disconnected from the prevailing situation.

This is a misleading depiction of what self-confidence is, and one that goes against everything this book represents.

Athletes are not, never have been, and never will be, passive victims of incidents in their sporting environment!

Let's take a closer look.

## Pathway Pitstop 2.2

Read the following situation, one faced by many golfers, and then answer the question posed at the end.

**A golfer is feeling assured and poised, after hitting a beautiful seven-iron over the brow of the fairway, towards the green. But all of a sudden, his confidence dips, as he sees that his ball has had an unfortunate bounce and come to rest under the lip of a greenside bunker. His deportment changes and his confidence fades.**

**Q.** Did the ball landing in the bunker cause this golfer's self-confidence to take a nose dive? A simple YES or NO answer will suffice, together with your reasoning.

| Response (circle) | Explain Your Response Below |
|---|---|
| YES | |
| NO | |

Now I'm hoping, particularly if you have read Chapter 1 on *The Frankenstein Factor*, that you circled NO and explained you answer thus –ish:

*'Of course the ball landing in the bunker didn't cause the dip in the golfer's confidence — he caused the dip in his own confidence, because of what he told himself about his limited capacity for coping with the next shot. It was his interpretation of the situation that caused it, pure and simple.'*

You will note that the power to succeed or fail lies within the gift of this golfer. As confidence is the belief that we can master a task, then the golfer has a choice to make as he stands in the bunker. He can choose the positive route of: constructive, self-affirming thoughts and images together with an in-the-moment focus; or he can select the negative route, and undermine his ability to perform the shot by predicting and picturing failure.

The choice is all his – never was anything else!

Self-confidence is a vital weapon in your fight against YouMinus infringement. But watch out for overconfidence and smugness. YouMinus can grab and twist your confidence into conceit. Boxing legend, Joe Calzaghe, reminds us that complacency leads to defeat:

> **"It's a fine line between being confident and overconfident. The day you become overconfident is the day you become complacent. The day you become complacent, is the day you get beaten."**
>
> *Raise Your Game - BBC SPORT website*

# BUILDING TOTAL SELF-BELIEF

For the remainder of this chapter, you will be asked to work through some powerful techniques and strategies that will really improve your self-esteem and confidence.

And consequently your self-belief.

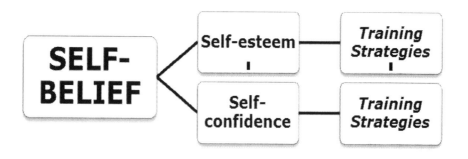

**Figure 2:** Developing your self-belief through training
(*After Jones and Moorhouse, 2008*)

You can see in Figure 2 that there are not only commonalities between the training strategies, as denoted by the link, but also an interaction between self-esteem and self-confidence.

There are bonuses to be had all around – if you improve one area, it can have a positive effect on others. Okay, let's get going. It's now time to develop your self-esteem.

# 1. INCREASING YOUR SELF-ESTEEM

We'll start straight away with an exercise. So fetch that pen or pencil again and complete Pathway Pitstop 2.3.

## Pathway Pitstop 2.3

### Those good and bad performances; and one really important question – why?

I want you to take a trip down Memory Lane and to select three of your standout performances and successes. Next, reflect on these triumphs and explain WHY you were successful on those occasions. Record your reasons below:

*Occasion #1:* I did well because

*Occasion #2:* I did well because

*Occasion #3:* I did well because

Let's now move on to those times when you failed to produce the goods. Isolate three occasions when you had a real off day, when nothing seemed to go right, and you lost. Examine these instances closely and explain WHY you were unsuccessful. Do this now, and record your responses below.

*Occasion #1:* I did poorly because

*Occasion #2:* I did poorly because

*Occasion #3:* I did poorly because

Having completed these two exercises, compare your responses and note down any differences in attribution. That is, do you explain your successes in a different way to how you explain you failures?

This is such an important exercise, as you find that those athletes with total self-esteem explain their successes in terms of their qualities as a person and performer. Their successes are down to them, not to 'Lady Luck' or some other fortuitous nonsense.

Instead they credit the good times to **their** sharp technique, physical endurance and mental strength.

Specifically, they may point to their quality training, the meticulous homework done on their opponent, or their own composure under pressure. Basically, they find personal reasons for their successes.

Interestingly though, when the self-assured athlete has an off-day, a curious but wise shift takes place. Instead of looking inwards and blaming himself, he attributes the off-day to *external* factors.

Now, not in a delusional way - where he may miss a learning point, but in a reasonable way that avoids beating himself up gratuitously. Athletes high in self-esteem understand that it's ludicrous to attribute any single loss to some inner frailty.

They know ability doesn't disappear overnight. To these guys the cliché 'You're Only As Good As Your Last Game' is total nonsense.

## What You Must Do

To develop your self-esteem, you must acknowledge *your* role in *your* own successes. Don't explain away your triumphs with such expressions as: "I got the rub of the green today"; "My opponent played poorly"; or, "I got the easy draw in the tournament". To do so wastes a prime opportunity to build up your self-esteem real estate.

If you attribute your successes to external factors then by and large you have handed your sporting future over to fate. And what does this do to your self-esteem? That's right – it undercuts it, big time. It also creates massive anxiety and uncertainty.

You're basically saying that in order to win again, your opponent must underperform, the weather must be favourable and that that black cat had better cross your path again on the way to the track!

How on earth can any athlete prepare for competition, when he perceives his potential for success as a hostage to fortune?

## Enough! It's Time You Took the Credit

You need to acknowledge that qualities such as your technical ability, strategic knowhow and inner resilience led to your good performance or win.

In this way, you start to believe that such successes can be repeated - after all, you have just come to recognise aspects of yourself that are enduring and under your control.

Right, let's collect more powerful evidence of your self-worth and competence and build up the portfolio 'til it's bursting at the seams!

## Pathway Pitstop 2.4

### Portfolio Of Evidence

To harvest more great evidence, I need you to look back over the years and list your accomplishments. Make sure these span all aspects of your life experience: sport, education, employment, as well as the interpersonal and social. Remember, self-esteem is about your inner value as a person, and as a person you are more than your role in sport. Once you are content that you've captured your key achievements to-date, I want you to set about mining for nuggets of self-worth and competence. To do this, I would like you to take each of your achievements in turn and to ask yourself this question: **What does this achievement say about my personal qualities and skills?**

Several clients have found this exercise quite challenging, especially when they reach the interpersonal side of their life. This is an area seldom thought of in terms of achievement. However, I encourage athletes to consider their relationships and significant events in life.

For instance, a top performer I worked with revealed that he was:

- in a stable and loving marriage
- a father to four children under twelve
- on-call 24/7 during his father's terminal illness
- always on hand to help his friends or family out with any personal problems
- a survivor of childhood abuse by an 'uncle'
- an active member in his church

This fine fellow, though incredibly modest, concluded that the nature of his relationships and life events, said much about his inner spirit, value as a human being and ability to withstand pressure. He recorded these onto crib cards, along with his achievements within sport and academia.

I strongly encourage you to do the same, and to:

- Log your accomplishments in life
- Drill down into each achievement and identify what it says about you
- Record the identified attributes onto cards

Keep these cards close to you at all times and read them frequently.

## The Case for the Defence

Given our tendency towards self-criticism, -doubt and -blame, you should view these crib cards as containing *the case for your defence*. The moment you recognise you're engaging in self-criticism, or worried about your ability to make progress in your sport, take out your cards and fight back!

## Get Connected to the Grid of Life
### - Develop a social network

While not a technique as such, it is important to have people around you who care and respect you for the person you are. Your worth as a human being will be reinforced as you receive that care and love and it will help you grow as a person.

We are after all social animals, which is why isolation is often a precipitant to low mood and self-esteem, as well as to anxiety and fear.

Often the best way to feel part of the world around you is to engage with it.

## 2. INCREASING YOUR SELF-CONFIDENCE

Great – now we're making good progress. You have already taken great strides to build up your self-esteem, by following the exercises in the last section. The central purpose of the exercises was to develop a portfolio of evidence that reflected your worth right back at you.

You trawled your memory bank, identified achievements, analysed why they happened and finally took credit for them. So now you know that you possess fantastic inner resources to meet your goals in life.

Building self-esteem is a work-in-progress, right throughout life. It's therefore important to keep on collecting evidence and crediting it to your self-esteem account. It will always be there for you to dip into on a rainy day!

Self-esteem and self-confidence are not mutually exclusive. Improving your self-esteem provides a springboard for enhancing your confidence.

Think about it. If you are pinpointing and appreciating your achievements over the years and accepting yourself unconditionally as a human being, then it stands to reason that this will stimulate confidence in your ability to perform and cope well. Doesn't it?

Nonetheless, you can't just rely on this. You must take deliberate action to boost your confidence way beyond its status as a mere by-product of your high self-esteem.

This section is packed with great techniques and strategies that will enable to you to do this very thing.

## Bringing Your Brain Back Home

The key to building up self-confidence is to take ownership of your ability to think great thoughts, to generate constructive imagery, to manage unhelpful emotions and to select positive memories. Do this and you'll feel you can do anything.

# Confidence takes you from
# the ordinary to the exceptional

You see, your thoughts, memories, feelings, behaviour and physiology are all interconnected and a positive change in any one will have a reciprocal affect on all of the others.

You can exploit this relationship to create a confident mindset. For instance, if you are a golfer faced with a downhill right-to-left putt to win a tournament, you may do some or all of the following to bolster your confidence in completing the task:

— Recall previous successes in similar situations.
— Act as if it is simply another putt, rather than a putt to win.
— Take a few calming breaths to settle your nerves and to ground you in the moment.
— Adhere to your ever reliable pre-putt routine to keep your mind focused on the process.
— Using vivid images to 'see' success, to see the ball do what you want it to do.
— Use positive affirmations to bolster your belief that you can finish the job off.
— Remind yourself that you were made for this moment and that there is nothing to fear.
— Accept the outcome unconditionally.

## Pathway Pitstop 2.5

### Thoughts, Feelings and Focus

Let's have a look at the make-up of your confidence. I would like you to reflect on those times, when your confidence has been **high** and to describe the types of *thoughts* you were having, the *emotions* you were feeling, and where your *focus* was directed. Then do the same for those times when your confidence was **low**. Next, note the differences in your thoughts, feelings and focus for the two categories of confidence. There's a difference isn't there? And the good news is that you have control over your thoughts, feelings and focus. What this means, is you can CHOOSE to be confident.

## Shop at the Confidence Store

It's time you became a mental consumer. It's time you browsed through your back catalogue of powerful, positive memories and used them to boost the credit on your confidence account.

### Pathway Pitstop 2.6

#### Fill Up Your Confidence Basket

You'll know that on *Amazon*, or any other on-line store, that when you search for an item and find it, you're then invited to 'Add to Shopping Basket'. Well, I would like you to browse through your memories and to place in your basket (i.e., record in your *Mental Game Journal*) those times when you demonstrated excellence under pressure. Do this now, and fill your basket to the brim. Build it high. Don't limit yourself.

#### *'Customers Who Bought This Item Also Bought...'*

Make sure to choose examples that cover as many of your skills as possible. In this way, you will have noted down powerful evidence of your competence across the critical components of your sport. For a rugby hooker, this could include memories of his superb lineout throwing; his strong moments of defensive play; and, those times when he took the bull by the horns and made great runs through the opposition. Whatever your sport is, select ONLY those memories that reveal your competence in key areas.

Once logged in your notebook, spend time consolidating each memory through imagery. If each occasion is replayed in the technicolour splendour and surround sound of the imagination, and you can actually feel that you're back in time executing the skill all over again, then this will have a profoundly positive effect on your confidence.

For instruction on carrying out effective imagery see *Pathway 5*, Chapter 8.

This Pathway Pitstop exercise is an excellent confidence-booster as it:

- Encourages you to focus on your strengths.
- Forms a stockpile of evidence confirming your competence.
- Reminds you, in vivid form, that you possess the ability to manage key moments effectively.
- Urges you to feel good as you replay your successes. As I overheard someone say: "Self-confidence is the memory of success"
- Is a form of rehearsal. By using imagery to rerun your successful performances through your mind, you are actually practising the skills and all from the comfort of your armchair!
- Makes best use of your time, attention and memory.
- Is a structured approach to overcoming self-sabotaging behaviour. The Frankenstein Factor tells us that the human default reaction is to dwell on weaknesses and failures. This is something we tend to do during times of solitude. This exercise provides a structured and powerful alternative to dwelling on the negatives. It is a particularity potent weapon in your battle against any YouMinus interference.
- Encourages you to be your own best M.A.T.E. as you are placing, in your confidence basket, great examples that prove your capability. It allows you to shout out,

perhaps for the very first time, a special and important truth:

## My Achievements – Top Evidence

- Provides a catalogue of memories that can be called upon in comparable performance situations. It is a stimulus for your confidence to know that you have mastered a similar situation before. The ensuing reassurance quells any interference and keeps you in the precious present. At last you will be using your experience to good effect.

One of my clients, Scottish and Ulster rugby star, Simon Danielli, works hard at this side of his mental game:

> **"I think key words pertaining to one's talents, and actual examples of these in past performances, are crucial for an athlete's self-perception and belief. I will often write down key words and examples of my best moments and this gives me confidence in the lead up to matches."**
>
> *Personal communication, 19.05.10*

And we can see the fruits of Simon's mental game work in his powerful performances for both club and country.

## Sit Your Mock Exams

We have all heard performers explain that their composure in a clutch situation was largely down to being in a similar situation, several times before. So, if you have previously closed-out a win, you can recall that particular experience to help you manage the existing one.

The technique above, *Shop at the Confidence Store,* has already encouraged you to build up such a memory bank of competence to call upon at critical moments.

But what if you have NO such experience to rely on? What then? How can you fortify your confidence *without* the nourishment of experience?

There is a way. Welcome to the world of 'mental inoculation', a mental game strategy that oozes quality if applied with intent. It is very powerful because it draws on a number of mental techniques.

## SIMULATION TRAINING

This confidence-building strategy is also covered in Pathway 4 (Chapter 7, Effective Focus) under the title *Go For The Jab! - Mental Inoculation*. It is an uber-strategy that straddles many mental game areas.

What we're looking at here is simulation training – the sports equivalent of sitting your mock exams.

To train under exam conditions is a vital part of developing mental toughness.

'Been there, done that' is profoundly reassuring to a performer, and while not all aspects of match day reality can be replicated in training, you can attain some pretty close parallels.

This really encourages a 'bring it on' mentality, come game time. Even if the proverbial kitchen sink is thrown at you, you know you can cope, retain focus and remain calm. This does wonders for your self-confidence!

There are two powerful methods of simulation training:

— **Physical Simulation**

— **Imagery**

## Physical Simulation

Here, you design your training sessions to be as close as possible to the real deal.

You could hire out a 'rent-a-crowd' to create the atmosphere of match day. Have them shout disparaging comments at you (within reason), make those inconvenient coughs or movements, or whistle and yell as you're about to take or make an important play.

As mental training is ultimately about training your mind to conquer your needy YouMinus, it is important to induce the feelings that come with being scrutinised and judged. Have an expert evaluator or two at training to inspect your performance and to offer up scores and feedback at the end. This allows you to get used to scrutiny and judgement and to realise that all you can control is your performance, moment-by-moment.

Why not have your family members come along or have your coach call the local media who can photograph or film one of your sessions?

Even better, introduce a rogue referee into your game to make some very dodgy decisions and see how well you cope. And if you don't handle it so well, learn a better way before match day arrives.

If the match you're preparing for is well above sea level, train at altitude. If you are going to compete in hot conditions, go warm weather training (if finances allow).

Given the vagaries of the weather here in Western Europe, you should also train when it's bucketing down, when pitches are muddy and when courses or tracks are windswept!

# Imagery

If you are playing or competing at a stadium new to you, then go and visit it. Get access to its locker room, arena or pitch and as you walk through it, suck in all the images and feelings. Take a few minutes, close your eyes and visualise being there on match day.

Here we have nature's gift - the ability to simulate competition conditions in the mind's eye.

Imagery is a very powerful simulation tool, one used regularly by the athletes I work with.

## Handball legend runs match day through his mind

The World No 1 handball champion, Paul Brady, visits the handball courts the night before a big game. He walks around and allows his mind to travel to competition day. He 'sees' and 'hears' the spectators as they anticipate his match.

He visualises himself warming-up, before then moving his attention to the game itself. He performs a range of great shots in his mind, from executing his trademark power serve, to hitting a brilliant winning strike off his backhand.

He sees, feels and hears himself stretching his opponent from one side of the court to the other.

So if you happen to meet this Sporting Great the day before a big competition, and he's sitting with his back against the wall of the court with his eyes shut, please don't disturb him; for he's in the middle of a game.

A mental one.

## 'Simulation Combo' Strengthens Your Brain's Pathways

Physical simulation training *and* imagery work best together than each on its own. In fact, your brain's neural network receives a thorough workout when you engage in this training combination. Your neural paths will be strengthened and messages speeded up to help you master your critical moments.

They will become like fibre-optic broadband channels in their efficiency and effectiveness.

---

### Pathway Pitstop 2.7

**Identify critical situations for simulation training**

I would like you to identify several critical moments in your sport and consider how you could use simulation training to master them. These will be situations that, up to now, you have considered outside the reach of preparation. Situations that you hope won't occur. Nothing damages confidence as much as this type of fear. So if you find yourself saying "I hope this or that doesn't happen" then 'this' or 'that' are situations you should consider for simulation training.

Be innovative with your ideas for reproducing competition conditions. Discuss these with your coach and work hard to find a way. And remember, your imagination can create *anything* you wish. So there is no excuse.

---

# Simulation Training in the 21st Century

In the summer of 2010, the sporting public learned of a revolutionary computerised training system for cricket batsmen – *ProBatter*. Based on what baseball players had been using for several years in the United States, ProBatter can simulate the specific bowling delivery of any bowler in the world. It also produces an image of the bowler running in to bowl. As English Cricket Board batting coach, Dene Hills, put it: "This (machine) will take practice up to another level...which can only help them when they encounter the real thing." (*Daily Mail*, 29, July, 2010).

In anticipation of the forthcoming Ashes tour, the English cricket team added to the simulation offered by ProBatter. Not only did they turn up the ambient temperature to mimic the Australian climate, but they also started to play loud rock music to help them focus better.

But Mail cricket correspondent, Paul Newman, reminded readers that "There is only one snag - the Aussies have a machine too, so right now, Ricky Ponting could be facing Stuart Broad in his garden. Virtual Tests anyone?" So, in this new millennium, we are now seeing competition in how top teams simulate reality!

# Engage In Quality Training and Preparation

### Deliberate Practice

Let me say it again – you must engage in purposeful preparation and quality training.

As we've already covered deliberate practice in Pathway 1, Chapter 4, I'll not repeat it here, but feel free to flick back now and reacquaint yourself with the topic. Gaining mastery over a task is *the* source of inner confidence.

### Plan Your Training

As a preliminary step, it is important to know your role, inside-out. You need to profile your role as an athlete across all the dimensions of your sport - the technical, physical, mental and tactical.

It may be useful to consider these dimensions as four modules of your sports examination and that, to perform with distinction, you must have sufficiently mastered the contents of each subject. Two times European Tour winner, Michael Hoey, views each round of golf as an examination of his technical, physical, tactical and mental abilities, and prepares for these four modules meticulously.

The parallel with preparing for academic examinations is useful. Think about it. If you have a pretty good idea of what questions will come up in a test and you've thoroughly revised for them, then you will feel confident and ready to give it your all. You've studied hard and gathered detailed knowledge and understanding of your subject. You've left very little to chance and feel you can master any question asked of you.

Now, isn't this the way you want to feel leading up to competition?

Confident and ready to rock?

Well, top international judoka Lisa Kearney thinks so.

She approaches her fights in an almost forensic manner. Her total confidence is a product of looking at the evidence in favour of her ability to fight well:

> **"My confidence comes from knowing how well prepared I am and that no one is better prepared than me. Knowing how hard I have trained. Knowing my strengths, ability on the mat and my wide range of techniques. Knowing my fight plan. Knowing how great my hunger is. Knowing I deserve it. Knowing, when it comes down to it, I have the right mentality, which I think is more important than anything else."**
>
> **Lisa Kearney** – *Personal communication, 13.05.09*

Retired champion boxer, Joe Calzaghe, holds a similar view to Lisa. Calzaghe never fooled himself in the pursuit of excellence in the ring and would ensure that his preparation was total. Nothing was left to chance. He entered fights knowing that he could not have trained any better. And this knowledge was both a comfort and a source of confidence:

> **"If I go into the ring without preparing properly, I'll be going in there with a false sense of security. If I've prepared to the best of my ability, I can put my mind at ease, knowing that if I perform to the best of my ability, I'll win the fight"**
>
> *Raise Your Game* - *BBC SPORT website*

## Engage In Constructive Performance Reviews

I remember as a youngster (around 10 or 11 years of age) loving goalkeeping so much that after playing football, be it competitively or in the back garden with my mates, I would return home, fetch my 'Goalie Jotter' and sketch out my best saves that day.

I would draw the goal posts, then the trajectory of the shots, say one heading for the bottom-right-hand corner, and then draw myself stretching across the goal to turn the ball around the post. I was no Picasso, but that isn't the point of course. To this day I can still recall the cosy satisfaction and excitement that came from carrying out this exercise.

Back then, I didn't know I was carrying out reviews of my performance that any world class athlete would do. I didn't know that by selecting the best bits, feeling good about them and committing them to memory I was strengthening the neural pathways responsible for making those great saves.

I hadn't a clue about all of that stuff. I simply did it because I enjoyed it and it motivated me to be the best goalkeeper ever. My goalkeeping dreams were born there.

Do you do anything similar? Have you a routine for assessing your performances? Do you ensure that you recall, reinforce and gain confidence from the good aspects of your performance?

Or instead do you tend to dwell on the errors, the defeat or the disapproval of your coach? Are you more emotionally aroused by memories of your poor performances, than by those elements of your display that were masterful? Or is your review much more balanced than this? Can you extract moments of proficiency from an otherwise poor performance? Or are you adept at finding a droplet of mediocrity in an ocean of excellence?

These questions are all important, so please spend some time reflecting on them.

How you evaluate your performance has a profound effect on your confidence and subsequent displays.

It is useful to remember that a performance review is the **beginning of your preparation for your next game**.

## Develop Your Review Process

Make sure you allocate time to evaluate your performances. An ad hoc approach is next to useless. Have a regime that becomes natural to you.

Each review session should follow a format. I suggest you begin with the positives from your performance, before then acknowledging that certain areas of your game still need worked on. You must fight the urge to dwell on the bad stuff and beating yourself up. You'll only sabotage yourself and your efforts.

Start off with the positives and stay there until they sink into your mind. Now, a cursory glance at these goodies is no good. I want you to record the best segments of your performance and FEEL GREAT ABOUT THEM.

Be passionate! Passionate responses commit the good performances to memory and you can retrieve them more easily when you need to boost your confidence.

Moreover, attaching a positive emotion to the memory of a great shot or play is a pleasurable experience. And let's face it, human beings are driven to repeat pleasurable activities.

I really recommend you keep an *Evidence of My Ability* journal to note down things like: great shots, committed tackling and passing, excellent driving and wedge play, accurate, flowing serves, fantastic volleying and passing shots, precise line-out throwing and valuable ball-carrying, composure in the clutch, adhering to routines and game plans, staying focused for the entire match...and so on, depending on your own particular sport.

You want to train your mind to remember all the good performances with the type of excitement and passion that ensures their repetition. Soon your mind will have a library of great displays and your confidence will start to soar.

While you reinforce the sparkling aspects of your performance with *strong positive emotions*, you should study the poorer aspects with a *dispassionate eye*. Here, you become the unflappable clinician looking at a set of blood test scores and circling the dodgy looking readings.

The doctor doesn't get emotionally involved with these readings, but instead puts in place a plan to address them. Perhaps the patient needs iron supplements or an antibiotic.

Whatever it takes, he does it.

His energy isn't wasted on 'what if' thinking and anxiety, as such emotional distractions will not help the patient.

So, it's the same for you and your poor 'readings' on the pitch. Mentally circle them, acknowledge their existence and accept them. Then deal with them. Chat to your coach and devise a training plan to improve the identified skills over the coming week.

This is what London 2012 prospect Lisa Kearney does. She knows her judo can only improve through honest and even-handed post-fight reflection with her coach Ciaran Ward.

It's only human to recoil from scrutinising one's errors, but Lisa accepts that progress is built on recognising and weeding-out the bad habits and nurturing the good ones. In the past she would have been very hard on herself, but now she approaches her performance reviews with much more enthusiasm and an eye to fairness:

> **"Me and my coach always sit down and talk about my fight and look at the video. It used to be quite negative, but it's more balanced now. I let go by looking at the good things and, with the bad things, I identify something to change, avoid or fix. In the past I didn't reinforce good aspects."**
>
> *Personal communication, 13.05.09*

When you have had some particularly poor performances and all seemed a total mess and a dead loss, I urge you take a step back and to do the following. Identify **three** skills or passages of play that contained at least some positives, no matter how small.  Learn to do this.

In fact, top athletes practice this fine art. They zoom-in on their poorest shows and locate positives; the two percent of their performance that wasn't actually that bad and, in many ways, was pretty darn good.

Down it goes in their journal and immediately it goes into their mental library.

## Control the Controllables

Once it hits you that you're not all-powerful and that there are things outside of your control, that's the moment you free yourself from unnecessary and confidence-draining worry.

There are only so many 'what ifs' you can conjure up and only so many contingency plans you can prepare.

This mental game area is also vital in your pursuit of effective focus and distraction control (*Pathway 4*). Lisa once again:

> **"I try to focus on things only inside my control. If it's a recurring thought, I might write it down and really go through it."**

Double Paralympian gold medallist, Jason Smyth, also recognises the simple truth that focusing on what he *can* control, is an infinitely superior strategy to worrying about those things he can't.

Interviewed after his history-making race in Barcelona 2010 (Jason was the first Paralympian to compete in the mainstream European Championship), he revealed that:

"I wasn't really nervous; I was concentrating on the race ahead – reacting quickly out of the blocks, concentrating only on myself and not worrying about others beside me."

## Pathway Pitstop 2.8

### 'My Controllables'

Split a journal page into two columns and head them up 'My Controllables' and 'My Uncontrollables'. Then list those aspects, before and during performance that are within your control and those that fall outside. Under **'My Controllables'** you will have a list of critical factors that you can master in advance of competition. For instance, if you record that you have complete control over your tennis serve, then, in the name of goodness, become the best server ever! It's in your control after all. Indeed, all of your controllables should be approached in this manner. In fact, what you should do, if not already completed, is to profile and prioritise these controllable elements and design awesome training programmes to develop them.

Okay, let's have a look at your **'uncontrollables' list**. Here you will have recorded those things – like poor decisions by officials, unfavourable weather – that you have no control over. Well, not in the traditional sense, of either preventing them occurring or eradicating them once they happen. But there is one control mechanism up your sleeve, one many athletes forget about – the ability to *interpret* the event positively, once it occurs.

How good is this for your confidence? Knowing that you can still influence the most unexpected of incidents by reacting to it in a positive way? You have the final say. Now that's control. A constructive reaction to an unforeseen distraction puts you back in the game.

It is important to remember this - playing sport is *meant* to be challenging and enjoyable. And part of the excitement is fuelled by its inherent uncertainty; just like life itself.

I mean, if every facet of sport was controlled and certain, then very few of us would be motivated or sufficiently focused to compete.

As Voltaire said, "Doubt is not a pleasant condition, but certainty is absurd". He's right you know!

# Contingency Planning

## Tom, the no-nonsense salesman

Tom is a 32 year old self-employed salesman, who supplies customers with his products across the whole of the British Isles. As you would imagine, he often finds himself driving huge distances and frequently through desolate, unpopulated terrain. He has always enjoyed the driving part of his job, unless time was particularly pressing.

One day last year Tom was heading for Inverness. The journey was ticking over nicely when, out of nowhere, a thought popped into his head: "Oh my goodness. Hey - I hope I don't break down out here. I wouldn't know what to do!" Eighteen months in post, and fourteen years driving, Tom thinks this thought for the very first time.

It transpired later that the pressures of new sales targets had been playing on his mind. This had prompted the entirely reasonable thought that if he was stranded on a roadside in the Highlands of Scotland, he wouldn't be able to meet his customers and achieve his targets.

So, there he was, in his Ford Mondeo Estate, finding that his focus had shifted onto worrying about his car playing up. He felt it inevitable that the very thing he didn't want to happen *would* happen.

In fact, he began to find evidence to support his prediction - "What's that noise? I haven't heard that before. Must be something up with the engine. I just knew it" or, "Oh heck; I sure hit that pot-hole really hard - that's bound to damage the tyre!"

This went on for some time.

His anxiety and 'what if?' thinking only subsided when he neared his destination that day. He arrived relieved but mentally drained and found dinner with his clients later that night a real struggle. In other words, he underperformed.

Tom woke up early the next morning and immediately felt very annoyed at being so anxious the previous day. He realised it had interfered with his meeting and that he really must do something practical to address it.

He'd found the whole episode exhausting and didn't want to go through it again. Yawning through dinner was simply not professional. Time to take action.

Tom turned off *Daybreak*, made himself a cup of tea, and took a notepad and pen from his brief case. He jotted down the following thoughts:

*"I now realise that my anxiety didn't really stem from whether or not my car would breakdown. It stemmed from the fact that, if it did, I was incapable of fixing it. I had no plan. No plan, no confidence. There was a gap in my preparation for the journey, and therefore a gap in my preparation for my clients. As I make these journeys on a regular basis there is a greater chance that one day the car will play up.*

"Therefore my best strategy right now is to plan to enrol in a car maintenance course and empower myself with knowledge and skills. This'll allay my 'what if' thinking and boost my confidence, as I'll then know I can cope with whatever crops up. As a Plan B – a 'to be sure to be sure' strategy – I will also join the RAC. Sorted!"

"What this all means for me, is that I can get back to chilling out and enjoying the drive and conserving my energy for meeting my clients later in the day. After all, seeing my clients and meeting their needs is the purpose of these trips"

From this simple analytical exercise, Tom became inspired to give even greater thought to his role as a salesperson. He set time aside later that week and asked himself a few tough questions.

For instance:

"If a client was especially demanding, or rude, or inappropriate, or, God-forbid, became seriously unwell in front of me, would I really know what to do? Am I equipped to deal with such critical moments?"

"Can I tighten-up my repertoire of interpersonal skill-sets to improve my sales performance? What extra training could I do?"

From this period of self-examination, Tom was sure that he had stood still for far too long and had become stagnant. In response to this, he set goals for the next 3, 6 and 12 months.

Within a year and-a-half, and after a lot of hard work from Tom, he became the top salesperson in his company for the first time, and won a trip to Orlando for himself and his family. And all because he had the wisdom to act upon a 'what if?' moment in the wilds of Scotland!

## Pathway Pitstop 2.9

**Develop Contingency Plans**

Tom, a real example from the commercial world, demonstrates the corrosive effect of being ill-prepared to deal with the unexpected and inconvenient. It also shows the confidence boost to be had from contingency planning.

While not every 'What if?' scenario can be catered for, I suggest you identify those situations in your sport that, if they occurred, would throw you completely. As a broken down car would've done for Tom.

List the scenarios and run them past your coach. Next, plan to deal with the situations, should they take place. In many ways, this is akin to having already studied well for a history exam at school, but then a few days beforehand thinking: "What if a question crops up on The Battle of Hastings?" While you know this subject rarely featured in previous papers, you decide to spend an hour, or so, revising the key points around the Battle. You do enough to feel in no doubt that if a question did come up, you could answer it sufficiently. So, instead of worrying about it being asked, you did something practical to cover that base. As a result, your confidence increased, and your anxiety eased.

*Pathway 4* (*Effective Focus*) also covers this mental game area. Identifying and preparing to manage potential pitfalls and distractions, enables you to maintain focus when it really matters. As I've said for many years: *An athlete caught off-guard is asking for trouble!* Don't be that athlete!

Plan your way out of surprise and into control. It's much better for your confidence and composure.

## Go Visit a Champ

If you need to understand what getting to the top involves, then consult a champion. He or she will describe what it takes.

You will also notice that they are normal, down-to-earth people. There is no genetic code to their success. They train hard and with purpose, stretching the boundaries of their abilities bit-by-bit.

They follow a robust goal-setting system, are driven from within and will persist in the face of setbacks. They will also have a strong support team around them.

These athletes are calm, confident and determined to progress.

## Pathway Pitstop 2.10

### Learn From The Best

Right, who would you really love to speak to? Name this person right now and then find out how to meet him or her. Write them a letter requesting a meeting. Do not just email them or their management company. Make it personal and heartfelt. You are on a mission to be the best, so you want to learn from the best. Explain this in your own way.

Bring a notebook with you and have questions prepared. Make sure you get as much out of the meeting as possible. If you are given permission to do so, you should record the conversation. Ask them about confidence:

*What is their definition of this mental game factor? How did they develop it? How do they think, feel and behave when their confidence is high? What tips would they give you in this regard?*

A more removed way to learn such intimate and important knowledge is to read some autobiographies. While choosing a performer from your own sport is obvious, you should also read the success stories of people across other sports and from other fields such as business, entertainment and science. You will find common themes in all of these areas. Note these down, understand them and start to apply them.

# The Simple Power of Affirmations

I can *never* run a sub-four-minute mile
I can *never* run a sub-four-minute mile
I can *never* run a sub-four-minute mile

What do you think **Roger**?

I **can** run a sub-four-minute mile
I **can** run a sub-four-minute mile
I **can** run a sub-four-minute mile

Both of these statements were accurate for those who held them at the time. The first represents the prevailing opinion, in 1950s athletics, about the impossibility of a human running a mile in under four minutes.

Many athletes would have believed this and repeated it over and over to themselves, paving the way to a self-fulfilling prophecy - failure!

The second statement represents Roger Bannister's view of reaching this milestone. And the rest, as they say, is history.

You'll know the story, I'm sure.

On 06 May 1954 Sir Roger, as he is known today, became the first athlete to run a sub-four-minute mile. After this achievement, other milers began to think that they too could run the distance in under four minutes.

And guess what? Many did.

Though I present this in a fairly tongue-in-cheek way, there is a very serious point to be made. If you repeat a statement or affirmation to yourself frequently enough, it begins to seep into your psyche and shape your behaviour.

It's no different to being told by a bully on a daily basis that you're ugly, or by a parent that you'll never amount to anything. Same process, same product. Unless challenged, you'll become that opinion.

Now, if the mind works this way, how can you capitalise on it? What sort of things could you say to yourself that you would love your mind to soak up and use to shape your future? In other words, what affirmations could you create to increase your confidence and improve your preparation and performance?

*Words are the most powerful thing in the universe...*

*Words are containers.*

*They contain faith, or fear, and they produce*

*after their kind.*

**- Charles Capps**

---

**MENTAL MONSTER:**
**"NOBODY else from Northern Ireland can win a Major."**

**"Well, I can."** (Graeme McDowell)

**"So can I."** (Rory McIlroy)

**"Me too."** (Darren Clarke)

---

### Right, what *are* Affirmations?

Constructive affirmations are personal, positive and pithy statements of belief. Their purpose is to alter your attitude about your ability to succeed in specific situations. They can also be more general than this, and focus on your attributes as an individual.

Whether they're specific or general, frequently repeated affirmations will boost your self-belief and confidence. They will download into your mind the belief that you can master what's ahead of you. Through time your behaviour will match the belief.

An affirmation is an amazingly straightforward mental game tool. It is a clever and simple way of convincing your mind to sculpt your future.

## Pathway Pitstop 2.11

### How To Create Your Own Affirmations

Given that we have roughly 50,000 thoughts a day, it would be sensible to have a positive influence over at least some of them! Creating your own affirmations offers you that chance.

Follow the steps below and you'll be arming yourself with a valuable mental skill.

**Step 1:** Identify a positive quality or behaviour you wish to possess or display.

**Step 2:** Once identified, write a statement telling yourself you already possess the desired quality or behaviour. So though you wish to be incredibly confident (future desire), you write an affirmation that confirms its existence in the present - "I am always incredibly confident in competition"

**Step 3:** A well-designed affirmation is:

- **Written in the first person** ("I...")
- **Worded in the present tense** ("I am..." "I have..." "I persist..." "I always... ")
- **Written in positive language** (Rather than "I will not choke", write "I am always calm and composed at critical moments.")
- **Sincere and matters to you greatly.** As you read your affirmation, you should feel emotionally connected to it
- **Succinct**, expressing precisely what you are doing, or what quality you're displaying that's moving you towards your goal. Each affirmation should deal with one issue. Steer clear of stuffing an affirmation full of qualities and

behaviours. Stick to one message per affirmation.

- **Written in 'your voice'.** The affirmation should feel right in your head. It needs to feel authentic. Having said this, though, an affirmation that feels a bit alien to you initially, should bed-in after sufficient repetition.

- **Realistic.** An affirmation that is too far-fetched will not be readily absorbed, even with frequent repetition. If you truly don't believe in what you're saying to yourself, then the affirmation needs to be adjusted to a more reasonable level. It's a bit like a salesman trying the sell a product he simply doesn't believe in. No matter how often he goes through the spiel with a customer, he feels he's fooling them, and himself.

**Step 4:** Have a look at the sample affirmations, below, (kindly provided by several of my clients) and get a feel for what your own list could look like. These examples are simply to prompt thought. Your affirmations must be personal to you and devised by you. As I said, you must feel that each affirmation has your stamp on it; that you care about it so much, it tugs at your emotions.

### Sample affirmations:

| | |
|---|---|
| *I am committed to my goal of reaching the top.* | *I feel at ease with myself.* |
| *I value and respect myself.* | *I always feel ready to play.* |
| *I always practice with a purpose.* | *When I step onto the pitch, I own it.* |
| *I trust my training.* | *I always remain composed in the changing room.* |
| *I really like myself.* | |
| *I always defeat my inner critic.* | *I belong on Tour.* |
| *I treat myself compassionately.* | *I'm in control of my emotions.* |
| *I am a confident person.* | *I feel confident on all putts.* |
| *I perceive anxiety as a sign that I'm ready.* | *I excel at free-kicks.* |
| | *I am dynamite in the box.* |
| *I always reach my ideal state for performing.* | *I enjoy the challenge of a big game.* |

**Step 5:** Begin to write your affirmations following the instructions above. Create affirmations that target *individual attributes* (e.g. your self-respect, self-control, confidence and determination), as well as your ability to master *performance-specific situations* and critical moments (maintaining

composure in putting or free-throwing when the scores are tight, and so on).

**Step 6:** Record your key affirmations onto cards and keep them close to you. You are going to be taking them out and reading them repeatedly. Some of my clients have laminated their affirmation crib cards and keep them safe. I have one guy, a well-known footballer, who treats his cards as he treats the money in his wallet. They remain close to him at all times and represent his mental currency to 'buy' confidence and composure.

**Step 7:** Find time, on a daily basis, to read these affirmations to yourself and out loud if you can. The affirmations that relate to your personal qualities should be read several times throughout each day. Once memorised, you have the freedom to recall them at will. Those affirmations, relating to sport-specific situations, should be repeated before training sessions and competition. Once absorbed, they can be employed at the appropriate moments during performance.

To be effective you have to repeat your affirmations until they stick. As with all the mental game skills presented in the book, affirmations need purposeful and continuous practice so that you can automatically have the qualities you need - when you really need them!

> *Act as if very thing you desire is already here...*
> *Treat yourself as if you already are what you'd*
> *like to become.*
>
> **- Wayne Dyer**

Where an affirmation is the *cerebral* tool to induce the qualities you want, acting 'as if' is the *behavioural* tool to achieve the same end.

They complement each other beautifully, so use them together to maximise your result.

These two clever little techniques are a perfect example of body and mind working together for performance enhancement.

---

### Pathway Pitstop 2.12

**Developing The Art of Acting 'As If'**

Acting 'as if' begins by establishing what follows those two little words. So perhaps you'll want to act *as if* you are *confident and assured* or *in full control and fearless*. Whatever attributes you wish to exude, gain a clear understanding of what they actually mean. Your work on constructing affirmations will have helped you in this regard. But as we're 'skinning this cat' from the behavioural end, you need to appreciate how a confident or fearless person acts.

I suggest you create an image in your mind of how you would like to behave. So, if *confidence* is your goal, run and re-run images that shout out, "I am confident!" To help you do this, identify a role model, preferably from your own sport, who oozes confidence. Zoom-in on his posture and facial expressions. Is he a 'head-held-high' sort of guy? Stands tall, shoulders back? Does he make appropriate eye contact and meet and greet with a firm handshake and a welcoming smile? Do these behaviours seem forced to you, or natural? How does this confident guy dress? When he chats, is it all about him, or is he a modest sort of chap who has no need to verbalise his CV?

---

## Do 'a De Niro'

Like all great actors, you need to research your role and work hard to 'become' it. We all know of the extremes Robert DeNiro goes to, to nail a part. While we mightn't be talking about such extremes here, the principle is still the same. What way do you really want to behave? And what qualities do you wish to display?

Can you actually see and feel that 'person' in your mind? Yes? Good - you have now just identified the part you want to nail.

Your job is to act in the manner of that part until *you become* that part. At every opportunity to act confidently, you should behave as a confident person would. You should exude the quality you want to develop. As with the absorption of affirmations, you need to repeatedly act '*as if* confident' until your brain gets the message.

Eventually it'll not be acting any more – it will be you – and a confident you at that!.

American psychologist and philosopher, William James, knew about this mental game skill over a hundred years ago. "If you want a quality, act as if you already had it", he said.

James recognised that the mind and body had a reciprocal relationship - that you could train the mind through behavioural change and in turn enhance the functioning of the body through mental training. What an amazing species we are!

Incidentally, if you have ever watched the movie, *Catch Me If You Can*, you'll witness one of the most proficient exploiters of the 'acting as if' technique. His name is Frank Abagnale Jr., played in the film by Leonardo Dicaprio.

While still in his teens, Abagnale Jr. conned many people when he acted *as if* he was a Pan Am pilot, a physician and a lawyer! If you get the chance, watch the film!

# Be Self-Compassionate

Several years ago, I spoke at a large gathering of coaches. All was going well with my presentation, until I referred to the mental game area of *compassion*. There was a significant intake of breath and then a few hands went up. The coaches who spoke all concurred that there was simply no room for compassion in the cauldron of competitive sport. But they had missed the point.

I took one of the coaches on, and our conversation went something like this:

**Coach:** "There's no place for such softness. Compassion has its place in the world. But definitely not in sport"

**ME:** "Okay, can you actually give me an example then of where compassion is appropriate?"

**Coach:** "Sure. Em, whenever your child cuts his knee and is crying; when you visit someone in hospital. Erm, all those charity advertisements on the world's starving millions. That kind of thing Mark."

**ME:** "So compassion is something you offer OTHER people?"

**Coach:** "Yes, I suppose that's right."

**ME:** "But *why* would you offer compassion to these people?"

**Coach:** "I guess you're trying to show you care, that you want the suffering to stop and if you could stop it, you would"

**ME:** "Fair enough, that's a good way to put it. You seem to see compassion as a forerunner to solving problems - *other people's* problems. You see that something isn't right, that people are in pain and you're moved by it. So much so, you'd take action if you could, to ease the pain. Right?"

**Coach:** "Yes, that's it"

**ME:** "Okay..."

**Coach:** "Well, er...yes. Oh, I've got you now Mark! You're saying that if it's right to be kind to others when *they're* suffering, then why can't we show ourselves the same compassion? So my players should forgive themselves if they mess up on the pitch and stop torturing themselves?"

**ME:** "Yes, you've got it. We should be kinder to ourselves and cut ourselves some slack when problems arise. We are human and we will make mistakes. Compassion is the direct opposite of softness. It is right to offer it to other people, but don't forget yourself! There is strength in this."

I built on this breakthrough by explaining that self-criticism interferes with performance. It very seldom yields any reward. The coaches agreed that if criticism from other people can erode confidence and esteem, then *self-criticism* must be even more harmful. They conceded that compassion did indeed have a place in sport.

Athletes, as part of their repertoire of mental game skills, should disarm their inner critic through self-compassion. In this way they can maintain their self-belief.

## Mournful Malcolm

A golfer I work with – let's call him 'Philip' - personifies his inner critic. In fact, he has even given it a name - *Mournful Malcolm*.

He sees Mournful Malcolm as having a lugubrious face and a nervous, shuffling gait.

As far as he's concerned, Malcolm is to be pitied, not feared. As soon as Mal embarks on a verbal attack, Philip diffuses the diatribe by offering 'him' some compassion and understanding:

**Mournful Malcolm**: "Dreadful shot!! Your short game is crap. It's an easy Par 4 and you're going to bogey it now. You're useless..."

**Philip**: "Okay Mal, you are hurting right now and I realise that you're striking out at me. I do understand, but it's serving no useful purpose you know. Now if you don't mind, Malcolm, I've a pre-putt routine to be getting on with."

**Mournful Malcolm**: [SILENCE].

At other times, Philip will challenge Mal vociferously, when compassion is thin on the ground.

Either way – through compassion or disputation – Philip limits his distraction to mere seconds and can refocus on the task-at-hand.

And so can you.

## Pathway Pitstop 2.13

### Disarm Your Inner Critic Using The Power Of Compassion

Your *Inner critic* is a component part of your mental monster, YouMinus. As such, it is a method of self-sabotage. Beating yourself up, blaming yourself and telling yourself off are all features of your inner critic. It shows up hot on the heels of an error on your part or some other 'catastrophe'. And boy, your critic can overwhelm you – if you let it.

The **first step** in disarming your inner critic is to identify, monitor and record your self-criticisms. What precisely do you say to yourself, when in self-attack mode? Pay particular attention to your choice of words and note if they chime with verbal attacks from the past.

For instance, a client I treated for depression often called himself a "useless pillock" and told himself that he'd "amount to nothing". Only through thought monitoring, did this man realise that the phraseology he used was his late father's and not his own. He put it well, when he said that he had turned into a ventriloquist's dummy and that his father was still 'working him' from beyond the grave. So who's working you?

**Secondly**, many athletes I work with find it useful to embody their inner critic, as Philip did above. To this end, reflect on what your own version of Philip's *Mournful Malcolm* would look like. Perhaps your critic will be the person from your past whose terminology you now use to beat yourself up. Or maybe, you'll see your inner heckler as the mental monster it is.

Whatever embodiment you settle on, describe it in detail, give it a name and then show it compassion. It's amazing how this mental game tactic can neutralize the inner critic's authority, allowing you to retain your confidence and composure.

To help you construct your compassionate self-talk, refer back to Philip's response to *Mal's* attempt to vilify him. Record a few compassionate responses on some cards and read them often until they are engrained in your mind. Only then, will such responses flow freely during training and competition.

# Unnamed Law:

## 'If It Happens, It Must Be Possible'

The fact that there are elite performers in your sport proves that it is possible to become great. This is indisputable.

If it happens, it must be possible. Just ask the guys that came after Sir Roger Bannister. While attaining greatness involves hard work, resilience, motivation and support, *you* can achieve it.

For me, this 'unnamed law' is as important and reliable as any law of physics.

# Case Study Update – Aaron

## Aaron Makes Progress Along Pathway 2
### Solution to Aaron's Pathway Problem

You first met Aaron in Chapter 3. This **24 year-old professional rugby player's** main problem lay with his rapidly unravelling self-belief. So much so, that he rated his self-belief as a **one out of ten**.

Aaron was back near the beginning of Pathway 2.

Briefly, Aaron had signed for a Championship side in England. The club saw the young fly half as a standout investment. After all, he had achieved highly in his sport, having played for his country at Under-18 and -20 levels and had been team captain at his former club.

The scene seemed set for yet more success.

However, things deteriorated rapidly for Aaron, as his once resolute self-assurance evaporated.

Following a mistake in his debut game, Aaron became increasingly fearful of failing and started to try far too hard to remedy the situation. He tried to force a good performance, but he simply piled more pressure on himself.

Anxiety and self-doubt gripped Aaron's mind and stole his focus away from the process of training and performing.

It didn't help that he fixated on what his club and its supporters where making of their new signing.

If you require a refresher on Aaron's case, **turn to Chapter 3 now**, before returning here to find out how he overcame his mental game problems and began to perform with a renewed and solid self-belief.

## Sport Psychology Intervention

By the time we met, Aaron had lost all heart and couldn't comprehend why his world had imploded so quickly. He had never experienced such an avalanche of self-doubt and self-criticism before. But then he'd never taken such a big step up in his career before. This move would have startled his YouMinus and primed it for action. As an ego-protector, it detests the discomfort and threat that comes with change and uncertainty.

It was during our initial session that I introduced Aaron to the Frankenstein Factor and his mental monster, YouMinus. He needed to know that the source of his mental game difficulties lay within himself - not with rugby.

Rugby hadn't changed at all. Instead, it was his perception of the game that had changed!

As such, he needed to learn the truth of what was happening to him and to realise that the power to overcome it was entirely within his control.

Aaron soon realised that his mental monster lay behind the corrosion of his self-worth and confidence. He came to understand that he had become far too focused on what other people were thinking of him; and that this unhealthy distraction undermined his match preparation and performances.

He also realised that a mistake made during a match didn't cause him to feel anxious or despondent. Rather, it was his negative interpretation of the error that lit the blue touch paper of unhelpful emotions.

So, part of Aaron's mental game work was to dig beneath his destructive reactions and see what he was really fearful of.

This proved to be very helpful for Aaron. He discovered some deeply-held beliefs about himself, other people and the world around him. And like anyone, these beliefs were the rules that governed Aaron's life and fuelled his reactions to certain things.

Let's take a closer look.

### Aaron's (Old) Rules:

*Rule 1*: "I am my achievements. Therefore when I fail *I am* a failure, a loser"

*Rule 2*: "It is a tragedy to let myself down in front of other people"

*Rule 3*: "It is wrong and stupid to make mistakes"

*Rule 4*: "In sport I must meet the expectations that other people have of me"

The next step was for Aaron to challenge the rigidity and downright destructiveness of these and other beliefs and to replace them with more balanced and useful rules for living and performing.

### Aaron's (New) Rules:

**New Rule 1:** "I am much more than my achievements. I am massively more than a fly half, brother, son and fiancé. I am not my mistakes, failures or losses. I AM ME, a person with unlimited potential."

**New Rule 2:** "Okay it's not pleasant making mistakes in front of others, but it's certainly NOT a tragedy. Being human brings uncomfortable moments, but the key is to manage them positively."

**New Rule 3:** "It is inconvenient to make a mistake, that's all it is. While I'd prefer not to make any errors at all, it's ridiculous to demand that they don't occur."

**New Rule 4:** "While it would be nice to meet the expectations of other people, this is a totally unrealistic and energy-sapping expectation in and of itself! Instead, I'll set my own expectations of what I want to achieve, making sure they are realistic, challenging and within my control. Now by doing this, I'll likely be successful and make a lot of people happy in the process. But that's just a bonus. I'm in the driving seat now."

Aaron printed these new, constructive beliefs onto record cards, laminated them and kept them close-at-hand.

To complement this work, I encouraged Aaron to shop at the 'Confidence Store' to build up a portfolio of evidence that demonstrated his worth as a person, and his capability as a rugby player.

It was time to seal those cracks in his self-esteem and confidence.

He recorded clear and detailed evidence of his ability and self-worth in his mental game journal and backed it up with dates and times.

And he learned a powerful lesson...

He had talent. He was a worthwhile human being. There was evidence to back it up.

As part of this exercise, I also asked Aaron's mother and father and his fiancée Vicky to each send him a note, telling him how much they appreciated him as a person, let alone as a son and soul mate.

Aaron committed this evidence to memory.

Day after day, he read the evidence, absorbed it, visualised it, felt good about it and, importantly, kept adding to it.

Slowly but surely his mind began to move in a positive direction. Helpful beliefs emerged, newly shaped, and these became the lenses through which he now interpreted events and experiences.

With Aaron's permission, I asked Ray, his coach, to have a one-to-one with his new signing. I wanted to bring a dose of reality to Aaron's negative interpretations of Ray's behaviour towards him. During this session Aaron was reassured that he had a big future at the club and that his coach had every faith in him.

Within just two weeks of our meeting Aaron was, as Vicky put it, "getting back to his cheeky old self".

You must always remember that mental skills are just that, skills. The more you work on them, the stronger they become. And Aaron had put in considerable effort to strengthen his self-belief. He built up a case to support his worth as a person (his self-esteem) and as a rugby fly half (his self-confidence).

It was also important Aaron recognised that the only time that ever exists is the present, and it was therefore futile to flick between the past and the future; particularly in the throes of a rugby match! As a former Philosophy student, Aaron took to this rationale like a duck to water.

To back this up, I also made sure he devised a robust refocusing strategy to allow him to lock back into the present, should he become distracted during a match.

I re-emphasised that one of YouMinus' greatest tactics, was to place the human mind anywhere, but in the present.

I asked Aaron to describe his pre-kicking routine. It seemed solid enough, with a neat structure to it. But the acid test of any such routine is seen in how useful it is. In other words, does it bring the athlete's focus to the task-at-hand, eradicate over-arousal and ensure high accuracy?

Aaron explained that the routine had served him well for years, but that the stress affecting him over recent weeks had brought an urgency to his kicking.

He said, "It got to the stage where I just wanted to get the penalty kick out of the way".

In reality, Aaron *had* changed his pre-kick routine. It was quicker than before. He explained that he was so gripped by self-consciousness and anxiety, "that everything just seemed to speed up, as if all I wanted to do was to run off the pitch". Aaron admitted that "for some kicks I was so nervy, I thought that my boot wouldn't even connect with the ball. So I just hit the darn thing, ready or not".

This situation needed prompt attention, before it grew into a chronic problem. It was important for Aaron to go back to basics and to enjoy kicking again.

He had always loved the challenge, so it was likely this would return if he set himself some goals and became driven by the challenge to improve.

As his difficulties were relatively recent and therefore not greatly embedded, I had high hopes that with a concerted effort, he would make rapid progress.

As homework, I instructed Aaron to physically *and mentally* rehearse his goal-kicking. I wanted him to speak to his kicking coach and for the two of them to set sufficient time aside each day to allow Aaron to get back into the groove.

I also insisted that he get a bag of balls and go practise on his own after training. To spice up his technical drills a little, I suggested he ask one of his teammates to try putting him off as he took his kicks.

True to his word, Aaron did this and reported the 'distraction exercise' particularly challenging, but incredibly useful. With practise, he found he could nail kick-after-kick, despite the best efforts of his strident teammate.

As a result, his confidence soared and a sense of mastery returned: "I'm still a brilliant goal-kicker. My ability hadn't disappeared. I know I can kick under any circumstance now Mark!"

I made sure that Aaron supplemented these physical drills with short sessions of mental rehearsal/imagery. In these sessions, he would see himself excelling in match situations and coping with those more challenging moments.

For instance, he would spend his three to five minutes of imagery securing 20 kicks from different angles and at different stages of a game. As with his technical work in training, this exercise also boosted Aaron's confidence: "You know what? I could score sixty great points in my mind's eye before heading off to bed!"

We also examined Aaron's pre-match routine. It was important that he stuck to a regime that kept his emotional state at a level appropriate to his needs, culminating in his 'personal ideal performance state' just before kickoff.

He had been feeling far too anxious before games; an emotional state fed by self-doubt and predictions of failure.

In fact lately he'd been retching in the toilets en route to the tunnel.

Aaron's ideal state had always been one of "nervy excitement" and a readiness to meet the challenge head on. However, when questioned, he couldn't tell me how he reached this state: "It just sort of happened Mark. I was always ready, but not anymore."

But at least he knew his ideal state, which meant he could learn techniques to reach it. I therefore taught him some very simple breathing exercises which he found extremely useful at quelling troubled nerves. He also employed imagery of past successes and motivational self-talk to inspire him. I wanted him to turn fear of failure on its head and to replace it with a desire to be "the best I can be" out on the pitch.

Aaron knew he was making progress when, in training, he felt a lightness of spirit returning and a flow to his drills and team play. Indeed Ray singled Aaron out for special mention at a team talk, following a Thursday morning training session. By the Thursday afternoon, Aaron found out he was in the starting fifteen for that Sunday's game.

I watched the match and Aaron played really well, notching up 17 points from the boot and marshalling his line completely. Though missing two kicks at goal, Aaron simply got on with the game. The kicks were history and anyway, he was "not his failures, nor his achievements".

He was a man with endless potential - as long as he had a plan and performed in the present. With this approach to his game, there was simply no room for YouMinus to survive, let alone grow. Aaron's team romped home 32-21 that day and Aaron was ecstatic after the game.

We parted that evening, agreeing to meet up again in three weeks' time to check on his progress. I stressed the need for Aaron to maintain a mental game regimen throughout this time.

## Distance travelled

Three weeks and two matches later, I met Aaron again. I knew from the media that he had continued to play well, so I expected no major problems. Aaron greeted me at his apartment with a great big smile on his face. He was a happy young man again, back in love with his rugby and performing free of interference.

He had accumulated a massive 40 points over the two matches!

Aaron produced his latest Profile sheet from his folder, showing his up-to-date ratings for the six pathways. And for Pathway 2, Self-belief, his rating had increased from an initial 1 out of 10 up to **8** out of 10. He was back in control.

Given the pivotal nature of self-belief, all of Aaron's ratings showed an increase.

I continue to work with Aaron, who has since moved on to an even bigger club. He is performing well, after some four months out of the game with a knee injury. And he has hopes of senior international recognition in the near future.

## Key Points from **Pathway 2**

■ Mentally tough athletes possess high self-belief. They respect and value themselves and approach specific sporting challenges with a 'bring it on' mentality. They give themselves credit for their achievements and remain positive in the face of adversity.

- Your mental monster, YouMinus, casts a dark shadow over your belief system and manipulates it to ensure you do two things:
  - That you perceive yourself as worthless and pathetic.
  - That you perceive specific situations as threatening and insurmountable.

- Self-belief is made up of self-esteem and self-confidence.

- Self-esteem is about how you see yourself as a person; about how you value, trust and accept yourself.

- Self-confidence is the extent to which you back yourself to be successful in specific situations.

- There are numerous ways to overcome the influence of YouMinus on your self-belief:
  - Give yourself credit for your successes.
  - Accumulate evidence to affirm your worth.
  - Recall previous top performances and skill mastery.
  - Learn from the best in your sport.
  - See your circumstances in as positive a light as possible.
  - Use affirmations.
  - Focus on what you *can* control.
  - Devise contingency plans.
  - Engage in simulation training.
  - Carry-out performance reviews that are balanced and constructive.
  - Engage in deliberate practice.
  - Act *as if* you are confidence personified.
  - Be self-compassionate.

# Chapter 6

## PATHWAY 3

# PATHWAY TO

# WORLD CLASS THINKING

Beliefs are the determinant of what one
experiences. There are no external causes.

**- David Hawkins**

By the end of Pathway 3, you will have:

- Understood the link between your thinking style and mental toughness.
- Discovered an amazing secret about the true nature of reality.
- Found out how your mental monster contaminates your self-talk and powers of interpretation.
- Learned powerful techniques that will enable you to think like a champion.
- Caught up with Taylor, a case study from Chapter 3.

This chapter contains information that will change your life forever. It will shape ALL the facets of your being and, of all the pathways, is the quickest route to mind mastery.

The way you think about yourself, other people and your experiences in sport and life, profoundly affects your motivation, emotional state, focusing ability and self-confidence.

It is not an exaggeration to state that interpretation is the way in to mental toughness, a successful sports career and a fulfilling life.

# MONSTER WATCH

## How YouMinus Attacks Your Thinking Style

As you discovered in Pathway 2 on self-belief, YouMinus targets our belief systems, as it knows that how we think about things governs our self-esteem, confidence and a whole lot besides.

YouMinus sucks the blood out of our ability to interpret things in a positive way, and shapes the meaning that we attach to the events in our lives. So whenever you make that mistake on the pitch or court, your mental monster insists you interpret it as negatively as possible. In this way, it gradually trains you to believe that the error caused your reaction and that you have no control over such things.

YouMinus spreads this tactic right across your life and before you know it, you are nothing more than a brittle being, whose emotional state is at the beck and call of events. Event X occurs and you always react with anger. Event Y occurs and you always feel self-conscious and embarrassed. Event Z occurs and you always feel worthy and valuable. Through YouMinus manipulation and repetition, you end up behaving like a lab rat.

You stop thinking for yourself and fail to recognise that no one event can cause you to feel anything without your say-so.

As you'll know by now, the ultimate goal of YouMinus is to create the mental equivalent of an autoimmune disease. It wants you to attack yourself from the inside and so snuff out your incredible potential in a blaze of self-criticism and frustration. And it hisses, *You're c**p, aren't you?!!*

By running your belief system and interpretative ability, YouMinus shapes your reality. Through time you start to believe it's the only version of reality that can exist. That it represents *the* truth about you, other people and the events in your life. But it's an illusion, a deception. The time has come for you to take a step back, see the spin for what it is – total lies – and set about shaping your *own* reality, ensuring that it's positive, enjoyable and successful.

# Creating Your Own Reality through the Power of Interpretation

## I, Robot

Before I knew otherwise, I accepted that my emotions and behaviour were governed by whatever was happening out there in life itself. It definitely seemed that way. Events would occur, situations arose and as a result I would experience feelings and act in certain ways. There seemed to be no join between event and reaction. This gave me the impression that situations *caused* my reactions.

I have named this concept the 'I, Robot Response'.

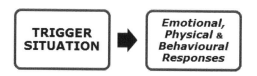

**Figure 3:**  The 'I, Robot' *Response*

What's your view on this? Have you ever felt this way: that your emotions and actions are controlled by events, and not by you? Do you feel that you are a passive receptacle of whatever life throws at you? Reflect on this issue now and jot down any examples to support your view: times when you seemed to react automatically to an event – as if the event itself had caused the reaction.

I truly hope you're not living this way – it is such a fragile and unfulfilling existence. Its effect upon your esteem and confidence will be negative in the extreme.

To place the control of your emotional well-being and sporting future in the hands of fate, is a hopeless way to live - and totally unnecessary! Because the truth is this:

# **Life** isn't 'out there'.

# It's been **inside you** all along

**You think you're HERE**

**But actually you are HERE!**

What this means, is that **you can control your life**. It doesn't have to control you. As a human being, you have been born with the gift of interpretation and choice.

## I, Human - Free To Interpret

What do we mean by life being *inside of you* and not *out there*? Well, here we're getting to the crux of this entire book. Every situation you face in sport and life is meaningless until you interpret it.

So an error is a neutral event until you spin it, for good or ill. And by *spin it*, I'm referring to the meaning you give to it. Now, it may not feel like it (because you're using it negatively right now), but the ability to interpret is **the greatest of human freedoms**.

## Frankl's space

Viktor Frankl, an Austrian neurologist and psychiatrist, was well aware of the liberating power of interpretation, even in situations of complete cruelty and evil:

> **Between stimulus and response there is a space. In that space is our power to choose our response. In our response lies our growth and our freedom.**

He's right of course. Within the space he speaks of, is life itself. And by the way, Viktor Frankl was a Holocaust survivor. If constructive interpretation can enable a person to survive pure evil, then, my friend, it can help you to manage a mere mistake on the football pitch or golf course. Let's get real here folks. Aim to be a lot more grateful and stop finding threat where none exists!

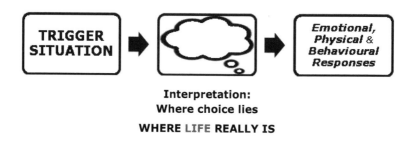

**TRIGGER SITUATION** ➡️ ➡️ **Emotional, Physical & Behavioural Responses**

**Interpretation: Where choice lies**
**WHERE LIFE REALLY IS**

**Figure 4:** Your reality lies in your interpretation of events

While we were born with the facility to interpret (a meld of language, memory, emotion and intellect), we were not born interpreting events in the negative way most of us do. We have learned to do this and it's a process that gave birth to our mental monster, a subject covered in Chapter 1. As interpretation is a skill, it is vital that you monitor your interpretive or explanatory style, to see if it is for you or against you; if it's a help or a hindrance.

For instance, does your interpretation of things typically:

- Undermine your self-belief, or boost it?
- Lead to more worry, or to greater mental ease?
- Dampen your enthusiasm, or increase your determination to succeed?
- Inflame physical tension, or lead to relaxation?
- Distract you from the task-at-hand, or enable you to remain fully focused?

How many of us do ourselves a huge disservice through faulty thinking? How many of us place a ceiling on our chances of success, by interpreting our ability to succeed as low? And how many of us underperform in our areas of work because we predict failure, or worry about leaving our comfort zones and embracing change? Millions of us, I'm sure.

But those at the top of their field know better. They know that their success is guided from the inside. They know that a positive mental attitude is everything.

And what is a positive mental attitude (PMA)?

It's simply CHOOSING to interpret the prevailing situation in a helpful and constructive way. So when you hear athletes talk about PMA, that's all it is – a well-practised habit of thinking in the most productive way possible, no matter what the circumstances are.

Just as Holocaust survivor Viktor Frankl did in Theresienstadt concentration camp.

*They can... because they*

*think they can*

**- Virgil**

## Monty's Mind

It'll not surprise you that golfing legend Colin Montgomerie knows that success comes to those who 'think they can'.

Monty, one of the greatest golfers from these shores, is an eight-time European Order of Merit winner, as well as a Ryder Cup player and captain. His fantastic accomplishments didn't come about by chance though. Of course not. Rather, they were fuelled by a tough mind – Monty's mind!

Here's what he has to say about PMA, and how important it is to respond constructively to events:

> **"Attitude is everything. It's not what happens to you, it's your reactions to it. We're all talented and we all can play the game at this professional level, but at the end of the day it comes down to how you react to certain situations."**
>
> *Raise Your Game, BBC SPORT website*

## Brady's World

You don't become a multiple world champion without being able to create your own positive reality. This is exactly what world handball No 1 Paul Brady does.

Paul and I have worked together for several years now, and one of the key learning points for this awesome athlete, was his realisation that nothing on or off the handball court can unsettle or distract him without his permission.

Paul makes full use of 'Frankl's space'.

If he makes an error, he gives it a mental shrug, remains really positive and focuses on the next point. With practice, he is now able to flip any irritation on its head within seconds. Being able to conserve mental energy in this way means that Paul can remain fully engaged in his matches until the very last point is won.

By creating his own reality on the handball courts of the world, Paul has become a living legend in his sport. As a prescient journalist once wrote:

**"The world is what Paul makes it."**

And I couldn't agree more - and it's the same for *all* athletes. Which means that you too can create *your own* positive reality.

SO DO IT!

## Rick DiPietro - Privilege, not entitlement

New York Islanders goaltender, Rick DiPietro, experienced a very difficult time over a twenty-month period from early 2008. This involved him undergoing several surgical procedures on his hips and knees.

Not a good situation to be in for any athlete, let alone an ice hockey goalie. But DiPietro, as all great athletes do, plucked positives out of the experience - he interpreted the situation as something he could cope with and learn from.

Instead of cursing providence – which would have been understandable – DiPietro did what John Keating urged his students to do in the movie, *Dead Poets' Society*.

You may remember that Keating, played by Robin Williams, encouraged his class to stand on top of their desks to gain a new perspective on the world.

Well, DiPietro stood on a metaphorical desk and interpreted his misfortune in a constructive light.

He would no longer take things for granted. Instead, he would view playing for a top team in the NHL, as a privilege, something to be cherished:

> **"In some ways you can probably look at it as a positive. It gave me the opportunity to step back and get a better perspective of how lucky I am to be given this great honor to be a professional athlete."**
>
> **Chuck Gormley**, NHL.com correspondent, February, 2010

This 'attitude of gratitude' (to coin Camilo Villegas' term from earlier in the book) had a positive influence on how DiPietro approached his daily training.

Despite his recent hardship, DiPietro knew he would enjoy his success much more, now that he had a different attitude. He returned to the rink determined to work hard:

> **"...how I come to the rink every day is a lot different now that I've gone through that. I keep telling myself that when you work that hard and go through that much, the end result will be that much more satisfying. It's true what they say about anything worth getting is worth working for."**

Aside from having greatness in common, Montgomerie, Brady and DiPietro also share the key to that greatness – *world class thinking ability*.

Would you like to think like a champion? It would be great, wouldn't it?

Well, now you can.

And this next section shows you how.

# HOW TO DEVELOP
# WORLD CLASS THINKING SKILLS

### "Hush! Check Those Words"
### *Sophocles*, Ancient Greek Playwright

So, now you know. What you say to yourself about **yourself**, about **others** and about **situations** has a direct influence on your emotions and behaviour. There is a powerful interrelationship between your thoughts, feelings and actions. This relationship underpins the practice and techniques of a very effective intervention, called cognitive behavioural therapy (CBT). There is a particular technique in CBT that I would like to share with you now, as it is a powerful tool for developing excellent thinking ability.

# The ABCDE Model
# of Constructive Thinking

We are not robots governed by life's events. Rather, we have the ability to shape our own experience of life in profound ways. We are free to interpret what occurs in our daily life and, for you, within and across your sporting experience. Please remember this!

Psychiatrists, Albert Ellis and Aaron Beck, founding fathers of CBT in the 1950s and 60s, discovered that their depressed and troubled patients interpreted situations in a highly negative and unhelpful way. These patients viewed themselves, and the world around them, through the lens of mistaken beliefs, with the content of their self-talk containing many instances of what I call 'buckled thinking'.

Now, as your thoughts or interpretations influence your feelings and behaviour, it is clear that negative, unhelpful thinking is going to bring about negative and unhelpful consequences, including:

- Reduced self-confidence and –esteem.
- Increased worry, anxiety, and stress.
- Increased frustration, irritability and anger.
- Reduced concentration.
- Decreased energy and motivation.
- Quitting in the face of adversity.
- Over-arousal/too hyped.
- Under-arousal/flat mood.
- Underperformance.
- Despondency after a defeat or poor performance.
- Unhappiness and feeling low.
- Remaining in comfort zone/risk-averse.

The ABCDE technique encourages you discover for yourself, that a situation (**A** - activating/trigger event) cannot cause you to feel anything negative. Instead, it is your negative interpretation or belief (**B**) *about* the situation that creates your unhelpful emotional and behavioural responses. These are the 'consequences' (**C**).

Once you have established this cognitive daisy-chain between situations, interpretations and emotional, physiological and behavioural reactions, you will then move on to mastering the art of disputing (**D**) your negative thoughts. By challenging your thoughts and replacing them with more helpful ones, you will notice that your emotions and actions become much more positive. These are the new effects (**E**).

Right, let's have a look at the ABCDE technique in action.

## Europro Tour Golfer knows his ABCs and Ds & Es

'Justin', a 23 year old professional golfer on the Europro Tour, was kind enough to offer up an example of the ABCDE technique in action. This particular illustration, set out below, was part of Justin's preparatory work for the new season. He had been keeping a 'Thought Diary' for a while, and had identified many trigger points that tended to trip him up badly on the course. One such trigger was when Justin faced, what he called, "a well dodgy putt".

These were short, but 'makeable' putts, occurring at critical moments. But as Justin missed more than his fair share of these putts, he realised it was time to tackle the mental interference that accompanied these moments. The ABCDE technique helped him to turn things around.

## Justin's ABCDE Example

**A**ctivating Event (*the trigger situation*)*:* tricky five-foot putt for bogey on the Par 4, seventh hole.

**B**eliefs (*the negative thoughts or interpretations of the event*): "Typical of me to leave myself the type of putt I hate and for bogey as well"; "I'm *bleepin'* useless at these. I can never read the line correctly"; "Miss this, and that's another two shots gone – why me?"; "Damn, there's a cameraman. What if my mates see this?"

**C**onsequences (*the unsettling effects of the negative thoughts and interpretations*): anxiety, bodily tension, fear of failure, outcome focus, non-adherence to pre-putt routine, rushing the shot, running the ball beyond the hole, leaving an equally tricky putt back.

**D**isputing (*challenging and changing the self-sabotaging thoughts and interpretations*):**"STOP! That's enough of that thinking. That's my inner saboteur talking, not me. I can**

rise above it. I wouldn't accept my caddy saying all this to me. So, there's no way I'm going to take it from myself. Look, I have no evidence that I'm going to miss this. Just because I have had trouble with these putts in the past, doesn't mean I will miss this one now"

"And as for my mates, I have no evidence they even really care about my golf career, let alone that they're even watching this right now!"

"Remember your routine and stick to it. Step back, take a couple of deep breaths, pick your line and see the ball drop before hitting it. Trust yourself mate, you're a great putter. Now let's do it"

**E**ffect (*the positive consequences of having challenged and changed the negative thoughts*): anxiety and tension eases, optimism rises, increased confidence in nailing the putt, focuses on routine, hits the putt with perfect feel – right into the middle of the hole!

Justin became a master of disputing his inner critic. He became 'barrister-like' in his approach and his performances soared.

His coach said he wasn't at all surprised at Justin's prowess in this regard, as he was "an argumentative little *bleep anyway!"*

Transferable skills eh? Well, whatever works!

Right, let's break the technique down into two manageable sections.

We'll begin with the ABC connection, before then identifying the skills you need to learn to be able to challenge and dispute (à la Justin) and to create new constructive thoughts.

## Pathway Pitstop 3.1

### Do Your ABCs

What I'd like you to do now, is to fetch a brand new jotter and to draw three columns per page, for the first 21 pages (see layout below). This will enable you to note down your As, Bs and Cs, over a three week period. You'll find that many of your recordings will be made in retrospect - after a training session for instance, or post-performance. But this is not just about you and sport - it is about you, period. So, please record your ABCs for any situation when your emotions have been particularly intrusive.

Remember, preceding these interfering feelings are thoughts or interpretations of a situation. No feeling is an island. It has its genesis in your thoughts, which are no more than your interpretations of situations. The ABC part of your investigation will unearth these connections and provide you with a sense of control. You'll no longer feel besieged by emotions that seem to magically appear 'out of the ether'.

| ACTIVATING EVENT | BELIEFS | CONSEQUENCES |
|---|---|---|
| **DAY 1** (Date) *Describe the trigger situation* ↓ **DAY 21** (Date) | *Record your negative thoughts/interpretation of situation* | *Record your emotions, bodily sensations & behaviour* |

Record you ABCs for 21 days and you will begin to join the dots between your interpretation of events and your feelings. And like a twist at the end of a Hitchcock movie, you will discover that all along you had been causing your own angst and performance difficulties. That it's only been you placing restrictions on your progress. *(Appendix 2 contains an 'ABC' Worksheet for photocopying).*

Okay, now the next step is to learn an incredibly important skill – **challenging and changing your thoughts and interpretations**.

*A wise man proportions his belief*

*to the evidence*

**- David Hume**

## Pathway Pitstop 3.2

### Challenge Your Negative Self-Talk

Having monitored and recorded your negative thoughts, you will then set about challenging their veracity, by using penetrative questioning. At this stage, it may be useful to conjure up in your mind an imaginary *'Judge Judy'* to take your negative interpretations to task. Show no mercy - grill them thoroughly. Here are some questions to use:

- Where is the evidence to support this interpretation? Am I using any thought distortions? (See the **Gremlin 6-a-side team**, later in the chapter).
- Does thinking in this way support me or hinder me?
- Is there a better way to think about this situation?
- How would I advise a friend to deal with this thought?
- Will this matter to me in a week's time, or even in 5 minute's time?
- When I thought like this before, did it serve a useful purpose? Or did it distract me?
- Why am I accepting this criticism from myself, when I would NEVER accept it from anyone else?
- Am I being arrogant, believing that my thoughts are always the correct version of reality?

## Google Earth it!

You could also ask yourself this:

> *If I was to 'Google Earth' my problem, how significant would it look? Do my thoughts look reasonable from 'out there'? Particularly when I look across at Somalia or Malawi?*

I have asked athletes to mentally zoom out – as with Google Earth – to gain an enhanced perspective on their worry or problem.

Many clients have found this brisk technique to have a profoundly positive impact on their subsequent interpretation of their 'catastrophe'. As a rugby player quipped to me once, "Hey, look, you can see my problem from space. Put that in your pipe and smoke it, Great Wall of China!" He employed this one-liner during matches as a sarcastic retort to his inner saboteur. In fact, he become so adept at this technique that he created a repertoire of retorts, using scorn to fight back against his inner critic and bully.

> **"Whoa, Double M [Mental Monster], your insight is awesome! I am indeed useless, after making ONE mistake, in ONE moment, in ONE half, of ONE rugby game, on ONE Saturday afternoon, on ONE bit of green grass, in ONE city, in ONE country, on ONE ball of rock, in ONE universe! Yeah, right, Double M!! Go catch yourself on, you bully, you saddo. Go stick your head in a bucket. "NEXT PLAY!"**

## Now do your Ds & Es

Once you have challenged each negative interpretation by putting it to the sword of scrutiny, then, as with our rugby player and golfer, you should construct counter-statements that are much more helpful to you and allow you to get back-in-the-game.

Spend some time on this as you need to find a new interpretation that works for you. Record these constructive interpretations in your 'D' column.

| **ABC** (Completed above in Pathway Pitstop 3.1) | **D**isputing | **E**ffects |
|---|---|---|
| *DAY 1 (Date)* ¦ ¦ ¦ ¦ ¦ ↓ *DAY 21 (Date)* | *Challenge your negative thoughts about **A** - be your very own Judge Judy – and **come up with alternative interpretations** that are positive and will advance your lot* | *Note how your **new thinking** about the situation makes you **feel and act*** |

Next, you can transcribe your helpful statements onto record cards and keep them in your wallet or kit bag. Practice these responses each and every time the triggers at 'A' crop up again.

This way, you get rid of those habitual negative reactions you once had to these events. (*Appendix 3 contains a 'DE' Worksheet for photocopying*).

The mental game played well, is all about controlling the controllables, and with this ABCDE activity you are doing exactly that. You cannot control the occurrence of many events in your life, but what you can do, is control your interpretation of them.

Exploit this ability right away!

## It's What Confident Athletes Do

Confident athletes monitor, challenge and change their destructive thinking patterns and rehearse their new interpretations and statements repeatedly. Through this meticulous and deliberate process, these athletes are etching out new neural networks for their new thinking style. In turn, they gain greater control over their emotional state. And so can you. Record your progress in column 'E'.

By the way, when you are constructing new interpretations, please ensure they're realistic ones and hold personal meaning for you. Use your own style of language, so that the change, from unhelpful thinking to helpful thinking, doesn't seem forced or contrived.

This is exactly what the rugby player described above did. He used his acerbic sense of humour to overcome his unhelpful thoughts before, during and after matches.

## Paul Brady, Quality Controller

Paul Brady takes responsibility for his self talk. He realises that unchallenged negative thoughts can trigger an emotional state that interferes with match preparation and performance.

Paul 'quality controls' his inner dialogue. Thoughts, not up to his high standards, are challenged thoroughly and knocked into shape, or discarded altogether.

> "It's just a case of **constant monitoring** of my thoughts and quelling any doubts as they arise. The main thing is to be aware of these negative thoughts and feelings in the lead up to big matches. I usually acknowledge them, analyse them as truthfully and objectively as I can and then begin the process of

**finding something positive in any of the negative thoughts. I try to be as rational and realistic as I do this. Failure to acknowledge this negativity, in a truthful and rational fashion, could result in complacency, or the risk of an area needing urgent attention being overlooked."**
> **Paul Brady** - *Personal communication, 04.06.10*

## Ronan Oertzen, Mental Barrister

It is important to put your defeatist thoughts in the dock and interrogate them. Many of us simply let such thoughts flow through unchallenged. However, top athletes cross-examine their negative interpretations. They certainly don't let them off lightly.

Rising surfing star, Ronan Oertzen, is one such athlete. Ronan personifies his unhelpful thoughts and, as any competent lawyer would do, presses them for evidence. He finds this strategy extremely valuable and has yet to lose a 'case':

> **"Self-talk is so powerful. Sometimes when I am having a bad surf and I am not performing well, negative thoughts come into my mind (e.g. 'you will never turn pro', 'everyone else is better then you'). These types of thoughts really destroy your confidence. To gain my confidence again, I question my bad thoughts for proof that they are facts. Every single time there is never any proof."**
> **Ronan Oertzen** - *Personal communication, 04.03.10*

# TEAM GREMLIN

If we perceive YouMinus as a *body* of destructive habits, then *Team Gremlin* is its bile duct. These are nasty, bitter and highly destructive thinking patterns that are found in the interpretations and self-talk of anxious, worried and depressed people. And I'm not just talking about a clinical population here.

I am talking about all of us. We all employ these thinking distortions - and they contribute to our negative emotions and moods.

When you are challenging your negative thoughts and interpretations, notice if you are engaging in any of the thinking patterns described below. I have depicted them as a team of gremlins, for two reasons. Firstly, they most certainly are mental pests and will badger you throughout your life, unless you fight back. And secondly, they are a team, because they all have a role and interact with each other.

Now, if this depiction is not useful to you, then form one that is. Either way, these subtle distortions of thought exist. To make progress in your mental game, you must identify and address them. You must defeat Team Gremlin.

## The Gremlin 6-a-side team

### Gremlin Profiles: Roles and Purpose

**1. All or nothing thinking:** This creep can break you emotionally using his good-cop/bad-cop routine. This gremlin encourages you to divide reality into one of only two extreme possibilities. If we interpret experiences through this distorted thinking lens, we tend to see things as either: a total success or a total failure; good or bad; black or white; completely right or completely wrong, and so on. This is a tough way to live and no way to approach sport.

**2. Over-generalizing:** On the back of this gremlin's shirt are two words: 'Always' and 'Never'. This thinking distortion encourages you to be melodramatic. You don't make the team this week, or a disappointing performance occurs and you think: "That's it, I'll never make the team now"; or, "I always mess up playing on that type of course".

So, the key skill of this gremlin is to push you towards taking one negative experience, in one specific situation, and to generalise it to self-pitying proportions: "I'll never..."; "Everything I do is...;" "I'm always..."

**3. Mental filter:** A very clever gremlin indeed. It asserts, "Don't look at those, look at these". In doing so, it steers you away from a list of positives and urges you, instead, to dwell on the one or two negatives in a performance. A startling example of this gremlin in action came from a golfer I worked with, a year or two back. After a splendid first round of 7 under par, in a tournament in Asia, this golfer became fixated on the putts he'd missed and the extra shots he could have picked up. Basically, he was upset that he had failed to attain a new course record!

This particular situation really frustrated me as a sport psychologist. This gremlin was in such control that the golfer was unable to let it go and turn his mind to the startlingly obvious positives in his first round. It was no surprise that he shot a two over par 74 the next day and, from being in third place overnight, fell back to 44th on the leader board.

This nasty little gremlin urges you to pinpoint a grain of displeasure on a beach of pleasure.

**4. Jumping to conclusions:** This mental gremlin goads you to form a negative view of a situation, without having any evidence to support it. It's about mind-reading and fortune-telling:

**"After that performance, the coach will think I'm a waste of time, that I'm rubbish."**

**"Oh boy, I'm going to have a stinker today, I just know it!"**

**5. Rigid reasoning:** This is a particularly bullying gremlin. This thinking distortion involves you setting very rigid rules for yourself. Your self-talk will be full of "I should...", "I must..." and "I ought to..." It is about perfectionism, a style of thinking that will set you up for failure, disappointment and despair. It is 'demand-led', rather than 'preference-led'. It is a particularly effective form of self-sabotage.

**"I really shouldn't have made those mistakes."**

**"To reach the top, I must not make errors."**

**"Life should be easier than this."**

**6. "What if?/Ah, but..." thinking:** This toxic gremlin seizes your present-moment focus and whisks it away to the future. And, not to a successful future at that. Your self-talk will be stuffed full with worry. "What if I mess up my first touch?", "What if I'm drawn against a low ranked player and lose?" You are persuaded to look for and find threat, where there is none. Reassurance does little to assuage your anxiety, as you retort with an "Ah, but..." and continue to worry again. This thinking distortion is a mental vice that can crush your potential.

## Beliefs Are Mental Thermostats

Your mind will find evidence to support each and every belief you hold about yourself, other people and the world around you. That's its job; which is grand, if the beliefs you hold are supportive and constructive. But not so good if you hold negative views.

For instance, if you are a free-taker in soccer, Gaelic football or rugby, and consider yourself a poor exponent of this dead ball skill, then guess what? You WILL BE. You will execute the task poorly most of the time. And if for a while you perform well, nailing kick-after-kick, then your self-image as a poor kicker will rear its ugly head and act as a 'mental thermostat' to bring your ability back to where *you* believe it should be - to an erratic level. And it will always be this way, until you identify and address the underlying belief.

If you don't, then, through time, your underperformances will result in your coach taking you off free-taking duties. Your mind will then use this as further proof that you were right to see yourself as an inadequate dead ball player. And what does your mental monster whisper?  That's right – *Gotcha, Knucklehead!!* Yet, had you challenged your unhelpful belief and improved your thinking and interpretive skills around free-taking, you would have escaped your self-imposed restriction. Accordingly, your performance would have improved and consistently so.

## Pathway Pitstop 3.3

### Identifying Self-Limiting Core Beliefs

Core beliefs are those underlying beliefs that feed your self-talk. They are the well-engrained rules you follow about three facets of life: yourself, other people & the situations you face.

*Self-limiting* core beliefs are those mental rules that place a ceiling on your progress. They restrict your ability to be all that you can be. So underneath such self-talk as "I'm useless", or "I am pathetic", is a perfectionistic rule along the lines of "I must not make mistakes"; "It is unacceptable to mess up"; "I must be successful in everything that I do, otherwise I'm a failure". You can see how these rules restrict growth. How can you ever make progress when you can't make mistakes?

The purpose of Pathway Pitstop 3.3 is for you to tunnel a little deeper into your negative self-talk and identify unhelpful core beliefs.

In an earlier exercise, you were instructed on how to 'DO YOUR ABCs', part of which was to record your negative thoughts and interpretations over a 21-day period.

To identify core beliefs, you should now look across your negative thoughts and see if you can detect any themes.

Perhaps, from surveying your negative thoughts, you'll come across a common theme that points to your concern about what other people think of you.

For instance, you may find that certain negative thoughts are triggered in competitions, but not during training sessions. This disparity should interest you and prompt a bit of detective work.

Whatever themes crop-up, crystallise each one into a core belief and record it in your mental game journal. Without having a clear handle on the makeup of a core belief, you will not be in a position to challenge it sufficiently, if at all.

To challenge these beliefs, engage your mental *Judge Judy*. Cross-exam the beliefs, dispute them and develop alternative, more self-supporting ones.

Remember this, a sports career can falter and fail on the back of a negative core belief. An athlete, who deep down believes "I'm not the type to make it big", *will* find evidence to support this conviction at every opportunity.

And, sadly, he may be oblivious to the fact that by doing so he is engaging in one mighty self-fulfilling prophecy.

# Liberate Yourself from People Worry

**"It's irrelevant what other people think;
it's what I believe."**
***Olaf Kolzig***, *NHL All-Star Goalie*

When all is said and done, are you a people-pleaser; someone who doesn't like to let people down?

Someone who is overly concerned and anxious about how others see them?

Well if you are, I can tell you this - you shouldn't fear ridicule and embarrassment any longer. To do so presupposes people (beyond your loved-ones) actually give a hoot about you for any longer than a few minutes - maybe even a few seconds!

So, here's a novel belief for you, and it will take all of that 'people pressure' off you:

### You are not *that* important!

It's time to wake up and smell the truth. It's time to burst the 'Myth of Self Importance' that I spoke about in Chapter 1.

As Olin Miller counsels:

### "You probably wouldn't worry about what people think of you, if you could know how seldom they do."

He's correct of course. And you can add the following truth to that as well:

### You cannot feel embarrassed, guilty or any other negative emotion, without giving your consent.

# Case Study Update – Taylor

## Taylor Makes Progress Along Pathway 3
### Solution to Taylor's Pathway Problem

You'll remember Taylor's case study from Chapter 3, when we looked at the Pathways Profiling system. This **17 year-old elite tennis player** was having a wretched time pursuing her dream of tennis success. Although only 17 when we met, Taylor had already accumulated considerable success in the sport. But moving up a level to the National Academy had set off her inner critic. It never shut up and bullied her into near-submission.

For some time, Taylor had been the star of the show, but entering the Academy placed her on a par with several other highly ambitious and driven young players. The stakes had been raised and Taylor panicked.

In an effort to keep up with her peers, she became obsessive and perfectionistic.

Taylor's beliefs and thoughts became so narrow and rigid that she set herself up for failure. Compounding this was her perception that everyone else was coping well with Academy life and progressing with relative ease.

She became so good at picking holes in herself and her performances that her best friend jokingly called her, 'Nitpicking Nora'. But it wasn't funny! Severely self-critical and despondent, this young tennis player was tearing her tennis ability apart from the inside out.

You may also recall that Taylor rated her position along Pathway 3 as a **two out of ten**.

So she still had a great distance to travel.

If needs be, feel free to turn to Chapter 3 to jog your memory of this case. Otherwise, read on and discover how Taylor cracked the mental game code by developing a thinking style that supported her pursuit of excellence.

## Sport Psychology Intervention

There was a rigorous educational component to my early work with Taylor. She needed a rationale for her current mental game difficulties, particularly for the existence of her vociferous inner critic. There were times whenever she felt completely dominated by this mental heckler. I explained how the *Frankenstein Factor* shapes much of our self-destructive behaviour and that the way to overcome her internal monster was to engage in systematic psychological skills training.

Taylor learned that beliefs and thoughts were mere theories, not facts. That they needed tested out, and not accepted unconditionally. She became familiar with the *ABCDE Model* of thinking, feeling and behaviour, and got to work immediately on monitoring, challenging and changing her thoughts.

She also realised that she held many unhelpful core beliefs, such as "I must never fail" and "I must never let people down". These, she realised, were straight out of *Team Gremlin*. Her thoughts were so inflexible that they disturbed her emotionally and affected her performances on the tennis court. Taylor agreed with me that with beliefs like these, she didn't need enemies.

For instance, if she played poorly and lost, she believed she had broken her mental rules of 'never failing' and 'never letting herself down in front of other people'. As a result of breaking these rules, Taylor's thinking travelled down the usual tramlines.

She would criticise, blame and hate herself when she fell short of her unrealistically high standards. She would judge herself as an incapable tennis player as well as an inadequate human being. From exploring her early life and upbringing, Taylor became aware that she was simply carrying on her father's tendency to find fault in her. He was the first person to lay down the tramlines of criticism that Taylor now followed.

This insight brought a wry smile to Taylor's face, an acknowledgement of its cruel simplicity. Her fault-finding was a *habit*; her perfectionism was a *habit;* and her low self-esteem and confidence were the inevitable products *of* these very habits. It was that simple.

So simple in fact, that Taylor stood up in the room and said: "Right that's enough. No more strict rules. I want to move forward..."

Realising that she had been using her brain systems *against* herself, swept a wind of change through her mind. She'd had enough, and wanted to take back ownership of her own brain and use its systems to her advantage.

First stop for Taylor, on this voyage of discovery and transformation, was the *language and interpretive systems*. She set out to scrutinise her thoughts for negative bias, before then testing them out.

No way would she call herself "a useless tennis player" when there was abundant evidence of her great ability.

She agreed that just because she chose to ignore how good she actually was, didn't mean her talent didn't exist. In fact, as it was there in spade loads, she decided she would stop treating herself like a piece of dirt on her tennis shoes.

Taylor worked hard and her progress was outstanding. Triggers that typically troubled her were reinterpreted in a kinder fashion.

For example, making a mistake on court, particularly at a crucial time, would have bothered Taylor greatly. She would have had significant difficulty shaking it off and its effect would've reverberated for several minutes, by which time further errors had been committed.

But with practice, she changed all that. She came to accept that mistakes were part of the package deal of life and sport.

From then on, whenever she netted an easy passing shot, Taylor would maintain focus and optimism, by telling herself the shot was now history and that her next serve was *the* most important shot.

She would then take a couple of deep breaths and engage in her pre-serve routine. If receiving serve, she followed a similar ritual.

Having been introduced to YouMinus, her true opponent, Taylor personified the mental creature. This then allowed her to converse with it at those times when it tried to re-exert itself.

This strategy took various guises. There would be moments when she spoke to it with compassion, while at other times you'd find Taylor tearing its illogicality apart, like a High Court barrister.

In doing this, Taylor had tackled her inner critic head-on. She threw the harasser out of her mind, barring it for life.

But she wasn't going to be complacent. She knew that YouMinus lurked in the shadows and that she needed to keep on her toes.

In fact, she remembers driving to see her coach one morning, feeling great, very upbeat indeed, when all of a sudden a thought appeared out of nowhere: "Who are you trying to fool Taylor, with all this positive thinking? It'll not last you know!"

For several seconds, this deflated her mood and for a moment she believed her mental monster's spin. But she had its number.

Having worked so hard on cultivating constructive thoughts and combating negative self-talk, Taylor was able to swat this piece of pessimism away.

She put YouMinus in the dock and cross-examined it thus: "And where's the evidence that this will not last?"

With no reply forthcoming, she turned on the compassion tap: "Look, I realise 'Frankie' (Taylor's name for her mental monster) that your role is redundant and you miss knocking me. But your time is over!"

Taylor often found compassion to be her most potent weapon against her internal critic, much superior to aggression or becoming over-involved in an argument.

## Distance travelled

Taylor made fantastic progress. I can't say she skipped merrily along Pathway 3, because it was tough going at times.

It demanded repetitive practice, perseverance and above all patience with the new mental skills and habits.

She took to the training programme with enthusiasm and saw it as a project - 'Overcoming My Inner Critic'. She then worked on her mental game transformation in a unit-by-unit format.

Self-esteem and self-confidence were approached as modules.

She was the student and she would learn to apply, in a disciplined way, the recommended strategies and techniques.

Taylor regularly sought feedback from me, typically through succinct emails.

This activity in itself boosted her feelings of self-efficacy.

From: ▮▮▮▮▮▮▮▮▮▮
To: ▮▮▮▮▮▮▮▮▮▮▮
Subject: ▮▮▮▮▮▮
Date: Fri, ▮▮▮▮▮▮▮

Hello Mark,

Sorry, another question! I've been having some difficulty using the positive affirmations we looked at on Monday. The problem is, i don't believe some of them, so have changed them 2 sort of more sensible statements. What do u think? Should i think big, even if i don't believe what im telling myself?

Thanks again for ur help. Hope im not being a pain.

Taylor

This email alone sums up Taylor's approach to her journey along this Pathway. She didn't sit on a query and let it fester. Instead she sorted it out.

The example here is a terrific one. Affirmations should indeed be realistic. The ones like 'Every day, I will become a better and better person' don't really sit well with many people.

There's a vagueness with it (i.e. what does *better and better* mean?) and a distinct lack of realism (i.e. *every day*?). A more practical affirmation would be, 'Today I will challenge my inner critic the moment it speaks out'.

Using many of the strategies and techniques covered in this chapter, Taylor became a much more assured and non-judgemental person. Mental interference was greatly reduced and she began to put in consistently good performances on court.

She now valued herself and believed she could maximise opportunities in her personal and sporting lives. She wasn't going to see life as a struggle against malevolent thoughts and emotions and the outwitting of other people.

She was now open to constructive criticism from her coach and others members of her support team.

Above all, she no longer harangued herself.

While she would pep up her motivation by talking firmly to herself, it was all based on positive truths:

> **"Come on Taylor! Stay focused on the next ball coming back over the net. You have a great return. You're backhand and forehand are smooth, your focus is firm and your mind is strong. Come on, next ball!"**

Taylor eventually stopped worrying about people's opinions of her and quashed the urge to compare herself to her peers, unless it was to a constructive end.

Learning something useful from other people was a positive pursuit, whereas feeling envious about her rivals' successes was destructive.

Taylor also broadened her thinking and interpretive style to allow room for alternative explanations. This flexible mindset allowed her to accept mistakes and to move on to the next piece of play.

She also began to experience unconditional pleasure from good performances. It used to be the case that her degree of satisfaction was dependent on receiving external acclaim.

Clearly, her motivational coordinates had shifted to an internal location.

For a seventeen year-old girl, Taylor demonstrated considerable maturity. Liberated by the rationale behind her mental game difficulties, she made considerable and relatively swift progress along Pathway 3.

Eleven weeks into the programme, Taylor reassessed her position on the Pathway from the initial two to a **nine out of ten**.

One year later at follow-up, she had maintained the progress made.

Commenting at the time, Taylor described herself as her "own mental coach", that the techniques were "straightforward, easy to use and it was just a matter of keeping at it, not getting complacent".

She went on to say, very kindly, that:

> **"...working with you Mark, was also straightforward. You told me like it was. That I needed to overcome my habits, that I was doing it to myself, you know, criticising and beating myself up. Despite the urge to condemn myself for having beaten myself up in the past, I resisted this, knowing that this was my**

**YouMinus being very sneaky, trying to suck me back into bad habits! So I gave up the victimhood thing, forgave my father, absolved myself of any guilt and got on with what you taught me...Oh, and I won at the weekend! Nearly forgot to say!!!!"**

# Key Points from **Pathway 3**

◼ The world's best athletes think in distinctly different ways to their competitors. They challenge and change their negative thinking and learn to perceive situations in ways that give them an advantage.

◼ Mental toughness is about understanding that:

- Reality is an 'inside job'.
- Negative beliefs place a ceiling on our potential.
- Nothing in the outside world can affect any of us, without our consent.
- Situations are 'emotion-neutral', until we think about them.
- Positive interpretation is the pathway to self-confidence, emotional control, effective focus and peak performance.

◼ Your mental monster wants you to see the world through *its* eyes. It wants you to buy-in to *its* version of reality. By seizing control over your interpretive ability, YouMinus convinces you that the world is a scary place, that you should avoid failure at all costs and that you are incapable of greatness. In this way, it places you in a prison of fear, anxiety and helplessness.

◼ Backing up YouMinus' assault on your interpretative system is Team Gremlin, a batch of highly destructive thoughts.

■ World-class thinking ability is within your grasp. Apply the principles of deliberate practice to the strategies in this chapter, and you will free yourself from a life of frustration and limitation.

# Chapter 7

## PATHWAY 4

# PATHWAY
# TO EFFECTIVE FOCUS

Attention makes the genius

**- Robert Aris Willmott**

By the end of Pathway 4, you will have:

- Come to appreciate, that effective focus is *the* must-have ability of the ambitious athlete. That it lies at the heart of what mental toughness is all about and is the lifeblood of peak performance and sporting success.
- Discovered how your mental monster seduces your attention away from the task-at-hand and on to irrelevant matters.
- Gained a comprehensive understanding of what effective focus is and how to attain it.
- Identified your own focusing fault lines – those times when you become sidetracked by internal and external distractions.
- Learned how to deal with your distractions and to refocus in the 'here and now'.
- Learned how to let go of errors promptly and to get back in the game.
- Discovered how to develop a quiet and focused mind for competition and to perform in *The Zone* - the sporting heaven inhabited by the best athletes in world sport.
- Caught up with Iain, a case study from Chapter 3.

Effective focus is the key to peak performance. Whether you're an actor, singer, fire-fighter, surgeon, student or athlete, you need to attend to the relevant aspects of the activity-at-hand, for the duration required, and without becoming distracted.

Distraction pollutes concentration and chokes performance. Such mental diversion is the psychological equivalent of a flesh-eating bug. Without adequate strategies to combat it, distraction will eat your performance up, from the inside out.

For you the athlete, those hard yards that you complete day-in and day-out to hone your technique, physique and fitness, can be wiped-out by a nomadic mind. Wiped out, because you don't know how to direct your mental energy towards what matters on the pitch, track, court or course.

There is no doubt that the ability to focus is the most vital mental skill in sport. Being able to attend to each facet of your game as it unfolds, is a prerequisite to performance excellence. This chapter provides comprehensive information and instruction to enable you to harness your focus for sporting success.

# MONSTER WATCH

## How YouMinus Attacks Your Ability to Focus

Any enemy, worth its salt, will attack where it can cause greatest damage and exert maximum influence. And so it is with your inner enemy, YouMinus. It attacks your ability to focus, because without effective concentration you cannot train and compete at your peak.

This mental saboteur knows that if you are incapable of pursuing your goals with full focus and commitment, and have problems performing in the present, then it has got you all sown-up. It knows that without the ability to focus on the right thing at the right time, you have no chance of realising your sporting promise. Your potential will be nothing more than a mirage on the horizon of your sport's career. It'll all be over.

So how does YouMinus go about sabotaging your focus? Well it's easy, really. This spawn of the Frankenstein Factor, turns you into a human meerkat. It has you looking left, right and centre for threat. For instance, it convinces you that making mistakes and failing, particularly in front of other people, are tantamount to sinful acts. It makes embarrassment, ridicule, guilt and ignominy, the big cats of the modern age. As a result, YouMinus will have you acting like some kind of modern day caveman, scanning your sporting environment for these threats. It seduces your purpose away from positive goals and onto the negative goal of avoiding failure and humiliation at all costs. And 'all costs' can be the end of your career!

And your monster mutters, *Oh! This is way too easy!!*

## EFFECTIVE FOCUS

## The Slippery Eel of the Mental Game

If concentration was a person, it would be Baroness Orczy's fictional character, Sir Percy Blakeney: or as he is better-known, *The Scarlet Pimpernel.* Sir P. is a mysterious character, hard to pin down, difficult to describe, but essential to find. Now, isn't focus a bit like that? All athletes know they need it to perform at their best, but struggle to define what it is and even where to find it. And when they do find it, how to keep it. Or better still, when they've lost it how to retrieve it!

### "Elliott!  Concentrate in class!"

I remember at school that my Maths teacher, frustrated by my lack of focus in class, would often be heard bellowing, "Elliott, yes you boy, con-cen-trate!!" In fact, so often was it hollered, that I thought I had a quintuple-barrelled surname: I was 'Mark Elliott-Yes-You-Boy-Concentrate'. This man became so irritated with my lack of corrective action that his veins literally stood out on the side of his head!

Eventually he resorted to sending me out of class to stand in the corridor; or to visit the Principal for a good thrashing.

But whatever punishment I received, the message was always the same - my lack of focus was entirely *my* fault. I was told to concentrate, I didn't do it, and therefore I was to blame. Or so I thought.

Former world number one tennis player, Martina Navratilova, knows that without a trained brain, a 'focus-on-demand' strategy is hopeless. For this tennis superstar, effective focus is always the product of effective practice.

> **"You can't be out there in the middle of a tough match pleading to yourself, 'Concentrate!' The concentration that you need has to come way before your match. You must mentally treat your practice sessions as matches, concentrating on every ball you hit."**
>
> *sonyericssonwtatour.com*

As I hadn't been taught *how* to focus effectively, then I simply couldn't be *asked* to do so by the Maths teacher. It was something I had to work on; something I had to understand, learn to do and practice regularly.

## Effective Focus is a Skill

Concentration is a limited mental commodity and as such needs to be eked-out appropriately during a performance. Now this takes skill.

Remember, it's an absolute nonsense for a student, athlete or offspring to be expected to concentrate, just because a teacher, coach, or parent demands it of them.

Instead, a more strategic approach is required to help them increase their focus. Focusing well is a skill and can only be improved with systematic training and practice.

Given the tendency of coaches to tell their athletes to focus, I strongly suggest that if you're not sure how to, TELL YOUR COACH. Then do something about it.

The same goes for any aspect of your mental game.

Advise your coach that you're reading this book and working on all parts of your mental game, including focusing skills. After all, you two are a team.

It's difficult to learn how to focus well for competition if you're unsure of *what* specific things you should be focusing on, *when* to do so and *how* to do it.

## Effective Focus, Defined

Effective focus is:

**The ability to direct appropriate mental attention to the important task-at-hand, for as long as is necessary to complete the task, while, at the same time, remaining unruffled by internal and external interference.**

Phew! I know, it's a bit longwinded, but it's essential that you understand the apparatus of focus in order to learn how to use it properly.

If you examine this definition, you can see that **direction, selection, duration** and **distraction** are all key elements of focus. The term 'appropriate mental attention' refers to the adjustable width of the lens of focus.

For example, a goalkeeper aiming to pluck the ball out of the air, amidst a crowded 18-yard box, should adjust his lens to a narrow focus setting.

A netball player surveying her options on court will initially adopt a broad focus, before then tapering her focus-lens to select out her wing attack to receive the pass.

We will examine the key elements of effective focus later. By the way, a more succinct definition of appropriate focus could be:

> The ability to keep **the main thing** the main thing... *(after Stephen Covey)*

> ...So long as you know what the main thing is of course!

Okay, let's look at what effective and ineffective focus looks like, starting with the latter.

## What Ineffective Focus Looks Like

An athlete with poor command of his focus will be:

- easily distracted by external factors irrelevant to his performance
- sidetracked by internal factors irrelevant to performance
- consumed by mistakes, unable to let them go
- overwhelmed by too many stimuli at critical moments in performance
- weighed-down by over-analysis

- excessively anxious and worried, prior to competition
- seduced by feelings of complacency or overconfidence, prior to performance
- preoccupied by the outcome of a performance, rather than by the process of performing

It has to be said that an athlete who focuses poorly during competition, is really an inadequately prepared performer. But this is GOOD NEWS as it places the control over focus at the feet of the athlete.

So it stands to sense, if poor focus is a product of poor preparation, that excellent focus is down to first class preparation and planning.

## What Effective Focus Looks Like

An athlete with excellent focusing ability:

- knows what he needs to focus on – what is relevant and what is irrelevant to preparation and performance
- can switch focus as and when required
- is able to deal with the predictable distractions that come with his sport
- is capable of bouncing back from unanticipated incidents
- accepts that errors are part and parcel of the performance package
- possesses a preference-led mindset, rather than one that demands perfection
- parks mistakes and moves on
- performs in the 'now' moment, the ONLY moment that ever exists
- controls the controllables of preparation and performance

- is good at controlling his emotions to a facilitative level
- is sufficiently self-assured to not concern himself with other people's opinions
- is process-driven and does not obsess over results
- identifies positives within setbacks, learns and moves on
- is able to detach himself from any ongoing problems in his life and to commit fully to the process of performing
- lives a balanced life, allowing his mind and motivation to refresh and recharge themselves, away from the high-end intensity and rigour of competition

An athlete who consistently focuses well during competition is a thoroughly-prepared performer. His ability to focus when it matters is neither due to good fortune, nor good genes – it is designed, planned and prepared for. Like all skills that have been mastered successfully, it's all down to deliberate practice.

## Pathway Pitstop 4.1

### You and Your Focus

Hand-on-heart, how skilled are you at keeping focused on the relevant aspects of your performance?

Do you possess the ability to perform in the present moment? Or do you suffer from a mind that jumps between the past and the future – you know, dwelling on a mistake and then worrying about the result?

Are you skilled at regulating your attention throughout a match? For instance:

- Do you know what to focus on?
- Are you aware when you've become distracted?
- Are you swift in regaining focus after a mistake, or some other distraction?
- Can you adjust your focus to meet the task?
- Can you sustain your concentration for the duration?

In other words, when your coach tells you to concentrate, do you *really* know what to do and how to do it?

If you have answered no to any of these questions, don't despair. Because through instruction and committed practice, you *can* acquire the necessary command over your concentration.

## Effective focus in the Heineken Cup

I have had the great pleasure and privilege to work with Rory Best, Ulster captain, for the past six years. He is the consummate professional. He works very hard at every aspect of his game and has particularly benefited from mental training.

Within six months of starting to work together in 2005, Rory had progressed from back-up to first choice hooker for Ulster and to gaining his first cap for Ireland, against the All Blacks. And as I write this book, Rory is on the cusp of his second World Cup.

One key facet of Rory's mental game training was learning how to move on after an error. Of course this takes practice. Routines need to be devised on how to park an error and maintain focus. Rory developed this ability well and to such a degree that journalist Peter O'Reilly observed:

> **"Rory Best doesn't seem to dwell at all on what's done, be it good or bad. He wants to know what's coming next."**
>
> *The Sunday Times, 03.12.06*

While there are many examples of Rory's ability to remain in the present after a potentially distracting incident, for me, the greatest example of all came in Ulster's game against Saracens in the Heineken Cup, in late 2005.

## Ulster v Saracens - Friday 9<sup>th</sup> December 2005, Ravenhill, Belfast

The game was just a quarter of an hour old, when Rory's lineout throw was gathered up near the Ulster line by Saracens' Simon Raiwalui, and, despite Ulster's defensive endeavours, the ball was recycled to Glen Jackson, who scored the first try of the game under the posts.

Rory's reaction to his overthrow and to the ensuing try was to park the error, by sticking to his planned routine for such times. He employed verbal and physical cues to lock his mind back into the 'now moment', and on to the next piece of play from the restart. The game unfolded.

With twelve minutes left on the clock, Ulster led by two points. It was a tight match and it looked like the next try would win the contest. Then this happened.

Ulster's Isaac Boss punted the ball down field and, in the subsequent rush to gather the ball, who should win the race and score? Only Rory Best himself! David Humphreys' conversion settled the match and Ulster ran out 19-10 winners. But more importantly, from the mental perspective, here was a clear demonstration of the reward to be had from learning to deal with a setback, the moment it occurs. It's an illustration of the psychologist's mantra that 'the only thing you can control is the next piece of play'. Rory did this with aplomb and it culminated in his match-winning try! As Peter O'Reilly said - all Rory wants to know is what's coming next!

## THE 6 KEYS TO EFFECTIVE FOCUS

The fifteen factors described in 'What Effective Focus Looks Like' can be distilled into the six keys, listed below. These keys will help to unlock your focusing ability.

**KEY 1 -** Dealing With Distraction

**KEY 2 -** Managing Mistakes

**KEY 3 -** Performing In the 'Precious Present'

**KEY 4 -** Shifting Focus Seamlessly

**KEY 5 -** Controlling Only What Can Be Controlled

**KEY 6 -** Maintain Perspective and Balance

Before we move on to examine the six keys and learn the strategies and techniques to acquire them, I would like you to complete Pathway Pitstop 4.2. As with the previous Pitstop, this is also a self-awareness exercise.

## Pathway Pitstop 4.2

**When I Focus Well *Versus* When I Focus Poorly**

I would like you to reflect on two types of experience:

- Occasions when you have concentrated well in competition; when your performance seemed to flow seamlessly from moment-to-moment; and,
- Occasions when you have focused poorly; when you struggled to perform anywhere near your potential.

As you consider and compare these two experiences, I want you to jot down any differences in your thoughts, emotions and the direction of your focus. So, when you have concentrated well, what were you focusing on, thinking of and feeling? And when your concentration was poor, what were you focusing on, thinking of and feeling?

Also, consider any differences in your mode of preparation across these two scenarios. When you focused well and your performance was seamless and fun, was your preparation fundamentally different to those occasions when your concentration was lacking and you underperformed?

Well, how did you get on? Were you able to identify any important distinctions that could explain why you focus well on some occasions and not on others?

I'm sure you did and I hope you have noted them down. It's vital information.

All right, let's move on with the process of unlocking your focusing ability, starting with the first key, 'Dealing with Distraction'.

# KEY 1 - DEALING WITH DISTRACTION

## Doing a Doug: A Cautionary Tale from the World of Golf

Although American pro golfer Doug Sanders had a great career, winning twenty PGA Tour events, he is remembered for one incident only – a missed putt in 1970!

Now, not any old missed putt, but a very short putt to win the British Open at St. Andrews. If ever there was an illustration of the need to develop and adhere to performance routines, then this is the one.

Let's listen in to Dudley Doust, of *The Independent*, as he describes Sanders' behaviour on the 18th green.

Sanders notices something:

**'Suddenly, he glimpsed a tiny impediment lying in the path from his ball to the hole. It was so tiny, so infinitesimal, that Sanders couldn't distinguish exactly what it was. A pebble? A bit of sand? Whatever it was, the damned thing took command of his mind. "Without changing the position of my feet," he later related, "I bent down to pick it up. It was a blade of dead grass." He tossed it away.'**

**As Sanders's shoes remained rooted to the ground, the fabled Ben Hogan watched the drama unfold on television in Texas. He felt a stab of misgiving. "Back off, Sanders," he implored his fellow Southerner. "Walk away from that putt. Relax. Resettle yourself." Sanders, ignorant of the advice being advanced from half a world away, sought again to pick out the line of the putt. The muscles of Sanders's forearms grew tense. He drew back the blade of his putter and, following a brief pause, stabbed it into the ball. "Mis-hit it," he realised. Then, in a gesture recognised by all golfers, he reached out his putter as if to rake back the ball for a second try. There was no second try: the ball curled slowly, agonisingly, and came to rest wide of the hole. The gallery's silence was followed by a soft, collective gasp.'**

*Dudley Doust*, The Independent, July, 1995

Doust interviewed Sanders after the event. Aside from Sanders' non-adherence to his pre-shot routine, Doust also learned that the golfer's self-talk had been highly presumptive, to say the least. In fact it had destroyed his focus - "As I stood over the ball, I wondered which side of the crowd I'd bow to first."

Wow! How human is that? Straight out of the mental saboteur's handbook! So, what *should* Doug have done? What corrective action should he have taken? Granted, the "tiny impediment" on the green disturbed him, but how should he have responded? Ben Hogan has already answered this one, but I'd like you to place yourself in Doug's shoes.

## Be There

Actually, if you're interested, logon to *YouTube* and see Sanders' error in 'glorious' 1970s faded technicolour. Type in: *1970 British Open - Part 4 - Jack Nicklaus*. Approximately 3 minutes into the video and you find

Sanders approaching the final green. As you watch, see and feel it unfold through his eyes. And if you are a golfer, place yourself in Doug's position and do it better. Win the British Open in your mind. Consider this a type of mental game treat.

By the way, Sanders' miss led to an 18-hole play-off with Jack Nicklaus the following day, which Nicklaus won. I don't think Sanders was able to park the error. To this day, he tells us it intrudes on a regular basis: "I don't think about it very much...Only about every five minutes of my life."

## Pathway Pitstop 4.3

### What's Your 'Dougie' Moment?

Have you ever done a Doug? Times when you thought it was all over, but it wasn't? Times when you thought you had sealed a win, but you hadn't? Times when you became distracted, and never regained your poise?

Record these occasions in your journal, and note how many of them are connected to worries over ridicule, loss of face, or shame. These, as you now know, are symptoms of an ill-at-ease YouMinus.

## Not Lost, Just Misplaced

Now, several years ago I worked with an older gentleman called Horace. He was living proof that with age comes wisdom! One day, just as we were about to head off to an important meeting, I noticed that Horace was looking for something in his office.

"You've lost the car keys, haven't you Horace?" He looked me squarely in the eye and said, "Mark, they're not lost. They're only mislaid and I just haven't found them yet!" His searching was logical and assured and it was no surprise that he very quickly located the keys.

And so it is with concentration. You haven't lost your focus - only misplaced it.

Your focus is always on, in the same way that Horace's keys were always there. His keys were just in the wrong place for the task-at-hand, and many times so is your focus. It is directed to irrelevant cues in your sporting environment. We call this distraction.

Distraction is therefore not an absence of focus; rather, it is an inappropriate use of focus.

## Distraction – Ye Olde Dependables

The more I go through life, the more I agree with the following verse from the book of Ecclesiastes:

> **'What has been will be again,**
> **what has been done will be done again;**
> **there is nothing new under the sun.'**
> *Ecclesiastes, 1:9*

It may appear as a fatalistic observation by Solomon, but my own interpretation of it, is entirely positive. If most things in life are predictable day-after-day, then you can prepare for them and not be surprised by their occurrence. And generally that is the case for the athlete. Most performances are about executing the basic skills well, free from mental distraction. It's not about flamboyance; though those great moments do happen. It's about repeating the hardy annuals and managing *Ye Olde Dependables* of distraction.

Time and again, you'll find that your performances are interrupted by the same sort of things. Now, if you're not sure about this and haven't examined this part of your game yet then do so now, by completing the following Pathway Pitstop task.

**Pathway Pitstop 4.4**

## <u>Your</u> 'Olde Dependables'

What are the dependable distractions in your sport? The ones that seem to crop up week-after-week - the ones that are expected. List them below and record in your journal. Then note to the right of each distraction, your current strategy for countering it. (*Appendix 4 contains a Distractions Worksheet for photocopying*).

| My Usual Distractions | Current Strategies to manage the distraction |
|---|---|
|  |  |
|  |  |
|  |  |
|  |  |

Many performers I work with tell me that this exercise is like seeing an examination paper ahead of time. It provides them with a sense of control over what seemed to be unmanageable events. By knowing what to prepare for and having the means to deal with it, boosts their confidence and reduces their anxiety.

After completing this activity, several athletes were astonished by the huge gap between their knowledge and their action. These clients usually left the second column empty. They were amazed and annoyed that even though they knew about their distractions (some for years) they did little or nothing to address them. Until now. Let me reassure you, this awakening is common. You will find many such landmarks on the road to self-development! Accept things as they are now and feel good that you are going to do something about the situation.

Right, let's dip into a range of athletes' diaries and discover those internal and external distractions that disrupt their performances (see Table 4). An external distraction has its origin in the environment you're in, while an internal distraction resides in you. As you read these excerpts, place a tick beside those that are familiar to you.

**Table 4:** Internal and External Distractions: Some examples

| EXTERNAL DISTRACTIONS | INTERNAL DISTRACTIONS |
| --- | --- |
| Cacophony of noise/kaleidoscopic colour in the stadium | Thinking about the result, before the game is finished |
| Game covered on television | Preoccupied by a mistake |
| Coach shouting at you from the sidelines | Dwelling on being favourite going into a match |
| Unfavourable weather | Worrying about losing |
| Mum/Dad/girlfriend/boyfriend at the game for the first time | Wondering what the coach/media/TV pundits will make of your performance |
| Sledging from an opponent | Overanalysing technique |
| Poor officiating | Fixating on bodily symptoms of anxiety or tiredness |
| Sudden noise in the crowd | Worrying about letting people down |
| Sudden movement by a spectator | Unrealistically high expectations |
| Spectator yelling out above the silence | Worrying about ill family member |
| Flashes going off | Looking at the leader board |
| Trains, planes or automobiles roaring past | Dwelling on the score/forecasting the result |
| Poor pitch/course/track conditions | Preoccupied by argument with partner before you left the house |
| Announcements over tannoy | Experiencing a twinge in a muscle and worrying about it |

Let's keep building up your awareness here – it's Pitstop time again.

---

### Pathway Pitstop 4.5

**Mapping Out Your Distractions**

Okay, now I'd like you to take some time out to examine in greater detail, the types of things that distract you in competition. Refer to Table 4 to facilitate your reflection, as I want you to categorise your interference into **external** and **internal** distractions. Record your responses in your journal. Also, make a note of *when* the distractions occur across the performance cycle; ie, before, during or after competition.

---

Great stuff; well done! You have now mapped out your distractions across your sporting experience. You know the genesis of the interference that draws you away from the task-at-hand before, during and after competition. This is an incredibly important base for improving your focusing ability. Knowing your enemy – interference – and when and where it strikes, is invaluable knowledge. It sets you up nicely for the next step - developing powerful strategies and tools to deal with your distractions.

# Dealing With Distraction - Strategy # 1:

## Know Your Role, Intimately

It is one thing to know what distracts you, but another to nail down what you *should* be focusing on. What is your role as an athlete? What should you be concentrating on before, during and after competition? What are those critical moments that can make or break a performance, depending on how you deal with them? Think about these now, and note down your thoughts.

The message within this strategy is this. If you know, and I mean *really know*, what your role is, including all those nooks and crannies of performance, then when competition time arrives your mind is primed to focus on what matters.

It is less likely to be influenced by irrelevancies as it's so heavily tuned-in to what's going on. "Know your role" is often advised, but I've seldom met a performer who is steeped in it enough to keep distraction at bay.

## Deliberate Preparation- Being at One with Your Role

Several years ago, I was invited to work with an Irish League team – Larne FC - to help them manage their minds in the lead up to a crucial Irish Cup game. It was 2005 and they faced their derby rivals Ballymena United in the semi-final. On paper, Ballymena were clear favourites.

But they hadn't accounted for a team who knew their individual and collective jobs and responsibilities. The Larne players had revised their roles continuously and were ready for their moment in the sun.

My first meeting with the team took place in their small changing rooms, on a clear and crisp March evening. Larne's manager, Jimmy McGeough, a highly experienced former player and coach, was fully behind my coming in and his enthusiasm had spread throughout the squad.

Ah! A sport psychologist's dream – a team willing to learn!

My first question to the team was this: "Do you believe you can beat Ballymena United in three weeks' time?" The squad answered with an unequivocal "YEAH, OF COURSE WE CAN!!" Using what is called *the downward arrow technique*, our interaction then went something like this:

**M.E:** "Great! And how are you going to do that? How are you going to win?"

**TEAM CONSENSUS:** "Play better, play well, score more goals than them"

**M.E:** "Okay. And how are you going to do that?"

**SOME PLAYERS:** "Train hard to make sure we play well"

**M.E:** "Sounds right - but how? What does playing well mean; what does it look like?"

[*Pause*]

**ONE PLAYER:** "It's our job isn't? It's what we do. And we must do it well"

**M.E:** "Good man yourself! That's it. And how can you make sure this happens?"

**THE SAME PLAYER:** "We need to *know* our jobs, our roles on the park"

**M.E:** EXACTLY! That's it. That's it. Now, lads, we're getting to the crux here. Hands up, how many of you know your role in the team?

[*All hands go up*]

**M.E:** "Good. Now I'm going to ask for three of you to describe your role in detail. Let's go to the spine of the team. We'll have the keeper, centre-half and centre-forward."

These three players described their roles to differing degrees of depth and detail. I was particularly struck by the keeper's analysis of his job as a goalie. He broke it down in specific detail and, when asked to describe it visually, he was clearly tuned-in to what was expected of him.

This young lad was so keen to prepare well that he would text me to seek advice and clarity.

I asked several other players to describe their jobs in as much detail as possible; and again there was great variation. One lad, who struggled to describe more than three key features of his position, was, nonetheless, able to relate in significant detail his job as a warehouse manager for a large retail outlet in Belfast.

Without being prompted any further, the player conceded that he needed to know his job for Larne in the same sort of detail that he knew his day job.

The entire team agreed that no player would be able to prepare or perform to the max, if he didn't know his role intimately. It would be an open invitation to distraction.

There was also a consensus that each player would carry out a task analysis, in consultation with their manager and coaches. These would then be recorded and read and reread on a daily basis.

They would also engage in daily imagery of the key skill-sets and situations described in these role analyses. Doing this, together with their physical, technical and tactical drills, meant they would become much more at one with their roles on the pitch, come semi-final day. Nothing was left to chance.

'What if?' scenarios were identified and contingency plans drawn up. For the younger guys, the unique feelings that come with such a big occasion were discussed with those who had been there before. This helped to inoculate the rookies against the unexpected.

An intense focus was put on the process of preparing and performing, and any loose talk of winning was clamped down on. Their concentration was on the 'now moment', with players advised to ask themselves "what could I do right now, however small, that will move me towards performing well?"

These lads were modern day heroes. They were working hard in their various day jobs and positions – we had electricians, teachers, technicians and students – and spent their remaining waking hours immersed in their football jobs.

By the time match day arrived, Larne FC had a squad of players focused only on those things that mattered. Distraction was going to have a hard time permeating these minds! Their brains were wired to keep their focus on the game on a moment-to-moment basis. And they did, running out 1-0 winners on the day, after a superb performance built on grit and a 90-minute focus. It truly was a team effort, with every man executing his role brilliantly. It's a day I'll never forget.

Now, while it may seem unfair to pick a Man-Of-The-Match from what was an excellent team performance, there was one player whose performance was nothing short of exceptional. To this day, I have yet to witness such a display of goalkeeping prowess.

Alex Spackman was Larne's keeper, and it was no coincidence that he was one of the players who took to the mental training programme with enthusiasm. Just as a researcher becomes steeped in his subject, Alex became steeped in his goalkeeping role. He took responsibility for it. He mapped it out clearly, using imagery to galvanise his technical ability and to run through situations that were likely to arise, throughout the match. He was focused only on what he had to do and on what he could control. And it showed through in a dazzling display, free of distraction. I thought it telling that after the match Alex revealed the following information to the awaiting reporters:

> **"At the end of the day, I just did my job... I just kept thinking about the next ball which was coming in"**
>
> *Larne Times, 07 April, 2005*

Now, what about you? Are you *at one* with your job? Do you prepare in a deliberate and purposeful way? Do you know your skill-sets thoroughly? Are you proficient in them all? Are you working on your weaknesses, as well as topping up your strengths? Have you taken time to sit down with your coach and discuss your role? If so, are you both in agreement as to what is required?

Cutting to the chase, DO YOU KNOW WHAT TO FOCUS ON, AND WHEN? For example:

- During your time in the locker room getting ready for the game?
- During your warm-up on the pitch or on the track?
- During performance?
- During downtime?
- After performance?

Please reflect on these questions. It is so important to record your responses, so you can refer to them later.

# Dealing With Distraction - Strategy # 2:

## Develop Refocusing Routines

Every minute of every day, right across the world, there are millions of people demonstrating the power of a focusing cue - the ringtone of the mobile phone.

With the skill of a gunslinger, we reach into our pockets in a heartbeat and slide open our phones to talk, type and send.

We are all technological Billy the Kids!

Wouldn't it be great if you could develop a refocusing cue as effective as a ringtone?

Well you can. Just as you learned to react to the ringing phone through constant repetition, you must develop your own cue for refocusing in competition - then practice it repeatedly.

Do this and it will have the desired effect – bringing you back to the present and into the game.

Now, this cue or trigger has to be personal to you.

Just as your own ringtone stands out above all others, your cue to refocus must be sufficiently distinct to pull you away from distraction.

## "Somewhere Over The _____ "

You said *rainbow* didn't you? Why?

Because the combination of the three preceding words led you to it. And it did so instantly, as the phrase has been ingrained into your mind over time.

Well, an effective refocusing routine follows the very same principle.

When you become distracted, you need to have a succinct combo of cues or triggers that will lead you back to full focus on the task-at-hand.

That leads to your mental rainbow!

The refocusing routine of a European Tour golfer I work with, involves these steps:

- **Step 1:** He recognises that he has become distracted (e.g., noise or spectator movement; thinking about his place on the leader board).

- **Step 2:** He steps back from the moment and takes two or three deep breaths. (The advantage of this simple routine is that he cannot breathe in the past or future – only in the present). A few deep breaths will therefore bring him back into the now moment.

# When you focus on **YOUR BREATHING**, you *will* focus in **THE PRESENT**.

- **Step 3:** Then he firmly says to himself "ENOUGH ALREADY!" Simultaneously, he will brush his mental depiction of a gremlin off his left shoulder, as you would with some dandruff.

- **Step 4:** His closing sequence is to place his right foot down on the 'fallen' mental pest, putting it out like a cigarette, before then straightening his back, lifting his head high and turning his attention to the shot-at-hand.

Through constant repetition of this routine – with a few refinements along the way – this talented young golfer found that his mind would release distractions almost straight away.

Speaking to him about this part of his mental game, he underlines that the routine only works because:

- – It is personal to him, and

- – He has had the patience to practice it, until it stuck.

## Pathway Pitstop 4.6

### Create Your Own Refocusing Routine

You will have noted from the golfer's routine that it comprised of several neat steps:

- Recognition of distraction.
- Stepping back from the moment (physically and mentally).
- Deep breathing.
- Engaging in constructive self-talk, complemented by a prearranged physical action.

From earlier exercises in this chapter, you should now be aware of the typical distractions in your sport. As a result, you are better placed than ever, to recognise when you have become sidetracked during performance. It is important that you develop a routine to turn that recognition into refocus. While your routine must be personal to you, I recommend that it is brisk, particularly if your sport is fast-moving or time-bound.

I also suggest that you follow the STEP BACK/BREATHING/SELF-TALK/PHYSICAL ACTION approach that framed the golfer's distraction drill, above. Your self-talk will, of course, be down to your individual preference, as will the physical cues you use. The bottom-line is this: the routine you develop should free you from the grip of distraction, allowing you to re-engage in what matters, and quickly.

# Paul Brady – Refocusing when it matters most

### BRADY vs. HEALY
### The 2008 US Nationals Open Singles Final, Kansas City, Missouri

In 2008, world handball champion, Paul Brady, faced Tony Healy in the final of the US Nationals Open Singles. The 'Nationals' is a massive event in the handball calendar. While Paul was the favourite to win, he knew that Healy would be a very tough opponent. The 'best of three games' match was going to be a lot closer than most pundits had thought.

Healy won the opening game 21-17, Brady the second, 21-14. In keeping with the rules, the final would now be decided on a tiebreak (first to eleven points would win the title). The first eighteen points were shared, in what was a thrilling game. But then, with the score locked at 9-9, something really bizarre occurred. Something that would surely test Paul's mettle.

Having just hit a wonderful killshot to take a 10-9 lead (or so he thought), Paul was asked by the umpire to replay the point. Why? Because his shot was so powerful, that the ball burst on impact with the wall!

So, instead of sitting at match point, Paul had to do what most of us have great difficulty doing – he had to refocus, dismissing any thoughts about his bad fortune and its timing. It would have been all too easy to feel hard done by and to dwell on the incident.

But not Paul. No way. His trained mind knew exactly what to do.

> **"Shrugging aside his rotten luck, Brady managed to make it back to the service box and reel off a quick ace. At 10-9, the world champion executed a text book hook serve down the left, before rolling the return out in the right corner to seal a sensational win."**
>
> *www.hoganstand.com*

For the situation just described, Paul used a well-ingrained refocusing technique, based on the 'Step Back-Breathing-Self-Talk-Physical Action' method.

What's also important for you to know is that Paul, like all champions, accepts misfortune as part of the package deal of playing sport competitively. The ball bursting at 9-9 was interpreted by Paul as a mere inconvenience, not a disaster. By positively reframing the incident, he removed any annoyance, accepted it for what it was and refocused, as a matter of course.

## Louis Oosthuizen Discovers the Sweet Spot of Focus

If you are an avid golf fan, you will have been drawn to Louis Oosthuizen's great win, in the 2010 British Open at St. Andrews. The young South African golfer demonstrated fantastic mental toughness in his pursuit of the Claret Jug.

As I watched the closing stages of the event unfold with a group of friends, many around me were waiting for Oosthuizen to implode, particularly as he approached the last few holes. But the implosion never came. Instead, we witnessed a golfer in command of his mind, particularly his ability to focus on the shot-at-hand.

And you know what? He also appeared to be enjoying himself out there! In the end, Oosthuizen romped home seven shots ahead of the field.

It came as no surprise to learn that Oosthuizen had a refocusing technique up his sleeve to deal with any distraction. Well not so much up his sleeve, as on his glove!

To deal with distraction, Oosthuizen devised the simplest of refocusing cues - he painted a red dot on to his glove! This visual cue was seen by Oosthuizen every time he gripped his club to hit a shot. It prompted him to commit his full focus to the shot-at-hand. The rest, as they say, is history.

Ace rugby winger, Simon Danielli, uses an equally simple refocusing technique. He employs a verbal cue to lock his mind back into the game:

> **"I will say to myself 'NEXT PLAY' to ensure I get involved again straight away, as the worst thing that can happen, is not getting involved for ages and have that recent error, or other distraction, playing over and over in your head."**
> ***Simon Danielli*** **-** Personal communication, 19.05.10

Another of the athletes I work with is elite judoka, Lisa Kearney. Where Oosthuizen uses a visual cue, Simon Danielli a verbal one, Lisa prefers to use a physical signal, together with a verbal prompt:

> **"I say to myself "Next grip" and make a fist. This is what I do to regain my focus"**
> *Personal communication, 13.05.09*

# Dealing With Distraction - Strategy # 3:

## Devise Focusing Routines for Closed Skills

From the outset, let's define *closed skills*. These are skills executed in a stable and predictable environment. The athlete knows what to do, when to do it and how to do it. Closed skills can therefore be planned for, movement-by-movement. They are self-paced, with a clear-cut beginning and end to them. Closed skills are one aspect of an athlete's performance that can be controlled right the way through, without interruption from anyone else. Except yourself, that is!

Top performers realise that distraction is likely when they perform in front of other people. Accordingly, they develop strong routines to ensure effective, uninterrupted closed skill execution.

The penalty-taker in football, the tennis or handball server, the dart or javelin thrower and the free-thrower in basketball, are all athletes that can make great use of the brain's love of routine and pattern-recognition.

Sports performers should develop routines for such closed-skills as, free-throwing in basketball, serving in tennis, penalty-taking in rugby, hockey and football, and for every golf shot!

---

### Pathway Pitstop 4.7

**Routines For Closed Skills**

Take a few moments to identify the closed skills you perform within your own sport. Note them down and rate how accomplished you are. For instance, what is your success-to-failure ratio? Are you improving? Or, are you inconsistent and feeling frustrated right now? Do you become easily distracted during these critical moments? Does the hoop seem ever so small at free-throws? Does the goalkeeper suddenly appear huge in goal, as you prepare to take a penalty kick? Does the hole shrink when putting? Do you feel overly self-conscious, excessively anxious and exposed at these times?

Jot down your routine when performing closed skills. Is it fit for purpose? In other words, does it bring your focus to the job-at-hand? Are you composed, confident and fully committed to nailing the skill?

Do you follow the same steps before each and every closed skill? Is your focusing routine something you work on and refine, to ensure it continues to serve its purpose?

---

## Neal

I worked with a footballer called Neal to help him improve his penalty-taking. Part of his problem was that the routine he used wasn't personal enough to him. It had been 'handed down' to him by his coach and it didn't tie-in with his personality. A bit like how hand-me-down clothes seldom match the recipient's individual taste! Neal felt self-conscious and ill-at-ease every time he came to take a penalty.

We met up two years ago, a week before the soccer season's busy Christmas schedule. Neal had missed his last two penalty kicks and felt he was about to be relieved of his position on the team.

After an hour-and-a-half, we had developed a new penalty-taking routine that Neal was going to try out in training the next morning.

I advised him to tell his coach of his plans and to hijack a keeper for a couple of hours! As I had to be elsewhere, I couldn't make training. But by mid-afternoon I received a phone call from an excited and extremely happy Neal. He'd scored twenty successive penalties that morning.

His first competitive opportunity came the following Tuesday night. With the game poised on a knife-edge, Neal sent the opposing keeper the wrong way from the penalty spot. The ball nestled into the back of the net; his team went on to win three-one.

Let's look at Neal's routine. It's one he still uses to this day, give or take the odd tweak or two.

- ⚽ Neal receives the ball from the referee, rotates it to locate the logo and sets off for the penalty box.

- ⚽ Walks purposefully to the penalty area and places the ball on the spot, with the logo facing him.

- ⚽ Stands behind the ball and visualises it hitting the selected target (e.g., straight down the middle of the goal to an imaginary 'ball magnet' located in the netting).

⚽ He turns his back to the goal and takes his prescribed four strides, before facing the ball and taking a step to his right (he's a left-footed player).

⚽ He takes two deep breaths as he narrows his focus even further saying, "Through the logo".

Then off he goes! The sweetest of left feet connects with the emblem on the ball and follows through smoothly, as the shot speeds to its target. It takes a superb goalie or a fortunate one, to save his penalties these days. This made to measure routine orientated Neal's attention to the task-at-hand. By repeating the routine over and over again, he became oblivious to the crowd, the occasion, the moment in the match, the score, and so on. It was just him, the ball and the target. Now, who does this remind you of?

## Here comes Jonny

**'The hands, he said, are like a barrier erected against the outside world, helping him to cut out the tens of thousands of opposing fans, who are likely to set up a barrage of whistles and jeers, in an attempt to disturb his intense concentration. "As I got more into kicking," he said, "I became more involved in looking at other aspects, and one area I looked at was focusing from the inside, slowing down the breathing, relaxation, 'centring', which is a way of channelling my power and energy from my core, just behind my navel, down my left leg and into my left foot to get that explosive power. When I was doing this, the position with the hands happened to be the one I adopted'. (*Richard Williams*,** *Guardian News & Media, November, 2003*).

Have you worked out who this kicking sensation is? Yep - none other than England Rugby World Cup hero, Jonny Wilkinson.

You will be familiar with his meticulous pre-kick routine. It is so well rehearsed that you could take fifty videos of it, superimpose them, play them all in one go and hardly see the join!

These types of routines are like signatures. They remain pretty constant over time.

# Dealing With Distraction - Strategy #4:

## Prepare For Those *What If?* Scenarios

By knowing you role inside-out and identifying and preparing for your expected distractions, you will significantly restrict the number of interruptions to your concentration throughout competition.

So that leaves those 'What if?' moments that can occur at any time - "What if *this, that* or *the other* happens?"

I have no doubt that we can eliminate the fear associated with *'What if?'* situations by preparing to meet them head-on. This is a win-win strategy.

If the 'What If?' situation doesn't occur, then great – no worries.

If it does, that's not a problem either, because we've prepared for it and can deal with it in-situ.

To avoid repetition, Pathway Pitstop 2.9 ('Develop Contingency Plans') in Chapter 5 has already covered this important strand of mental preparation.

# Dealing With Distraction - Strategy #5:

## Go For The Jab! - Mental Inoculation

Also covered in Pathway 2 (*Total Self-Belief*), simulation training is an extraordinarily versatile mental game method.

Here, you practice in conditions that approximate those of competition.

In this way, you tick several mental game boxes. Carried out effectively, simulation training can boost your confidence, familiarise you with the stresses of competition and enhance your ability to concentrate effectively.

I often describe simulation training as a type of mental inoculation. In terms of your focusing ability, it offers you the opportunity, ahead of time, to fortify your mind against such psychological 'germs' as:

- performing in front of a large crowd, TV audience or the national selectors
- competing away from your home ground
- unfavourable weather and playing conditions
- fatigue and stress
- poor refereeing decisions

As you can see, these are all potential distractions that can lure your mind away from the task. However, you can learn to manage these situations with training that mimics the real event.

# Robert Green Receives the Boo Jab

Matt Barlow reported in the *Daily Mail*, that after Robert Green's infamous faux pas for England in the 2010 World

Cup against the USA, the West Ham goalkeeper had taken personal responsibility to prepare his mind for the forthcoming Premier League season.

The mental game strategy employed by Green was simulated practice:

> **"West Ham's players and coaching staff have been hurling abuse at Robert Green, in a bid to prepare him for the World Cup backlash expected from crowds this season. The goalkeeper was subjected to prolonged booing during a friendly match at Ipswich on Saturday, a reaction to his howler in England's 1-1 draw against the USA, when his handling error gifted Clint Dempsey an equaliser...Although West Ham insist that their goalkeeper is not haunted by the incident, they do not want the inevitable terrace taunts to distract him when the Premier League season begins on Saturday week. The Hammers are at Aston Villa on the opening day and Green will increase his normal concentration exercises with his team-mates encouraged to hurl insults at him as he trains. Green is a devotee of sports psychology as a way of improving his powers of concentration."**
>
> **Daily Mail,** *05 August, 2010*

There are two types of simulated rehearsal:

- **Physical simulation**, and

- **Mental simulation.**

These two strategies work best in combination.

I'm sure Robert Green complemented his physical simulation training with imagery. This would have allowed him to continue to practice away from the training ground.

## Pathway Pitstop 4.8

### Engage In Physical & Mental Simulation

Physical simulation involves the actual mock-up of the potentially interfering circumstances. Be creative. Have a good chat with your coach and, between the two of you, devise practice sessions that 'vaccinate' you against the wannabe distractions. So, you could invite a large group of spectators along to training. If you belong to a team, your Supporters' Club could offer up an eager audience. To replicate the feeling of being judged, you could always ask along the local media.

Training in front of your friends and family may also induce this "What'll they think of me?" feeling. To get used to dealing with unanticipated noise, you could have a photographer, or two, take ad hoc pictures, or have your coach encourage a few of the spectators to heckle you during training.

Visit the arenas you're going to compete at and take it all in. Have a tour of the changing and performance areas and engage your senses. What do you see, feel and otherwise sense in the stadium? Note these, as they can inform your imagery work, the second form of simulation used by performers.

Simulation using imagery is a neat and flexible way of complementing the physical mock-ups. Whether at work, at home, or sitting in the park at lunchtime, you can use imagery to place yourself in the situations you want to master. As the brain doesn't differentiate between a *real* and *imagined* event, what you have with the brain's imagery system, is a gift of a mental game tool. And one that is used regularly by the best and underused by the rest.

## Anxiety and Focus

Excessive anxiety can have a profound effect on your ability to focus effectively. But with simulation training (physical and mental), you have a strategy that enables you to prepare for such pressures. For instance, you can use imagery to place yourself under the cosh - to see and feel yourself mastering the moment. This moment could include stepping up to take a penalty kick, or feeling highly anxious in the locker room five minutes from kick-off.

Vivid, controlled imagery, can take you anywhere you want to go. Take your mind to those key periods before and during performance and master them. This will prevent you from being thrown by the situations, should they ever occur.

# Dealing With Distraction - Strategy # 6:

## Develop Competition Plans

With this strategy, we're talking about developing a *chain of activities* that links the before and during phases of competition. It's about programming your time in a constructive manner, allowing you to:

- Remain focused on important things.

- Manage your energy efficiently.

- Reach your PIPS* (Personal Ideal Performance State).

  *(Check out Pathway 6 for further information on your PIPS and for great techniques to attain this 'just right' state).

A great deal of confidence and encouragement can come from itemising the mental and physical routines you will follow in the lead-up to competition and beyond. You'll feel reassured that no matter what crops up, you have ways to deal with it.

To paraphrase the strap line of a famous mobile phone company, you'll be in a position to say to yourself – **"I have a technique for that!"**

## Pathway Pitstop 4.9

### Develop A Preparation Chain

I want you to bring together all features of your preparation for competition. Remember, the collective objective of your strands/links of preparation, is to bring you to a mental state *just right for you* and your performance. So list, in chronological order, the steps you will take in the run-up to game day and the routines you will follow on-site and during performance. Here are some prompts to help:

### Night Before Event

- Decide on a night-time regime that ensures you get a darn good sleep.
- Record the time you will go to bed/hours you will sleep.

### Competition Day

- Record your routine for the morning of competition, from waking-up to arriving at the ground or arena. Be specific.
- Consider your diet, what you'll eat and drink, and when.
- Schedule time to pack or check your kitbag.
- Schedule for your mental prep work.

### Departure Time

- Schedule your time to leave for the competition site.
- Record how you will travel and at what time you should arrive at the ground or arena.

### Now List Your On-Site Plan

- Record the mental and physical routines that will link your arrival, to the start of your performance. Be precise.
- Consider those controllable rituals. By all means, put on your kit in a certain way, if it helps, and have a precise warm-up routine that works for you. But don't complicate things.
- Note down the mental game routines you'll engage in.
- Record the expected distractions and your strategies to deal with them. Record your *'What if?'* scenarios, along with your contingency plans should they occur.
- Record the *where/when/what?* of your warm up routines.

Such meticulous preparation is important and is something you should discuss with your coach right now. Start with the end in mind.

Establish how you want to feel at the start of your performance and work backwards from there.

Pathway 6 is vital to you in this respect, as it tells you how to reach this desired performance state.

Okay, let's move on to Key 2. Here, you will learn how to accept and park errors rapidly and remain focused on the task-at-hand.

## KEY 2 - MANAGING MISTAKES

Many of my clients are at the top of their fields, and to a man and woman, they will say that the emotional half-life of winning, is too fleeting to hang their emotional hats on.

For them, the journey is the satisfying part. And what makes it satisfying, is that it involves overcoming setbacks, gaining mastery of situations and progressing.

It's about meeting a challenge head-on.

For the elite performer, errors are nuggets of learning, opportunities to discover a better way. It was Orlando Battista who said that "An error doesn't become a mistake, until you refuse to correct it".

This distinction is useful. It tells us three important things about how you should approach this part of your game:

- **Accept** that errors will happen.

- **Learn** from your errors.

- **Develop** a technique to park errors and move on.

These three principles form a strong base for managing setbacks during performance; and for that matter, dealing with them once the match is over.

## Accept that s*** happens

Making mistakes and meeting adversity are part of life. While uncomfortable, they are not to be feared. If nothing bad occurred in life, we would never appreciate the good. In fact, would we even have the words 'good' and 'bad' in our vocabulary? If everything was flawless, then that would be that, surely?

We'd have nothing to strive for. And let me tell you, it's the striving that's the best bit. Striving fuels growth.

# Learn From Your Errors

### Ireland 20 – Scotland 23 (Six Nations, 20 March, 2010)

Interviewed after an Ireland-Scotland international at Croke Park, Rory Best agreed that the lineout had been shaky during the game. While disappointed, Rory's thoughts had already turned to the remedy – hard work. He accepted the situation and was already planning to turn it into something valuable – learning.

> **"So that's just something I'm going to have to take on the chin and live with. I have to start practising again and show that it was a one-off, a blip. These things happen."**
> **Belfast Telegraph**, *22 March, 2010*

Learn from your errors. Be mature at post-game review, and identify the reasons for the slip-ups during the match, race or round. Tease out key development points to take into training, the following week. Was the error primarily due to a technical weakness, or was it a result of distraction? Were you tiring due to inadequate conditioning? Was it all of the above? Whatever can be learned, learn it. This way, good emerges from bad.

The best performers in world sport train their focus, and have learnt to put their mistakes behind them. They leave nothing to chance.

Let's listen-in to what Paul Brady has to say on the subject:

> **"As with all mental training techniques, I try to practice staying in the 'here-and-now' in training games, before I attempt it during matches. I try to put mistakes and setbacks out of my mind during my training and just concentrate on the next point. Unless I practice this in training games, then I won't be able to do this during pressure situations in competitive matches."**
> **Paul Brady** – *Personal communication, 04.06.10*

# Develop techniques

The inability to park errors instantly, is a common human failing and a universal reason for many poor performances. Dwelling on a badly hit pass or scuffed shot, takes your attention away from the ONLY time that exists and the ONLY time available to you, to exert influence on the game.

That time is the NOW, the present.

It is vital therefore that you develop mistake-management routines that enable you to let go of a slip-up and stay in the game. It is not part of your role to chew over the past, even if the past is only a matter of seconds ago.

As Brian Clough once said, "It only takes a second to score a goal". Clough's right of course, but the footballer needs to be alert to the scoring opportunity, in that second. He won't be, if his mind's elsewhere.

Managing mistakes, is ultimately about knowing and managing *yourself* better.

Here's how to do it.

## Stage One: Examine your poor responses to errors

Look back over recent matches or competitions, and note down those occasions when you couldn't let go of an error. Describe the scenarios. Are there commonalities across them? Are there certain types of errors that throw your focus off-beam? Does it depend when the mistake occurs and against whom?

Record your responses to these mistakes and use the 'ABC Model' to frame your analysis. You'll recall from Pathway 3 that: **A** is the activating event, the error in this case; **B** is your belief/interpretation of the error at A; while **C** refers to the emotional and behavioural consequences of holding the interpretation.

By the way, make sure you check your interpretations for 'thinking distortions' (see 'Team Gremlin' in Pathway 3), for this is likely to be where the *real error* lies.

This examination is invaluable. Perhaps, for the first time, you will realise that an error only ever becomes a distraction, when YOU let it. That's because you think, feel and behave in ways that aggravate the situation. While we often want to blame other people or events for our angst, the simple truth is that the blame lies much closer to home!

The insight you gain will then form the basis of the work you will do, in devising a suitable mistake-management technique. After all, if you know how you caused your own distraction, then you are well-placed to devise a remedy.

To help you on your way, you should use the A.I.M. framework as a guide.

## Stage Two: Take A.I.M.

To ensure a positive response to errors, you need to do three things:

✦ **A**cknowledge that the error has occurred;

✦ **I**mplement a technique that parks it in the past; and,

✦ **M**ove on with your performance.

As with all routines, the one you develop to park errors will be personal to you. Off the shelf ideas, seldom meet your needs and personality style. To avoid repetition, I suggest you revisit Pathway Pit Stop 4.6, 'Create Your Own Refocusing Routine'. It will help you to develop a brisk mistake-management routine. You may also get ideas from the following real world examples.

## Using the Mind's Eye

Imagery is central to Tommy Bowe's mistake-management routine. Rather than ruminating on the error, Tommy will acknowledge it, and erase it from his mind by 'taping over it' with the correct version of the skill.

> **"I see where I went wrong, then visualize doing it right and put it out of my mind then"**
> *Personal communication, 01.04.10*

Not only does this technique keep Tommy in the present but also, by imagining the skill executed well, he is laying down a blueprint for next time. You can be sure the error won't be repeated. His brain has been sent a powerful message.

Here are several more examples. Again, you'll note the personal nature of the routines:

### Squash the Gremlin

A rugby player I worked with a while ago, personalised an error as a gremlin on his left shoulder and, with venom, would squash it in an instant with his right hand - before then getting on with the game.

### Ouch!

I worked with a well-known poker player for a BBC documentary. One of the areas that he had difficulty with was maintaining focus. There is plenty of time to become distracted sitting round a poker table!

Just as simple as Louis Oosthuizen's strategy above, the poker player fixed an elastic band round his left wrist, twanging it when he found his focus wandering.

The subsequent minor *Ouch!* moment reminded him to refocus on the task-at-hand. As with Oosthuizen's red dot, the elastic band was always visible.

# KEY 3 - PERFORMING IN THE PRECIOUS PRESENT

*Time doesn't exist -*

***Clocks exist.***

## Excellence occurs in the NOW!

Life, let alone sport, is no more than a series of individual moments that when stitched together, produce what we refer to as *experience*. Therefore, to optimise what we can achieve in life, we need to manage each moment to the best of our ability, particularly those crucial moments. If we do this, then through time, enough of these individual instants will cluster together to bring us success and fulfilment.

Sounds simple, eh? - When you're competing, just stay in the moment you're in. However, this is not something we do well, for all the reasons provided in Chapter 1. Due to the Frankenstein Factor, we are seduced by the past and the future in equal measure, tossing and turning between the two. But the flip-flop mind has no place in a performance setting. Beyond the odd tactical decision, performers need to stay in the present.

This 'in-the-moment' philosophy has been adopted by top golfer, Michael Hoey. It is an approach that has enabled him to move up through the ranks of the Challenge Tour, and to consolidate his tenure on the fiercely competitive European Tour, by winning the Estoril Open de Portugal in 2009 and the Madeira Islands Open in 2011.

By way of illustration, look at what Michael wrote in an email to me, on the cusp of his 2009 triumph. It demonstrates that he was cultivating a process mindset, and was engaging in simulated practice. He was also learning from watching other elite players; in this case, Tiger Woods:

From: Michael ██████████████████████████████
Date: 30 March 2009 18:33
To: Mark Elliott ████████████████████
Subject: ██████████

Mark,
Another week and another chance to play with lower and lower interference. It's like anything, the more you reduce it, the more benefit and enjoyment you get, and the easier it is to do...I've told myself, go to Portugal, keep it simple, do what you're doing, it's working, and make your practice quality...Focus on short game, try to create pressure when practising, and make sure to practice acceptance during practice. And it's no different during the tournament.

I watched Tiger at the weekend and it was amazing the places he hit the golf ball, accepted it, put it behind him and trusted his ability and exceptional short game.

Just thought I'd let you know my thoughts at the moment and aiming to always play more freely and keep myself in the precious present.

Speak later in week Mark,

Cheers.

Developing a process mindset takes practice. You cannot wish it into existence; you have to work at it, using all of the strategies offered to you on Pathway 4.

Michael has to work hard at practicing and performing in the present. He strives to appreciate the moment he is in, knowing it is the only moment that really matters. He realises when he has become distracted and has learned to refocus rapidly. For instance, when an error occurs out on the course, he does his best to accept it and move on. He realises that an error is an historical event, albeit an extremely recent one! In fact, learning to accept errors and remaining in the present, helped Michael to win his second event on the European Tour - the 2011 Madeira Islands Open at Porto Santo Golfe. Leading by two shots, with six holes of the final round to go, Michael hit a poor tee shot at the Par 3 13th. As soon as it happened, he was beset with regret and a resignation that he had missed the chance to win. He recalls saying to himself: "That's it now; I've thrown this thing away completely". But Michael overcame the inner critic and was able to refocus within seconds.

He accepted that the shot had happened, preferring to deal with reality, than with ifs, buts and maybes. He then set about his well-honed preshot routine, which reassured his mind that all was well. Next he hit an absolute humdinger of a rescue shot! The subsequent bogey 4 felt like a birdie to Michael and from then onwards he sealed the deal, winning the title by two shots – his second win on Portuguese soil. It was a proud day for both of us.

## Pathway Pitstop 4.10

### What's Your Totem?

I thoroughly enjoyed the 2010 movie *Inception*. It's the one with Leonardo DiCaprio and the theme of dream-invasion.

If you have seen it, you'll recall that with all DiCaprio's hopping about from dream to reality, it was important for him to have at hand a totem, an object that would help him to differentiate between dream state and real life. For DiCaprio's character, Dom Cobb, his totem was a small metallic spinning top. As I watched this, I realised that there were parallels with the experience of my clients. This may sound strange, but bear with me. Let's say a golfer makes a mistake, or is otherwise distracted, he has *three* places to go, with only one of them reality. Can you think of the three? Exactly, the past, the present and the future. And the only real state is? Correct again – it's the present! To snap your mind back into reality, it would be useful to have a totem, a trigger or cue that wakes you out of the dream state. 'Dream state', in this context, refers to an athlete's propensity to dwell on the error and/or to worry about outcomes.

So what's your totem? What physical actions and verbal cues do you use to remain in the present?

# KEY 4 - SHIFTING FOCUS SEAMLESSLY

Top athletes can instantly switch focus during performance. They are adept at managing their mental energy, by focusing in the right way, at the right time, as a match unfolds.

In fact, they can do this so smoothly, you get the impression they're spreading their attention across several tasks simultaneously. But they aren't: they're shifting their focus sequentially. It's just we can't see the join!

When we talk of shifting focus, we're referring to switching between the four focusing styles available to us. Effective switching, according to psychologist Robert Nideffer, is a skill in itself and involves matching the most appropriate focus to the task-at-hand. If we are poor at this, then we end up depleting our concentration resource and wasting valuable energy. As a result many of us become distractible and tire towards the end of a performance.

 **Quick task:** Can you see the young woman and the old woman in this classic optical illusion? If you need some help, the eye of the old woman is the ear of the young woman. The old woman's mouth is the young woman's necklace. Now that you can identify the two women, I want you to focus on them both simultaneously. You can't really though can you? If you try to focus on both, your concentration is compromised. Neither image is seen with a full focus. To see them both optimally, you need to shift your attention sequentially, between one and the other. This is what you need to do when performing in your sport.

## Direction and Width - The Two Faces of Focus

At any one moment, an athlete's attention is placed or arranged in one of four ways. There's no fifth way. Each arrangement is a synthesis of two distinct dimensions: direction and width. *Direction* can be either internal or external; *width*, broad or narrow. The two dimensions crosscut, creating four focus orientations:

1. Broad-External
2. Narrow- External
3. Broad-Internal
4. Narrow –Internal

We'll now weigh-up the strengths and functions of each focusing style, with illustrations from several sports.

## 1. Broad-External

When an athlete adopts a *broad-external* focus, his attention is directed outside of himself and he is evaluating options. In the real world of sport, this could be a D-man in ice hockey, rapidly assessing the relative merits of his teammates' positioning, before then moving the puck hard and fast to his forward. A golfer surveying the layout of a hole is also using a broad-external focus to help him gather the necessary information (wind direction, bunker-placements, etc) to aid shot selection. When a soccer goalkeeper has ball-in-hand or a midfielder, ball-at-foot, they will both initially use a broad-external focus to rapidly assess the busy, shifting scene in front of them, before distributing the ball. Fundamentally, the broad-external mode of focus is used to swiftly and accurately absorb what is taking place on 'the field-of-play', before responding immediately and seamlessly with the appropriate action.

## 2. Narrow- External

As playing sport is a fluid experience, it is essential that sport performers learn to shape and shift their attention to meet the demands of the presenting circumstance. Take the above ice-hockey player for instance. In the blink of an eye, he needs to be able to narrow his focus, from the broad-external (used to scan the ice) to the *narrow-external*, to target his forward with the pass. Similarly, (though a tad more sedately than the hockey guy) the golfer, having scrutinised the layout of the Par 5 fifth hole, will narrow his focus to hitting the golf ball to the selected target. Whether passing, hitting, striking or receiving, the narrow-external focus is a vital point of concentration for the athlete who competes in ball sports.

## 3. Broad-Internal

As with broad-external, the *broad-internal* focus also places attention on assessing the bigger picture, but this time from an internal perspective. Emphasis, here, is on methodical planning through strategic, deliberate thought and imagery. For instance, a golfer will utilise a broad-internal stance to develop a game plan for his first round, in a forthcoming tournament. He will systematically analyse and mould his tactics to the demands of each hole. He will 'play' shots in his mind and record his ideas for the round. Basically, the broad-internal modality pertains to all sports. It would be a foolhardy manager, coach or athlete, who approaches a competitive encounter without having firstly focused on strategy. It's the fail to prepare/prepare to fail pitfall.

## 4. Narrow-Internal

The golfer, having devised his game plan (broad-internal focus), begins his round. Before each shot, he not only assesses the layout of the current hole (broad-external), but also, as part of his pre-shot routine, he visualises the ball travelling to the selected target. The use of imagery in this way requires a *narrow-internal* focus. Another example of this in action is the hooker who visualises the ball hitting the selected target at a lineout. Then, there is the free-taker in soccer, rugby or gaelic football who, as part of his pre-kick routine, 'sees' the ball split the posts or hit the top right-hand corner of the net. A narrow, inner focus is also adopted by the player who recalls positive memories to boost his energy and confidence, as well as by the nervous athlete, who engages in calming imagery and abdominal breathing.

## Pathway Pitstop 4.11

### Understanding The Attentional Demands Of Your Sport

In this exercise you'll be identifying the attentional demands of your own sport. Once completed, you'll have an enhanced understanding of where your attention should be placed at various times during performance. You will also identify the type of focus best suited to delivering each element of your role. To bring this information together, I'd like you to pair-off the skills of your role with each of the four focusing styles just described. Use the matrix below to catalogue the skill-sets and scenarios. A copy of the matrix can be found in *Appendix 5* for photocopying.

| Times when I need a broad-external focus: | Times when I need a narrow-external focus: |
|---|---|
|  |  |
| Times when I need a broad-internal focus: | Times when I need a narrow-internal focus: |
|  |  |

The insight gained in this exercise will enable you to develop the right focus for the right occasion during competition.

## Good v Bad

Having identified and categorised the attentional demands of your sport, you are now well placed to carry out a further layer of assessment.

To help you do this, I would like you to select two recent performances; one good, one bad.

Beginning with your high level performance, plot the course of your focus throughout the contest, by asking yourself the following three questions:

- Under what circumstances did I adopt each of the four styles?
- During the performance, did I generally apply the right focus to the right situation?
- When I look back over this performance, was there one focusing style that tended to predominate throughout? If so, which one was it?

Next, examine the poor display and ask yourself the very same questions. Once completed, compare your responses. Were there any distinct differences in your focus, between the good and bad performances?

I bet you there were. I'm thinking you probably noted more task/focus mismatches during your poor performance.

Times, for instance, when you were applying a narrow-internal style (e.g. dwelling on a mistake) to a situation that demanded a narrow-external focus, to lock you back into the game.

What's the key then? Simple. Find a way to repeat the focus you had during your top performances.

After all, these performances underscore the necessity to switch your focusing style, when required. They also confirm that you *can* do it!

It would be worth drilling down a little deeper into these performances to discover: how you prepared for these events; your readiness to perform; and, any techniques you used to stay in the present moment.

Doing this will help you to identify the key elements, common to high level performance.

# KEY 5 - CONTROLLING ONLY WHAT CAN BE CONTROLLED

**"Not being able to govern events, I govern myself"**
**Michel De Montaigne**

How many of us dwell on issues over which we have no control? Our search for certainty in life, fuels the desire to control things.

But life isn't that obliging. So we must weed out those issues over which we have no control and place our focus on those we *can* actually influence. This makes better use of our mental energy. Furthermore, letting go of *the uncontrollables* is surprisingly liberating.

## The Control Paradox

Becoming mentally tough is, paradoxically, a dance between gaining control and giving some of it up. It is about gaining control of what you can affect, in terms of your preparation and performance; and it is about giving up control and ACCEPTING those aspects of preparation and performance that you cannot influence.

# To gain control over your performance you need to **let some control go**

How many footballers have we watched haranguing a referee over an unfavourable decision? Too many! And how many times has a referee replied, "Oh, okay then. I'll reverse the decision. You have the free-kick instead"? Probably none at all. This is one example of wasted energy on something that will not change. It is also a burden on a player's finite store of concentration.

If not already completed, you should flick back to Pathway Pitstop 2.8 ('My Controllables'), in Chapter 5, and carry out the exercise. This assignment will enable you to identify what you can change, and what you cannot.

## KEY 6 – MAINTAIN PERSPECTIVE & BALANCE

In a reminder that life is happening as we speak, and that it is but a fleeting experience, I suggested to the footballers of Lisburn Distillery FC, of the Irish Premier League, that the number **888** would be a useful focusing cue for their forthcoming big cup game, against Belfast powerhouse, Linfield.

Mental training had been going well, and I had been searching for that extra focusing cue that could help the team perform for 90+ minutes, and reach their first cup final for many years.

I wrote up on the flip chart 888 and asked the players to consider its relevancy. Many very creative ideas where put forward, some repeatable, some not; but no-one considered it as anything to do with their mortality. Yet 888 represented their average mortality, in months. Males in the West live for an average of 74 years. Many of us in the room that night were already half-way there! The younger guys also began to calculate the months they'd been alive. A frisson of 'let's get going' flowed through the room, like a spiritual Mexican Wave.

We agreed that each player would felt-tip 888 onto the back of their hands, as a reminder to grab their opportunity against Linfield. The time was now, the underlying motivation - "If not now, when?"

The team went about their business against the mighty Blues and fought hard for every ball – and I mean *every* ball. They were fully committed to the process; they made the most of their chance. Life was too short not to. To a man, each player focused on his role, performed in the moment, batted away any distraction and, in the end, they won the match 2-1. Paul Kirk, Distillery's innovative and passionate manager, was overjoyed and paid tribute to the role of sport psychology, in the preparation of his troops.

In fact, here was a manager who believed that sport psychology was an investment. An intelligent and highly qualified coach, Kirk brought me on board for the 2003-04 season. By April 2004, Lisburn Distillery, the soccer alma mater of Martin O'Neill, qualified for Europe for the first time in 33 years.

The morning after the cup win, I had the BBC on to interview me about, "this 888 business". I was quick to remind the interviewer, that this focusing technique was merely the finishing touch to their mental preparation.

The success was the product of meticulous physical and mental training. Without this and without determination and commitment, you can write whatever you want on your hand, but it'll make little difference.

While this "888 business" was a technique for a particular occasion, what lies beneath it is a very simple truth held by the best in the sporting world - life is short and it must be lived. Many of us merely exist, rather than live. Truly successful athletes are rounded individuals, which is why they tend to be like the guy or girl down the street. They are not loud. They do not act in a way that cries out, "Hey look at me – I'm special". They do not exude an air of "don't you know who I am?" Indeed, they couldn't care less. They have their priorities right. Family first. And it really doesn't matter to them if some stranger fails to recognise them in the supermarket, or wherever.

They are internally driven to succeed and require few external reinforcements. They live their life from the inside-out. They are free, unshackled by the silly pressures of modern life. Worrying about what others think of them, or keeping up with the Jones's, are not on their 'To-Do' lists.

But, playing with their kids, spending quality time with their partners and visiting their parents, are high up on their list of priorities. For many top class performers, their faith is very important to them and they never lose sight of it.

Many others have hobbies that take them away from the hothouse of training and competition. Right brain, creative activities are often chosen – playing a musical instrument and painting, are two examples from athletes I work with.

Ireland, Lions' and Ospreys' winger, Tommy Bowe, knows that balance is important, not only to meet the other important roles in his life, but also to keep his motivation high and burnout at bay:

"I am trying lots of different things outside of rugby here in Wales. It is very important, in my opinion, to have other things going on so that you can concentrate when you're at training or within a match. You need to have something to keep your mind active away from the game or you will get fed-up and tired of it."

*Personal communication, 01.04.10*

In fact as I write this, Tommy is taking flying lessons, with the aim of getting his pilot's licence. So he'll not only be flying down rugby pitches, he'll be flying over them too!

## It's what The Zone is

Focusing on the process, staying in the present, moves you to that state, where body and mind meld and where athlete and environment become one – 'The Zone'.

For me, **the zone is our natural state**, but the ways in which we are educated and socialised, has moved our mental focus too firmly into the left brain.

The left brain is about analysis, detail and separateness; whereas the zone is about **silence, in-the-moment concentration and oneness**.

It is our left-brain orientation that has made it difficult for us to focus in the present, to stay with the process and to enter the zone on a regular basis.

## Paul Goydos Joins the 59 Club

In the first round of the John Deere Classic, in July 2010, Paul Goydos became only the fourth golfer in PGA history to play a round of golf in 59 shots. After his round, Goydos was asked to explain how it had happened. As is often the case, he didn't really know. But one thing he was sure of, he didn't over-think. There was a flow about his game, a sense of body and mind working together automatically:

> **"Yeah. Well, obviously I wasn't thinking. If I was thinking, I think I would shoot 74 or 5... They talk about being in the zone...My game just got better and better as the day went on. I think part of it was my subconscious and I kind of got on autopilot a little bit and stayed out of my own way. It wasn't a conscious effort to stay out of my own way. I just kind of did."**
>
> *pgatour.com*

Unfortunately, Goydos didn't talk of how he prepared for this event. Nor did he speak about his degree of confidence and emotional readiness to play in-the-moment. However, he did tell us that he got out of his own way; a clear reference to eliminating his YouMinus from his round. While he said he didn't consciously do this, he most certainly liberated himself from the monster's grip, by permitting himself to have fun and to not set restrictions on his efforts to perform. And he did *this* bit consciously.

> **"Let's enjoy it. Let's try to make the most of it and have a good time...And I kind of decided, let's have a good time and see what happens."**

This 'devil-may-care attitude' almost certainly freed Goydos up, keeping him away from worrying about the outcome and remaining in the process of hitting each shot. Remember too, that you cannot experience enjoyment anywhere else but in the current moment. Consequently, if you have *enjoyment* as a goal, you will be much more grounded in the present. Enjoyment and satisfaction can come from breathing in the air of the moment, feeling alive, recognising the privilege of playing your sport and, if you are a golfer, committing yourself to each shot. Find the equivalent in your sport and make enjoyment a goal.

## The Peak Performance Sandwich

### Think-Shush!-Think

The left brain does have a very important role to play, particularly throughout the preparation, planning and review stages; but we need it to butt-out during performance; we need it to Shush!

It is impossible to play in the zone when the left brain is chattering away, drawing us from the present to things in the past and future.

**So**, **yes**, learn from the past;

**And yes**, plan for the future;

**But** for goodness sake, live and perform in the present

The information contained across *all* of the six pathways, will enable you to play in the zone. But key amongst these, is the pathway you're on right now!

Effective focus is the key to delivering the type of high-class performance when you are at one with your game. One of the best descriptions of this state comes from ex-Belfast Giants' centre, Bobby Robbins:

**"When you are in a hockey game, you are in a different place. Your natural thought process is far too slow. If you attempt to rely on this archaic means of thinking, you will feel pain, and you will fail, and you will lose, and you will miss.**

**A heightened state is required, and some people refer to this as "the zone". In the zone, you do not think about the pass you are making, or the shot you are zipping toward**

the net, or the body check you are laying on a two hundred pound man...it just happens.

There are only so many drills one can come up with during a hockey practice. And we have all done them countless times, forward and backward. And you don't think about doing them, they simply happen. Your body somehow knows where to go and what to do, and you step back and watch your arms controlling the puck, and you look down and see your skates pumping piston strides, as the whites and blues and reds of the ice zip by.

Even when you aren't looking, you know a puck is coming. Somehow your ears hear the sound of rubber on ice, a perfect sliding disc projectile, and you put your stick out, and your brain maps out invisible algorithms and graphs and charts, and like magic, you place your stick exactly where you know the puck is going to be. And you catch the puck without breaking stride, and know which direction to take it."

*Bobby Robins - belfastgiants.com*

# Case Study Update – Iain

## Iain Makes Progress Along Pathway 4

### Solution to Iain's Pathway Problem

You'll remember, from Chapter 3, that Iain, a **25 year-old professional footballer**, had significant difficulty maintaining appropriate focus before and during matches.

Or, as Iain eloquently put it: "Hey Doc, I live in Distraction City and can't find the road out!"

I found this description telling, as it depicted Iain as trapped in a place he didn't want to be. He knew that he had taken many wrong turns and had become bogged down with irrelevant matters. Needless to say, his performances were suffering. He knew this, as did his coach, but neither had addressed the problem effectively.

So the problem got worse and Iain was eventually referred through to my practice.

What follows, is a synopsis of our work together. Here, you'll find out how Iain found his way out of 'Distraction City', by following Pathway 4. Now, if it's been a while since you read Iain's case and you would like to refresh your memory before reading on, then flick back to Chapter 3 right away.

## Sport Psychology Intervention

After I had explained to Iain what proper focus was, he shook his head and assessed himself as a **three (out of ten)** for this mental game area.

To place his assessment rating in a positive light, I put it to Iain that his score meant he'd *already* travelled about a third of the way along Pathway 4. While acknowledging this, he emphasised that it merely represented those few times when he had performed in the zone. However, he went on to stress that he had no idea why, or how, he played at his peak on those occasions. As far as Iain was concerned, performing in the zone was some sort of random event, or peak performance roulette.

As a centre forward, he had become acutely aware of his flagging goal-to-game ratio. Pressure was mounting, as he felt he was letting the manager down. After all, the gaffer had shown faith in him by bringing him to the club, the previous season.

At that time, he had been specifically tasked with solving the club's perennial goal-scoring problem. The team's

'Goals For' statistics needed a massive boost and Iain was the man to do it.

One of the first activities I asked Iain to do, was to identify what he *should* be focusing on across the performance cycle, but particularly during a match. This essential exercise enabled him to differentiate between, what was relevant to his role as a centre forward and what was patently irrelevant.

It was the first time Iain had *ever* been asked to do this. Iain had two lists at his disposal, with the headings: 'Things Relevant to My Job on the Pitch' and, 'Things Irrelevant to My Job on the Pitch'.

Next, he reflected on two types of performance: times when he played with full focus and played well; and, times when he was easily distracted and played poorly.

Even a cursory examination of these occasions told a story. When concentration was poor, Iain had let his mind wander to things extraneous to his job on the pitch (e.g. harsh refereeing decisions, fretting about what his manager was thinking, and dwelling on the mistake he just made).

When Iain played well, his mind was engaged in the moment-by-moment unfolding of the match. In these games, he seemed to play in automatic pilot mode. With little thought, he would be making great runs, finding space in the box, losing his marker on numerous occasions and, crucially, scoring or making goals.

I asked Iain to become his own personal scientist and to look deeper still into these examples. I wanted him to uncover any differences that existed at the preparation level. For instance, if he focused well in match A, but poorly in match B, I wanted him to identify how ready he was to perform prior to these two games. What was he thinking and feeling prior to matches A and B? Where was his focus? Had he reached his ideal performance state? Or was he too flat, or over-aroused and anxious?

By answering these questions Iain discovered the main factor that affected his focus, for good or ill. Its simplicity alarmed him, and he wondered why he hadn't cottoned onto it sooner.

The factor was: **the degree to which he was emotionally prepared**.

Simple as that!

Iain had no idea of his PIPS, his Personal Ideal Performance State. Again, no-one had advised him to work out his 'just right' state. He was playing Russian roulette with his ability to focus appropriately.

If, on the off-chance, Iain stumbled across his PIPS, then he was well-placed to focus effectively. However, more often than not, he was either under- or over-aroused, neither of which were conducive to his performance.

Under these circumstances, he was prone to making early mistakes, which then became distractions in themselves. Before he knew it, he became caught-up in a destructive domino effect.

The good news is that Iain identified his PIPS and developed techniques to control his emotions. He found deep abdominal breathing amazingly useful and conceded that the imagination was a woefully underused mental facility.

As a result, he stepped up to the plate and learned how to use imagery to enhance his preparation and performance.

Iain was baffled by one thing in particular. Why did he often perform much better in training than in competitive matches? Then, during our session on thinking errors and the power of interpretation, he worked it out for himself:

> **"I think and feel more positive before training. It seems that I glide more naturally into my PIPS for training sessions. I'm not as uptight about making mistakes. No-one is watching, no spectators, you know? Although I want to impress the coaches during training, it's totally different to that in actual matches. But I realise I place that pressure on myself. Nobody else does it... I'll say to myself before a game, "I must do this"/"I must do that", "So-and-so is watching" – all that sort of c\*\*p. This leads me to make mistakes and playing below expectations. Yeah Mark, I can see it more clearly now and what I have to do to prepare properly for matches and to be ready to play."**

I wanted Iain to have a toolbox of techniques and strategies to help him refocus during matches. While he now entered games ready to perform, there were still going to be times when his mind wandered and the unexpected happened. That's life after all; no matter how ready or prepared one is, stuff still happens.

Iain listed his potential distractions and devised a couple of refocusing routines that would work for all occasions.

Now that he knew what distraction felt like, he was well placed to act, almost instantaneously, to bring his mind back into the present and onto the next piece of performance.

He also worked hard on his thinking style, as he had become rigid in thought and belief. He had started to demand that things went his way: which meant that if they didn't, he was left feeling dejected instead of a bit disappointed.

His work on the mistake-management strategies opened the door to a more preference-led approach to sport and life; an attitudinal change that helped greatly.

## Distance travelled

Although our work together incorporated techniques from several of the remaining five pathways, if we tie Iain down to focus alone, we can see that he made tremendous progress in this area.

He developed a regimen for match day that worked a treat. In fact he became so aware of when to apply emotion-management techniques that it became *unusual* for him *not* to be ready to perform. What a tremendous turnaround in his mental game!

At the end of the soccer season, Iain had scored 32 goals. When we first met, he had bagged only four in ten matches. He was a fantastic person to work with - a real gem and now a real star on the pitch.

When re-rating his pathways several months later, Iain plotted his position along Pathway 4 at a **9.5**. As a result of the mental skills training he engaged in, he had travelled from a low rating of 'three' to almost the maximum rating on offer.

You need to know too, that his ratings improved by an average of two, for each of the remaining five pathways.

As I've said thousands of times to athletes and teams, there is a massive built-in bonus with mental game training: **progress in one area can stimulate progress**

**in others**. The six pathways intersect and feed off each another.

## Key Points from **Pathway 4**

- Mentally tough athletes focus on what is relevant to *their* preparation and performance, and shut out distractions. They know that concentration is a limited mental commodity that must be eked-out out wisely. Accordingly, they learn to:
  - focus on the process of performance and not the outcome
  - accept and manage mistakes and get back in the game
  - bounce back from unforeseen events
  - focus only on what *can* be controlled, during preparation and performance
  - instantly switch focusing style during competition
  - manage their arousal levels
  - park personal problems at home

- Top sportspeople know that effective focus is the pathway to performing in the zone.

- *The Zone* is that mental state athletes enter, whenever their left brain chatter has shut-up, and mind and body are functioning as one. During these occasions, focus is absolute and techniques are unleashed with excellence, moment-to-moment.

- By focusing on what you *don't* want, you actually attract it. So, if you focus on the mistakes you DON'T want to make, or focus on NOT missing the penalty kick you're about to take, then you substantially increase your chances of making mistakes and missing the kick.

- Your monster toys with your focus by bringing your mental interference to the boil. It knows that, with your mind elsewhere, you cannot make progress. It loves nothing more than distracting you with fear of failure and loss of face.

- No-one is born with effective focus. It is a skill, so it requires practice. Pathway 4 contains various techniques and strategies that, once mastered, will enable you to harness this most precious of natural resources.

# Chapter 8

## PATHWAY 5

# PATHWAY TO IMAGERY CONTROL

The Possible's slow fuse is lit
by the imagination.
**- Emily Dickinson**

Perhaps what we sometimes call 'genius'
is simply a refusal to altogether let go
of childhood imagination.
**- Michael Cibenko**

By the end of Pathway 5, you will have:

- Understood the positive role effective imagery plays in mental toughness, peak performance and meeting your sporting goals.
- Discovered how your mental monster hijacks your imagination.
- Learned what imagery is, how it works and why it is *the* most powerful and versatile of mental game tools.
- Learned how to use imagery to radically enhance your training and performance.
- Caught up with Natalie, a case study from Chapter 3.

Imagery is the effective harnessing of the human ability to imagine. As a mental game technique, imagery is like no other. It is incredibly versatile; capable in the right hands, or rather the right brains, of strengthening your self-belief, motivation, concentration and emotional control.

As such, it can toughen up your mental game in all sorts of ways, enabling you to become the athlete of your dreams. This Pathway is therefore extremely important to you.

# MONSTER WATCH

## How YouMinus attacks your Imagery System

As your imagery system speaks the language of your mind, it is little wonder that your mental monster exploits it to trip you up. In an effort to disrupt your progress, to stop you from realising your potential, YouMinus sends you vivid images of failure, disappointment and disapproval. It takes you to all sorts of scary places. As your mind accepts imagery as real, particularly clear, vibrant imagery, then you begin to think, act and feel as your inner bully would want you to.

So in effect what's happening here, is that YouMinus has engineered a hostile takeover of your brain's right hemisphere. With its grubby little hands on the levers of your imagination, it has now got control over many aspects of your mental game and therefore your potential to perform at your optimum.

And it whispers, *In your face, you waste of space!!*

## Rory Best

I have worked with Ireland and Ulster star Rory Best since June 2005. When we first met up, Rory was number two hooker for Ulster, with Paul Shields the first choice. I quickly realised that Rory was a young man driven to improve his performances and to make the hooker's position his own.

The one aspect of his role that gave him concern, was his lineout throwing. A technically difficult skill area, lineout throwing also attracted YouMinus to the party. You can see why.

Firstly, the hooker is on his own, with sole responsibility for lobbing an oval ball with precision, to an awaiting teammate. Lose a lineout and you lose possession; rather you give it away. No pressure there then! Secondly, lineout throwing, as with other closed skills, affords thinking time. And we know, don't we, that humans don't do downtime very well?

Even if it's for only 20 or so seconds!

Finally, all of this is played out in front of *other people*. We're not too fussed on this either. For Rory, lineout throwing had become a breeding ground for mental interference. He provided a glimpse into this, in an interview with Peter O'Reilly, of *The Sunday Times*, prior to a Heineken Cup game for Ulster:

> **"It got to the stage where I was hoping the ball wouldn't go into touch. I had to try something."**

*"I had to try something"* was a reference to our work together and, in particular, to his use of imagery as a rehearsal tool. Rory has benefited greatly from employing imagery. It has allowed him to practice remotely and to complement his physical training with imagery work at home and elsewhere.

As with any new skill, Rory initially found imagery difficult - "I couldn't do it at first. I'd close my eyes and see nothing" – but with perseverance and practice it got better, much better:

> **"But [Mark] said it was a technique that needed practising, like throwing itself. Eventually I got it and it did help."**
>
> *The Sunday Times, December 3, 2006*

You will hear more from Rory in a short while, when he offers you a powerful description of imagery in action; a technique that has helped him to become one of the world's best hookers. But let's take a step back for a moment; in fact, right back to our early years.

## Sweet Childish Days (Wordsworth)

As kids, we competed at the Olympics, played at Wembley and served at Wimbledon. In fact, I can still vividly recall those long summer days, during the 1976 heat wave, when

I graced my public tennis courts as if I was Bjorn Borg. The courts became Wimbledon and I took on the persona of the unflappable tennis legend. I also became Manchester United's Alex Stepney in my back garden, and adopted his goalkeeping mannerisms and technique.

For those indoor purists, I was the 'Crafty Cockney', Eric Bristow, playing in the World Darts' Final - against the inside of my bedroom door. I copied his posture and technique; and threw 'his' arrows with an air of cheeky confidence.

My inner rock god was sated in similar fashion. All I needed was a hairbrush, a mirror and my imagination - and voila - Freddy Mercury, live at Hyde Park, London!

We all did these sorts of things as youngsters, didn't we? It wasn't just me, was it?!

We took our minds to pleasant and exhilarating places. In doing so, although we didn't know it at the time, we were rehearsing skills, stepping outside of comfort zones and sculpting mental states. Yet no-one told us to do this; we just intuitively knew to use our imagination productively.

So clearly, using imagery in this way is our natural state.

However, you will know from Chapter 1, that the Frankenstein Factor corrupts our human gifts, using them for its own malevolent ends. By the time it does its dirty work, our natural gifts feel very alien to us. And, so it is with imagery.

Consequently, we need to reconnect with this ability. If this was a schmaltzy book, I would now be advising you to reconnect with your inner child. Yuck!! Okay, let's start somewhere near the beginning, and build from there.

# IMAGERY CONTROL, DEFINED

Imagery control, or mental rehearsal mastery, is all about the highly skilled recapturing and refining of the gift of the imagination, and using it constructively. It is about a structured approach to placing ourselves in different scenarios, by using our neglected right brain, the seat of our imagination.

## What is an Image?

Now there's a question. I like to think of images as our thoughts *polished*. They are the vivid, primarily visual, product of directed thinking. If I ask you to choose an item relevant to your sport (say, a piece of equipment – ball, racquet, stick - or even your team crest), and to direct your mind to see it in detail, you should be able to make a pretty good fist of it. After all, the capacity to imagine is an inbuilt mental tool and as with all tools, the sharper it is, the more effective it becomes. And how do you sharpen it? Through practice, of course!

Let's now examine one of the strongest relationships in nature; the relationship between imagery and your emotional state.

## Images and Emotion

I would like you to envisage, as vividly as possible, a particularly tense and emotional incident in your life, and use all of your senses to do so.

It could be a time when you were waiting by the phone for important exam or medical results. Perhaps, it was a time when a loved one was seriously ill, or passed away. It may be the anticipation of a team selection announcement, or it could be the morning of your first team debut.

Perhaps, it's the night you proposed to your girlfriend; or it could be witnessing the birth of your first child. Whatever the situation, shut your eyes, take a few deep breaths, and go back there now, noting your reactions as you replay the selected experience.

This exercise demonstrates the long reach of the imagination. It shows how you can recreate situations in such a powerful way, that you feel you're actually reliving it, in real time. And, as you imagined your selected scenarios, you will have rekindled the emotions of the time.

Sadness, joy, pride, excitement, wonderment and happiness, may well have been elicited by the vivid memories and images. You may also have experienced physiological reactions too, such as butterflies in your stomach, queasiness, or a lump in your throat.

Depending on the scenario, you could well have felt that hug, or the baby nestling in the crook of your arm, or the smell of the talcum powder, the perfume, or the liniment in the locker room. Perhaps a tear was spilt, or a smile crossed your face. Maybe you vocalised an 'I love you', or a laugh burst out, or perhaps you gave a resounding YES!, remembering that moment of good news.

Whatever your moment, private to you, your imagery will have led to bodily and emotional reactions and a sense of *being there*.

Yet you haven't left your seat, bed or wherever you are reading this book. The power of imagery is simply beyond words, literally!

Let me reassure you, using imagery, for performance enhancement purposes, is but a reasonably small and structured step away from what you have just done. You will be moulding this ability to *mind travel* in a systematic way and applying it right across the performance cycle. By doing this, you will be taking a massive stride towards becoming mentally tough.

# Imagery and the Brain

### That's a Wrap!

Want to hear something incredible? You do? Great! Here goes: **Imagery creates real change in your brain.**

Told you it was incredible. Put simply, your brain, your neurology, is stimulated by imagery, in the same way as the actual activity would excite it. You see, images in the mind - vivid, precise, multisensory images - are accepted by the central nervous system as real and, as a result, real change happens in the brain.

> **"The moment all our awareness converges on an internal representation and that picture becomes more real to us than the external environment, we begin to rewire new connections in our brain."**
> **Joe Dispenza**, *Evolve Your Brain, 2007, P405*

This change involves the brain tissue myelin. When any of us physically practise a technical skill over and over again, myelin wraps itself around the neural circuitry involved in the execution of the skill. And why is myelin such a big deal? Because it helps turn 'B-road' brain circuits into 'broadband-like' motorways. In other words, it helps to embed your habits and accelerate your response time.

The fantastic news is that this very same process occurs whenever we use *imagery* to rehearse the very same physical skill/technique. Myelin will wrap itself around the relevant brain circuitry, as if you had just practised physically!

# Mind and Body: You try spotting the join!

The following Pathway Pitstop contains a mind-blowing exercise. Please carry it out now, after which I'll explain how it works.

---

### Pathway Pitstop 5.1

### Mind & Body Connection  - *Pendulum Exercise*

Prepare to be amazed, all who have never walked the imagery path before. Try this exercise out now. Fetch a bulldog clip (there'll be one somewhere in your house) and tie it to the end of a piece of string, about 8" -10" long. Stand up, and using your dominant hand, hold the string between thumb and forefinger and dangle the clip with arm outstretched at right-angles to your body.

Once the string is steady (and with your eyes still open), place your focus on the clip and begin to imagine it moving from left to right. You are engaging your mind's eye here, and attempting to 'see' the bulldog clip moving, as requested. The more clearly you 'see' and 'feel' the clip swinging side-to-side, the sooner you attain the most miraculous of results - the clip starts to do as it's told. It starts to move, and WITHOUT you physically feeling you're making it happen. You are neither moving finger nor thumb; they remain static.

And, as you stay fully focused, plying your brain with clear visual instructions, you can make the pendulum swing to the width of *The Joker's* smile! Side-to-side to the horizontal plane. Amazing!

Please try this out. It WILL work and work well, with keen focus and practice. The more relaxed you are before visualising, the better the results. So, do it now, be patient and, if it's new territory for you, get ready to be astounded.

---

Right, how come the pendulum moved without you physically manipulating it? What on earth was going on? And should you call in Derek Acorah? Well, no, to put it bluntly. What's going on is 100 percent normal.

## Explanation

The images in your mind of the string/clip moving from side-to-side, send a type of 'e-video' to your brain. This e-video is accepted by your brain as real and responds by sending electrical impulses down your arm, through your hand, to the finger and thumb holding the string. These impulses are imperceptible to the naked eye, but are sufficient to get the job done. The string swings. It therefore seems that something magical is afoot; which explained why a young golfer, attending one of my mental game seminars, jokingly described the experience as "some sort of voodoo!"

I assured him that the pendulum exercise merely demonstrated an underused human ability and was entirely natural, as opposed to being supernatural.

# The Swiss Army Knife of Mental Game Tools

Imagery is your flexible, versatile and user-friendly mental game skill. It will help you to improve your ability across the technical, physical, strategic and psychological dimensions of your sport and can be used before, during and after competition and training. It truly is the Swiss Army knife of mental skills. Just take a look at all the things it can do.

# Imagery **Before** Competition:

Imagery can be used, prior to competition, to help you to gain a sense of mastery and control. It can help you to:

- Accelerate the learning, acquisition and refinement of your technical skills.
- Rehearse your performance.

- Picture, feel and sense success.
- Review and reinforce your game plan, strategies and routines.
- Rehearse and consolidate your contingency plans for those 'what if?' moments.
- Inoculate yourself against unsettling pre-comp anxiety.
- Psyche yourself up, when your mood is flat.
- Attain a state of relaxation.
- Raise your levels of motivation and commitment to training and performance.

## Examples from Elite Sports Performers

### The International Surfer

Top young surfer, Ronan Oertzen, employs imagery to sharpen his technique, prepare for performance and to refocus during performance. Let's hear what he has to say:

> **"I find that the imagery/visualisation technique is very helpful when I have to refine specific technical skills. I use visualisation every day and, even when I am in the water, to prepare myself, so when I get a wave, my mind and body are ready to perform. Sometimes you can get carried away and lose focus in the water. When this happens, I use visualisation to refocus so that I can perform better. I always visualise before a heat, so that I feel prepared."**
>
> *Personal communication, 04.03.10*

### The F1 Driver

F1 driver, Jenson Button, also incorporates imagery into his pre-race routine. It enables him to: negotiate the track ahead of time; deal with critical moments; rehearse key skill-sets; and bring his emotional state to an ideal level.

> **"I'll sit down on a Swiss ball with a steering wheel in my hands and close my eyes. I'll drive around the circuit, practising every gear shift. It's just a little bit of visualisation work to get me in the mood for it. Qualifying is just one lap, so you have to be on it."**
>
> *Raise Your Game, BBC SPORT*

## The Ice Hockey Goalie

Former Boston Bruins' goalie, Byron Dafoe, is on the ice long before the hooter goes for the start of a game. He knows that imagery is an amazing mental game tool, one that we should all use:

> **"In the afternoons, I just mentally run through the game, visualize myself making the saves, patting the guys on the head after a victory. Hey, the mind is a powerful thing. And we don't tap into it enough."**
>
> *mentalgoaltending.com*

I couldn't agree more!

## The Rugby International

One of my clients, Ulster and Scotland wing, Simon Danielli, has found our work on imagery to be invaluable. It has enabled him to prepare meticulously for matches. He knows that his mind can travel to any situation he chooses, and because of this he can rehearse particular skills and strategies ahead of a game.

Simon also uses imagery to *Shop at the Confidence Store* (see Pathway 2) and will rehearse, over and over in his head, great pieces of individual play.

"In a game of so many variables like rugby, as in most sports, many scenarios are going to be presented throughout the match. Knowing that you can cope with them and that you have the tools to deal with or exploit them is so important. How players arrive at this knowledge is totally individual, but many players like to visualise scenarios, many of which they have encountered in recent games and performed successfully. I like to play over a few of my 'best moments' in my head before games."

*Personal communication, 19.05.10*

## The Cycling Knight!

Triple Olympic gold medallist, Sir Chris Hoy, has benefited greatly from using imagery in preparation for competition.

This British cycling icon has employed imagery to subdue unhelpful thoughts and feelings, as well as to familiarise himself with his race plan.

"(I) used visualisation when I had a negative thought or anxiety. I would visualise the starting gate and each segment of the race. By race day I'd gone through it over 100 times."

*guardian.co.uk*

## The Boxing Champion

Interim WBA World super middleweight champion, Brian Magee, does what all great athletes do – he leaves no stone unturned in his pursuit of excellence.

As a result, he uses imagery to rehearse strategies for managing those moments that could distract him from the job-at-hand. He runs through his fight plan and sees and feels himself box his opponent in the ring. He will also absorb himself in the arena, using imagery to acclimatise to the surroundings:

> **"This is the most important tool for me as it familiarises me with my opponent, for example seeing myself fight him in the arena. If I've never been there before it limits the amount of surprises or upsets you have to deal with, up to and during the event. If you have imagined it, it's already happened. You've dealt with it and most important you did it with a positive outcome for yourself."**
>
> *Personal communication, 28.03.10*

## The Judo Player

Elite international judo player Lisa Kearney incorporates imagery into her post-training analyses. She consolidates her learning by replaying in her mind the techniques she's just worked on. Imagery therefore adds value to her training.

> **"I also use imagery outside of competition to go over techniques from training to know how it feels to do it correctly."**
>
> *Personal communication, 13.05.09*

# Imagery <u>During</u> Competition:

Imagery is employed during competition, to enable you to excel and cope.

## Closed-skills

Imagery can be used to rehearse a discrete closed-skill, immediately prior to its execution (e.g., before free-throws in basketball; penalty kicks in football; lineout throws in rugby; all golf shots; and serving in racquet sports).

US Open champion, Graeme McDowell, includes imagery into his pre-shot routine - "I'm swinging well and hitting the shots I see in my head" – while Rory Best always sees the ball land at its target, before he releases a lineout throw.

> **"I would be visualising the point, closing my eyes and trying to picture where the ball is going. Whenever the call comes in, I'll get myself ready and bring the ball back. I'll see that target in my head, a split second before I throw it, so I'll know where I am putting it."**
>
> *www.irishrugby.ie*

### Reinforcement

Top athletes also use imagery during competition to quickly remind their brain to store and repeat a particularly well-executed skill.

### Eraser

Imagery is an effective eraser. It can be used to tape over a mistake and replace it with the correct execution of the skill. A couple of seconds is all that it takes to 'tell' the brain that all is okay and that it's time to move on. Simon Danielli exploits this mental facility to the full:

> **"Imagery can help here. For example if you dropped the ball , you visualise having caught it and making a break for a try etc, or again remember something similar in past games that you did do well."**
>
> *Personal communication, 19.05.10*

## Imagery <u>After</u> Competition:

For this phase of the performance cycle, imagery is used to review, refine and reward. It allows you to:

- Carry out a constructive review of your performance. Remember, imagery is your personal *iPlayer*, so you can replay aspects of your performance over and over again.

- Reinforce the positives within your performance. Be sure to mentally fist pump these as you run them through your mind. This way, the brain will be inclined to repeat them next time.

- 'Tape' over the poor aspects of your performance with the correct version. This is something Ospreys, Ireland and Lions ace, Tommy Bowe, does in his post-match review:

> **"In sport, most people have felt what defeat is like.It is very important to find out what went wrong early and move on. I try to see where I went wrong, then visualize doing it right and put it out of my mind then"**
>
> *Personal communication, 01.04.10*

Reviewing your performance in these ways, allows you to isolate those areas of your game that need to be sharpened. It will fuel your discussions with your coach, and inform your training for the following week.

Imagery can also be used to aid your recovery from injury. How? Well it can:

- Accelerate the process of recovery and rehabilitation, through 'seeing' the affected body part healing.

- Help you manage pain. Here you are using imagery as a distraction technique.

- Enhance your psychological readiness for returning to training and competitive action. Imagery is used to rehearse your technical skills, build up confidence and encourage your body to 'just do it', once you are back.

So if you become injured, capitalise on the mind-body connection.

# Perspective -The Hokey Cokey of Imagery

### You Put Your Whole Self In, Your Whole Self Out

Imagery can be used from both an *internal* and an *external* perspective. When you use imagery from an internal viewpoint, you are imagining yourself IN the scenario you have chosen. You are in the situation carrying out the selected activity, seeing it through **your own eyes** and sensing it, as you would do in real life. Imagery from this first person perspective is also referred to as *associated* imagery.

External imagery involves the athlete **observing himself** performing, as if watching himself on a screen. This *disassociated* perspective allows the performer to examine his technical ability in detail and to pinpoint areas for improvement.

# So which is best: Internal or External?

Internal imagery offers a more sophisticated representation of the real situation. You can see, hear, feel, smell and taste the imagined experience, as if you were actually going through it. This surely puts internal imagery out in front in the contest between the two perspectives, doesn't it? Well, yes and no.

**Yes**, in terms of preparation for competition, but **no**, in terms of learning new skills and capturing an overall 'big picture' view. Here external imagery is the better way to go.

The external perspective allows you to observe and measure various elements of your performance from several different positions. You'll find too that you can correct errors in technique in a more dispassionate and clinical fashion than would be the case if you used the internal method.

As a rule of thumb, internal imagery is the perspective of choice for competition preparation (you have to be IN it to win it!), while external imagery is best for learning a new skill, as well as identifying and remedying errors in performance (you have to be OUT of it to see it).

But as with all broad principles, you should employ imagery in the way that suits *you* best - one that generates vivid, controllable images and provides you with the greatest value.

## Internal Perspective

### Real World Example

Ireland international hooker, Grand Slam winner and Ulster captain, Rory Best, describes his mental rehearsal for a forthcoming Heineken Cup game.

> **"I vividly experience the imagined situation as if I'm in it, seeing, feeling, and sensing it in the way I would in a match. I feel the rugby ball in my hand as I wipe it down with a towel. I hear the lineout call and then steady myself on the line feeling my feet nestling into the pitch ready to go through my pre-throw routine...**
>
> **I see the ball with the Gilbert logo facing towards me and I position the ball so that the valve is where I like it to be. There's a feeling of relaxation as I take a few deep breaths, adjust my jersey and I feel the movements of my arms extending over and behind my head. There is a**

**bitter breeze hitting my face and I can see the steam rising from players' bodies.**

**I see my teammates jostling for position with their opposite numbers in the line, and I select the target point for my throw. I then release the ball with ease, knowing it's going straight to the target. I see Johann's hands extending to the target point as he is lifted high. He catches the ball bringing it into his chest. I feel my movements as I reposition myself in preparation for the next play. I engage in the maul, and feel my body bind behind my fellow forwards."**

Rory's use of vibrant, realistic, positive and controlled internal imagery means he can rehearse his lineout technique on a regular basis in-between training sessions.

## HOW TO MASTER IMAGERY

The ability to imagine is a human gift, but like all gifts it is of little use if it's unwrapped, unused or misused.

In the same way that a human's ability to run doesn't transform into competitive sprinting without expert instruction and unswerving practice, the ability to imagine will not develop into the powerful mental skill we call *imagery*, without directed training and effort.

The following six principles - in the form of the acronym, **CREATE** – will show you how to turn your imagination into an effective performance enhancement tool.

## Calm the mind to clear the canvas

The ultimate purpose of imagery is to capitalise on the connection between mind and body. We know that imagery sends signals to the parts of the body relevant to what is being imaged. This is a great way to get additional practice in, away from the training ground or gym. However, in order to generate clear and vibrant images (i.e. to communicate as clearly as possible with the body) it is important for your mind to be quiet.

Very quiet!

Like an artist setting out to paint on a blank canvas, you must clear your mental screen before creating your imagined scenarios and running through them. If your mind is still showing re-runs of your domestic 'to do' list or college assignments, you won't be able to produce imagery worth talking about!

To quieten your mind, I suggest you engage in a simple relaxation exercise, such as taking several deep breaths. (If you wish, you could go to Pathway 6 now, which offers you a wide range of relaxation techniques).

Make sure you are in a quiet environment where you will not be disturbed. One day, with practice, you'll be able to use imagery against a backdrop of noise.

Once you have relaxed sufficiently, your mind will be at its optimum to receive imagery. It's then time to move on to generating vivid and lifelike images.

## Realistic

Given that you wouldn't revise for questions that *won't* come up in your college exam, you shouldn't generate imagery that is of little or no relevance to the realities of playing your sport.

Imagery needs to be as accurate and precise a representation of actual competitive situations, as is possible. By doing this, the communication between your mind and body will be at its 'loudest'.

Any weak or vague imagery is like a whisper being passed from mind to body. Your body will be going, "Eh! What's that you said? Hello, testing, testing. Have you started yet?"

So create imagery that makes you feel as if you are *actually there*, in the imagined place. To do this, you need to incorporate all of your senses.

While the visual sense dominates our experience of life, we also hear, taste, feel and smell. All of our senses create our reality. The smell of engine oil, the whiff of liniment, the scent of newly cut grass, the feeling of a warm breeze on your face, the stick in your hand, the ball underfoot, the butterflies in your stomach, the elation after scoring, the satisfaction from a well-executed play, the taste of blood in your mouth, all knit together with the associated visual experience.

## The 'I-Fit'

What I call an Imagery-Fit (*I-Fit*), is a structured way to build up a detailed description of how it looks, feels, smells, tastes and sounds, to play your sport across a series of situations. Two things are important here. Well, two questions, really.

One - **Do you know your job?** What are the components of your role across the performance cycle (before, during and after competition)? Two - **For each element of your role, what do you experience?** Better still, what would you like to experience? Next, build an *I-Fit* for each part of your sporting experience - these will then inform your imagery sessions.

Remember, in order to match reality, you need to feature as many of the senses as possible.

Your imagery sessions should be positive, with you performing in a consistently good way, or coping with an adverse moment in an effective manner. It is also important that you learn to control your imagery, as this too enhances the realism. You perform in real time, therefore you have to imagine in real time too.

## Research Your Sport

Become your own researcher. Know your sport inside out – literally! Use an *Experience Log* to record the sensations around particular scenarios. Describe the activity (e.g. free-kick, right-hand-side of opposing box...) and note down what you see, hear, touch, taste and feel (emotionally and physiologically). Some senses will be more relevant than others.

For any fresh experience, such as competing at a new ground, course, track or court, you should research it. If, for instance, you are a high jumper due to compete at an outdoor arena new to you, visit it as soon as possible as part of your preparation for the meet.

Once there, take a photo or video of it, including the locker room and the walk out into the arena. It might be empty, but ingest the arena's atmosphere, and top it up with two or three 'as if' exercises.

An 'as if' exercise for this high jumper would have him sitting in the locker room and imagining he's about to be called out to the arena. By doing this, he will experience all that goes with it - the anxiety and the eager anticipation!

Or he could walk out to the arena as if it really is Saturday morning and 'hear' the crowd, 'see' the competitors and 'note' the events going on around him. He could then walk over to the high jump zone and wait his turn!

He could stand there, as if anticipating his first attempt at making the height, and experience the emotions that go with it. He could also picture and sense his pre-run-up routine and a successful jump.

This on-site research will bring an athlete's mind so much closer to what reality would be like come competition time. As I've said elsewhere in the book, this is a bit like getting the exam questions in advance of the test.

## Enduring Practice

No surprise here! We can only ever become proficient at anything in life, by practising the necessary skills on a regular basis and in a deliberate way. And this of course applies to the use of imagery as a performance enhancer.

You should practice daily – spend about four minutes on each imagined scenario, until it is lifelike and vibrant. I suggest four minutes, as it seems neither too long to create ennui, nor too short to be of little value. As mental rehearsal is revision for your sporting exam, you need to focus on what is going to be asked of you in competition. But not to the point of tedium, which is counterproductive.

Equally, you don't want to under-revise, rendering your imagery practice almost meaningless. Strike a balance, based on your current proficiency in using imagery and your goal for improvement. Although four minutes is a ballpark figure for each situation you imagine, the key to effectiveness is the *quality* of your images.

It's important to prepare for each imagery session. You should know where you're going to carry out your session, what you want to achieve by it, and how much time you are going to allocate to it.

You should also consider writing out and recording imagery scripts to guide your sessions. This is when the research, referred to earlier, can really payoff.

## Assimilate

Elite performers combine virtual reality with actuality. That is, they let imagery inform their real-life practice, and vice-versa. So for instance, if they successfully perform a move or skill during a training session, they deposit it into their imagery bank by replaying it in their mind as soon as they possibly can.

Some sports more than others lend themselves to immediate mental reinforcement. For example, a golfer can readily replay a good shot in his head - feel and see it and commit it to memory. This in turn informs his I-Fit for that particular skill-set. It's a bit like writing a note in the margin of a page - it gives a particular paragraph enhanced meaning and brings it to life.

Imagery can also be employed to boost your readiness for training. If, for example, you feel flat as you arrive for a technical session, you could find a quiet place and run through your mind the big picture goal that gives meaning as to why you are training on a wet, cold Wednesday. If too hyped for training or competition, you can use relaxing imagery to bring your arousal down an emotional notch or two.

The *Circle of Enhancement*, below, is a very simple representation of the benefit to be had, from assimilating imagery practice with real world practice. It makes perfect sense to do so. After all, would you revise for an academic examination, but not attend class?

No, of course you wouldn't. Otherwise, you create an 'information void' and quite probably end up revising the wrong topics. There is a strict dance between real life training and mental rehearsal.

**Figure 5:** The Circle of Enhancement

# Top-Up

To keep your imagery lifelike (that you're 'in' the scene you're rehearsing) it is important to update/top-up your I-Fit information in terms of what it looks, feels, sounds or smells like to perform differing aspects of your role.

Moreover, as you improve technically, make sure you factor the progress into your imagery practice.

# Evaluate

As part of the process of mastering imagery, it is useful to evaluate the evolving quality of your mental movies. After all, you are the in-house director! So, you should monitor and assess the value of each imagery session.

As learning is incremental, you will be assessing progress from session-to-session and across several features, pivotal to effective imagery.

These include:

- The usefulness of your relaxation, prior to generating imagery.

- The degree to which you were using all of your senses.

- How immersed you were in the scene. (Did it feel real; as if it was actually happening in the present?).

- The level of control you had over the images. (Were you able to run the images at actual speed? Could you speed them up or slow them down, if needs be?).

- Identifying the images you found particularly difficult to recreate. And why?

This all presupposes of course, that you have set effective goals for each imagery session. Revisit the PUMAA system, in Pathway 1, to guide your objective-setting for your session work. You will be setting goals around the features just described and I suggest you rate your imagery performance on a simple ten-point scale.

While not wishing to clutter your sporting life with way too much paperwork, you should record your session-assessments in an 'Imagery Log'.

Imagery Log? Okay then, a small jotter.

I suggest you also read over the section in Pathway 1 on deliberate practice and apply its principles to imagery development. This will guarantee mental rehearsal mastery.

# Case Study Update – Natalie

| Natalie Makes Progress Along Pathway 5 |
| :---: |
| **Solution to Natalie's Pathway Problem** |

In Chapter 3 you met Natalie, a **20 year-old pole vaulter**, who used her imagery system to sabotage her preparations for competition. You will recall that she produced her own video nasties of the mind, in which she saw and felt herself failing.

She'd become skilful at using her imagination to counterproductive ends. Feeding this habit was an overanxious mind, moulded many years earlier by an overprotective mother, who saw the world around Natalie as a cruel and dangerous place. Like a mental baton, Natalie picked this message up and ran with it. Over time, her anxiety morphed into a fear of failing.

But she did very little to address it - topping it up instead with ominous imagery. Her mental rehearsal was technically good, but focused on the wrong subject matter – failure. To take account of her ability to produce clear and vivid images, Natalie scored herself **3 out of 10** for Pathway 5. The deficit of seven represented her inability to mentally rehearse productively; Natalie was great at creating *negative* images.

Although having quite a bit of ground to make up, I had high hopes that Natalie would make rapid progress along Pathway 5.

And she did just that.

Here's how.

## Sport Psychology Intervention

One of my initial tasks with Natalie was to introduce her to her inner monster, her YouMinus, and to explain its development. She needed to know that it had commandeered her interpretative and imagery systems and that it was currently polluting the intimate relationship between her thoughts, images, feelings and behaviour.

If Natalie was serious about meeting her goals, she had to regain control of her own brain. She had to start fighting back. Knowing that her true opponent was YouMinus, gave her a real boost.

I explained to Natalie just how magnificent the human imagination can be and that imagery was a highly effective channel of mind-to-body communication.

To illustrate the point, I asked Natalie to perform the pendulum exercise. She was astonished by it and was keen to know more. So I went into greater depth about how imagery works for the athlete.

She soon realised that if she continued to feed her mind with all sorts of defeatist images, then her body would follow suit.

She also came to understand that her negative interpretations were creating equally gloomy mental pictures. In fact, her worries provided the narrative and her imagination, the box-set of DVDs! These video nasties felt so real at times that she was sure her dark predictions would come true.

But now she understood! She had a rationale, not only for what had been happening to her, but also for the way forward.

There was a greater sense of purpose with her now and she was going to stand up to her inner saboteur. With Natalie, I had an athlete who responded strongly to the educational part of the intervention.

When I set out the list of functions that imagery served in sports preparation, performance and evaluation, Natalie really took note. She even described imagery as a type of 'mental Swiss Army Knife' that offered her multiple ways to defeat her inner monster!

The next phase of the intervention involved Natalie monitoring the supply chain. She identified her negative core beliefs and challenged them, before creating new, realistic and constructive ones.

She kept on top of her self-talk and recorded instances of unhelpful interpretations. Then she cross-examined these negative thoughts to test out their truthfulness. Like many who carry out this task, Natalie found she had a set of thoughts that served no useful purpose, and weren't even true. There was absolutely no evidence to support them.

Natalie became more adept at catching negative thoughts early and replacing them with much more self-supporting comments. She was amazed that she had thought in such a toxic way for so long, without ever checking the facts.

To improve her self-esteem, Natalie listed all her achievements and gave herself credit for them. She also looked further inwards and saw her value as a person, and that it was about time she gave herself a break.

She realised she had a lot going for her and that it was counterproductive to dwell on what was missing, particularly on  issues over which she had no control. It was time for an attitudinal change.

Accepting the uncontrollable aspects of life was a major mindset shift for Natalie. She could now place her full energies on what *could be* controlled and improved.

Given that she was already proficient at creating mental images, albeit negative ones, I was sure that she could turn this around fairly easily. However, as with her work on her thinking ability, it would require constant practice.

Natalie delivered. She followed the CREATE system, which guided her in a systematic manner to flip her negative tendency on its head. She drew up imagery scripts for every 'blade' of her mental Swiss army knife and as a result, her preparation for competition improved considerably.

As expected, Natalie's performances also improved. By taking back control of her mental game, she had cleared the way for her talent to shine through. I'll never forget the call I received from her coach, who expressed his delight at the change in his athlete.

## Distance travelled

Natalie made fantastic progress within just three months of our first session. Using imagery as a tool of mental rehearsal allowed her to become a 'virtual' winner.

By running positive images through her mind and seeing and feeling herself performing with confidence and excellence, Natalie was burning success into her neurology. It was almost inevitable that she would soon attain great things.

Natalie delivered! She set a new personal best within the first month of our working together and broke it once again, two months later.

In terms of distance travelled along Pathway 5, Natalie re-rated herself as **9.5** out of ten. As the intervention was holistic, she also experienced positive gains in self-esteem, confidence, concentration, motivation and emotion-management. In fact, her ratings across the remaining five pathways to mental toughness increased by an average of two units.

And all achieved within twelve weeks.

## Key Points from **Pathway 5**

■ When all is said and done, mental toughness is about training your brain to work for you when you absolutely need it to. It's about taking back control of your brain's extraordinary systems - and there is none more extraordinary than the imagery system.

■ Athletes, who deliver consistently high level performances, use imagery on a regular basis. It is integral to their preparation, and they employ it strategically, both during and after competition

■ Imagery is the most versatile of mental game tools. It can be employed to:
 – Practise and refine technique.
 – Rehearse performance.
 – Prepare for 'what if' scenarios.
 – Reinforce strategy/game plan.
 – Boost motivation.
 – Regulate emotions.
 – Increase confidence.
 – Improve concentration.

■ As a mental tool, imagery exploits the powerful mind-body relationship.

- An effective image should incorporate *all* of the senses.

- The brain cannot differentiate between a vivid image, created in your mind, and reality itself. As far as your brain's concerned, your image *is* reality.

- Imagery creates actual physical change in your brain.

- Imagery can be carried out from either the internal or external perspective. Each has advantages over the other, depending on the purpose of your imagery session.

- As imagery is a skill, you must put the work in. You must train your imagination in a structured way. The CREATE system will enable you to master this most vital and valuable of mental game tools.

# Chapter 9

## PATHWAY 6

## PATHWAY TO EMOTIONAL CONTROL

Some people took it upon themselves to interpret my extraordinary self-control as evidence of a lack of emotion. This struck me as pretty arrogant. I had emotions, all right, trust me on that; I just knew how to master them, and that was true on the court and off the court.

**- Pete Sampras**, *kysportpsych.com*

Anxiety is the space between the 'now' and the 'then.

**- Richard Abell**

By the end of Pathway 6, you will have:

- Understood that emotional control is central to mental toughness and an indispensible ingredient of effective preparation and performance excellence.
- Learned how your mental monster influences your arousal levels, by manipulating your thoughts and images.
- Discovered the intimate relationship that exists between emotions and performance; and, have laid bare the sources of your toxic anxiety.
- Identified your Personal Ideal Performance State (PIPS)
- Developed a toolbox of powerful routines, techniques and strategies, to help you control your emotions and to reach your PIPS, at will.
- Caught up with Grant, a case study from Chapter 3.

What often separates *great* athletes, from *very good* athletes, is the ability of the former group to seal the deal in the clutch: in other words, to manage their emotions when it really matters.

The best in world sport are mentally tough and have learned to handle their emotions in highly effective ways. They are quick to recognise when they've become overly anxious or flat and immediately set about adjusting their emotional state, to one more favourable to competition.

Elite performers know their emotional topography so well, that they never get lost for any length of time. While the occasional cul-de-sac moment still occurs, they don't stay trapped there, feeling increasingly anxious and scared.

Instead, these athletes turn their emotional state around and get back on track straight away.

This Pathway will help you to navigate your own emotional landscape. You will find a way to identify and negotiate those mental and emotional potholes that buckle your performance, and leave you stranded on the roadside of a great sporting career.

# MONSTER WATCH

## How YouMinus Attacks Your Emotional State

Here we see your mental monster's tactical deathblow as it sets about peppering and paralysing your mind with fear.

It fools you into seeing sporting competition as threatening. It turns you from a once composed, confident and focused performer, into a frightened and anxious worrywart. One who now frets about his results, status and reputation. Who has become self-conscious, risk-averse and anxious.

To achieve this shift in your mentality, your inner monster exploits the powerful relationship that exists between your thoughts, feelings and behaviour. It twists and turns your perceptions of yourself and your potential to perform well. Like a crack SWAT team, it seizes your focus with precision and moves it away from the process of preparation and performance and onto all sorts of frightening outcomes – the 'what ifs?' that haunt the uptight athlete:

- **What if I lose the match?**
- **What if I don't make an impact in front of the new manager?**

- **What if I'm substituted live on TV; I'll be so embarrassed?**
- **What if I make a mistake that gives away a goal?**

And on it goes. Worry after worry peppers the mind of a monster-munched athlete. These bleak predictions then generate a host of unpleasant emotions and physical sensations.

If right on the cusp of competition, these feelings will profoundly affect an athlete's ability to compete at his best.

In a wonderfully sneaky move, his YouMinus has set him up to underperform, which is the very outcome he had feared. And as it does so, it whispers in the athlete's ear – *This is too easy. Got you all over again – you no-hoper!*

However by following Pathway 6, you will have fought back, big-time, against your mental monster. You will have taken personal responsibility for your own emotional state and stripped YouMinus of its influence over your thoughts, feelings and behaviour; and, therefore, your life!

# EMOTIONS AND PERFORMANCE

When we speak of emotional control, what we're really talking about is *arousal* control. In particular, identifying and attaining the level of arousal that optimises your performance in competition.

Just like stocks and shares, your arousal can go up, as well as down. But one major difference is that *you* hold the reins to your emotions.

There is no gamble involved. You can manage your arousal levels, by raising or lowering them to a state conducive to your performance.

## "But What Emotions Should I Control?"

My answer to this question, from a real athlete, went something like this: "Modify those emotions that are *disruptive* to your preparation and performance".

So, if your anxiety is too high, then regulate it to a level that works for you. Alternatively, if you feel far too relaxed, then regulate it to a level that works for you.

Simples!!!!

In the former scenario, you will use techniques to reduce your arousal to your ideal state, while in the latter case, you will aim to psyche yourself up to a more conducive emotional level.

But, of course, this presupposes three things:

- That you know your ideal emotional state for competition.
- That you can recognise interference, when it occurs.
- That you have the skills and techniques to alter your state, when required.

If you want to get your hands on these three keys to emotional freedom, then this Pathway is for you.

Okay, let's take a closer look at the relationship between arousal and performance.

## The Arousal Continuum

There is a certain point along the arousal spectrum (depicted below), that maximises your readiness to go out there and perform. As with Goldilocks and her porridge-tasting, there is a level of arousal that is JUST RIGHT for you. And it is your job to locate it, work out its recipe and develop the skills to reproduce it for every game.

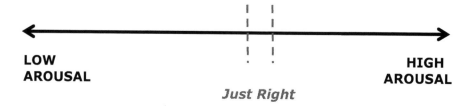

**Figure 6:** The Arousal Continuum

Emotions at the lower end of arousal include, feeling apathetic, down and uninspired; while, at the higher end of the continuum, we see such intrusions as over-anxiety, irritability and fear. Indeed, anxiety and performance can often have the type of dysfunctional relationship, only seen on *The Jeremy Kyle Show*. Picture the scene.

**Jeremy:** "Here they are, ladies and gentlemen. Please welcome to the show, 'Anxiety' and 'Performance'"

*[Mixture of heckling and cheers]*

**Jeremy:** "Thank you for coming here today. What's up in your relationship? 'Performance', we'll start with you. Why did you contact the show?"

**Performance:** "Fanks Jezza. It's just, y'know, sorta fing – y'know, 'Anxiety' disses me all the time. She's way hyped innit? Does m'head in. Can't focus - y'know what I mean?" *[Begins to sob]*.

**Jeremy:** "Bring the box of tissues on please Andy...Thanks mate. Okay, Anxiety, surely you can see what you're doing here? Performance is in a bad way, and you seem to be causing it. What have you got to say for yourself?"

**Anxiety:** "Oh, it's always *my* fault innit? Performance is such a wimp. If I say boo, he jumps. If I go quiet, he's then *waiting* for me to go boo, you know? I can't *bleepin'* win can I?"

**Jeremy:** "It's obviously a relationship in trouble. And no better man to help you both out, than our genius psychotherapist, Graham. Welcome Graham to the stage, ladies and gentlemen... [*Cheers of adulation*]...Graham, what advice do you have for Anxiety and Performance?"

**Graham:** "Well, Jeremy, here we have a couple at war. What they need to do, is to understand each other better. Only then, can they reach a state where they both get something out of their relationship. At the minute, there's just way too much tension about, and Performance is suffering badly because of it. Anxiety needs to recognise this. Right now, she is a destructive force in their relationship. But she mightn't know this."

**Jeremy:** "What can you and your team do for this couple?"

**Graham:** "Well, Jeremy, the first thing we need to do, is to encourage these guys to communicate better. In particular, I feel that Performance should tell Anxiety how she affects him, when she's hyper, irritable and agitated. She frets far too much, and dumps the worries onto Performance. When she does this, Performance is bound to go out of sorts. He has no chance. For me, Performance is suffering a lot in this relationship, and will continue to do so, until he stands up for himself and tells it like it is. Only then, can Anxiety adjust her ways to meet his needs. And she'll benefit too, as energy will be saved, and the relationship optimised."

**Jeremy:** "So what you're saying here, Graham, is that there's a balance to be struck?"

**Graham:** "Absolutely, Jeremy. I want to know about their good days together, times when their relationship dovetails perfectly, and all is well. They must find a way to replicate those good days. And we will help them do that. I think we have a couple, here, who'll have a lifelong relationship. It's important, therefore, that they find a way to get on."

**Jeremy:** "Terrific Graham.  Did I ever tell you, you're a genius?"

**Graham:** "All the time, Jeremy. All the time."

Of all the emotions referred to by athletes, anxiety is implicated as the major barrier to effective preparation and performance. But, what do we mean by anxiety? What is it made up of? What causes it? And, in particular, what does excessive anxiety do to an athlete's performance?

## THE ANATOMY OF ANXIETY

Anxiety is a natural reaction to threat and danger, in the physical environment. It alerts an individual to either fight the physical threat, or to run like the clappers from it. This is commonly referred to as the *fight-or-flight mechanism*. This mechanism is a simple and effective survival system, passed down to us through the Ages, from our primordial relatives

The fight-or-flight mechanism has kept the human species ticking over, for millions of years. Without it, our ancestors would have acted like lemmings and the human race would have expired. We should be grateful therefore to a small almond-shaped structure in the brain's limbic system, called the *amygdala*. This structure is associated with anxiety and fear and is our internal alarm. It is meant to 'go off', when there is *real* danger.

We can all think of times when this tiny mechanism has kept us safe.

In fact, I have a lot to thank my amygdala for. I remember I was about eight and crossing the road to a friend's house. I was full of expectation that day, as my mate's father had just bought him an *Adidas Telstar* football. (We were very easily pleased in the 1970s!).

I stepped off the kerb opposite my friend's house, took a few strides forward, before then noticing a car screaming towards me. In a flash, I felt a surge of adrenaline and hurled myself back onto the pavement to safety – and all in a split second. The amygdala was central to keeping me safe that day. It activated my body to do what was needed to survive the danger. The rush of anxiety propelled me to safety – making the amygdala an incredible piece of genetic kit!

But, there's a twist in the tale. The amygdala will also respond to *perceived* threat.

This means that you only need to *interpret* a situation as threatening and your inner alarm system will ring. It will accept your perception as reality and act accordingly: *Alert-Alert! Run or Fight!* And it will do this every time you dwell on some 'threat' or other. As a result, your anxiety builds up a head of steam and, unless addressed, will hamper your preparation and performance.

## 'Rep' - The Brain's Bouncer

The part of our brain concerned with survival is ancient. It is called the *R-Complex* – it is our reptilian brain, or *Rep*, as I have named it. Now, Rep is like one of those doormen or bouncers who you simply cannot reason with. You know the type, I'm sure. They throw you out on the street because they sense threat, not waiting to gather sufficient evidence before acting.

I recall an occasion a few years ago, when I was queuing up with a few friends to get into a nightspot. After a bit of a commotion at the head of the queue, we witnessed a young lad being frogmarched out of the premises. Very undignified, and the poor lad looked really frightened and bewildered. His friends were mortified too and had apparently tried to reason with the big, burly and frankly, thick bouncer – but, to no avail. It turned out that the bouncer had heard the young chap swearing and, in a blink of an eye, had seized him. It transpired that the lad had Tourette's syndrome! The threat wasn't real. It was a manifestation of a nervous bouncer's mind.

Rep is similarly trigger-happy and can wield its power at the most inappropriate times. It can perceive threat in the most benign situations, before then cracking the threatening nut with an emotional sledgehammer. This overreaction is precisely what's happening to you whenever you feel panicky and stressed before a big game - when there's really no threat to your survival at all.

You're not facing surgery, or a firing squad. In fact, it's quite the opposite of such trauma – you're about to play the sport you love! But something's happening; something's going on that's inviting Rep to stick its oar in. And it's this - **you are afraid of failing, of letting yourself down and of being derided**.

You're so used to being apprehensive, that come match day, Rep is wondering why the heck you continue to turn up at all. As a result, it is obliged to protect you, and will initiate the fight-or-flight response to help you get out of there and onwards to safety. Here Rep is merely doing what Rep does best. It's getting you away from danger, pronto. There is no time for reasoning; just fighting or escaping.

The amygdala is ringing and the exigencies of time demand an immediate response.

During these periods, Rep takes over the running of your brain. Great when actual threat to survival exists, as I found out as a kid, but not so good when it's merely our modern day versions of threat (e.g., the potential for failure, embarrassment and ridicule) - and it's only five minutes to kick-off! Under these circumstances, the bouncer's running the nightclub.

# Rep hijacks your brain and rides
## roughshod over the rational neo-cortex

Instead of guarding caves, modern man and woman guard their egos, often at any cost. Excessive anxiety is one of the prices they pay. So, it's important to reassess the alleged threat and see it for what it really is - **that it is not about a risk to your survival**.

> *If you treat every situation as*
> *a life and death matter,*
> *you'll die a lot of times.*
>
> **- Dean Smith**

By the way, if you would like a clear-cut example of Rep running the show inappropriately, then visit *Youtube* to see Zinedine Zidane's 'head-butt moment', during the 2006 World Cup Final. I think we can firmly agree that Zidane had not engaged his logical neo-cortex! Somehow he sensed danger in the middle of the beautiful game.

So, how's your amygdala? Now there's a question you're not asked every day!!

Nevertheless, it's an important query and one you can respond to right now by carrying out Pathway Pitstop 6.1.

## Pathway Pitstop 6.1

### Are You Abusing Your Amygdala?

Think back on your life and recall those times when your internal alarm system kept you safe. Times when your amygdala went off appropriately and the fight-or-flight response saved you from actual harm. In fact, kept you alive.

Once you have done this, and recalled the emotions you felt at the time, I want you to think about your sport and identify those times, before and during performance, when you have felt similarly aroused. Times when you were gripped by the same type of overwhelming anxiety and dread. After you've done this, answer the following questions:

- Were these sporting situations *truly* life-threatening?
- Was there clear and present danger in the locker room, or on the pitch? And, if not, then what on earth was going on? Why were you so uptight and stressed out?
- Is it possible you had been upping your amygdala's sensitivity level, over time? That for months and indeed years, you have steadily reset its dial to HIGH SENSITIVITY? That all along, you have been training it to react to triggers in your sporting environment, as if they were grave and catastrophic events? If so, it would certainly explain your choking at critical moments, the jelly legs in the locker room, and that detached, unreal sensation following a bad mistake. Incidentally, the same type of sensation experienced by those who've just been shot!!
- Could it be, then, that you've abused your amygdala over time? That you've unintentionally trained your inner alarm to equate performing in front of others, making mistakes and embarrassing yourself, with such genuine threats as a gun pointed at you, or a car racing towards you?

# When Anxiety Goes Bad

Ideally then, we want our inner alarm to go off when there is a *genuine threat* to our survival. That's its purpose. It's the same with our burglar alarms at home - we only want them to ring when an intruder tries to break in. We don't want the alarm ringing every time the wind blows!

But with our ability to interpret any situation as threatening, our amygdala can be in business 24/7, ringing every time we worry and engage in scary 'what if?' thinking. Anxiety at this excessive level is *toxic*.

# Toxic Anxiety and the Athlete

**"Anxiety is the poison of human life."**
**Tryon Edwards**

Anxiety shows up in three main ways – physically, cognitively and behaviourally. We will now examine the effects of excessive anxiety on each of these aspects of being human.

As you read the following three sections, you will be left in no doubt as to why acute anxiety/high arousal is toxic to performance.

# PHYSICAL EFFECTS

When anxiety is high and your fight-or-flight response is activated, your mind and body are interested in only one thing – your safety. To achieve this, your body goes through different changes, in preparation for running or fighting.

So the *actual* preparation you're involved in, when highly aroused, is for survival, *not* for sport. You can see the problem here!

One manifestation of intense anxiety is the effect it has on your muscles. You'll find that your muscles will tighten and that any finesse required will be absent. If your sport is say, snooker, golf, tennis, or darts, you will find excessive arousal having an extremely detrimental effect upon the more delicate skills. Muscles that need to be loose will tighten.

In the sports just mentioned, the performers may have difficulty executing pots, putts, serves, or throws with the necessary deftness and flow. Muscular spasms can occur that disrupt the snooker player's cue work, the golfer's smooth putting action, the tennis player's throw of the ball at a serve, and the dart player's release of his dart. What were once unthinking graceful actions become dismantled by acute anxiety.

Golfers, including Bernhard Langer and Ian Woosnam, have all been struck by *the yips*; the yips being the term used to describe this distressing manifestation of choking at critical times. Darts legends Eric Bristow and Jocky Wilson have been similarly affected. The yips have also been reported by cricketers (especially by bowlers), by pitchers in baseball, and by free-throwers in basketball.

It is no coincidence that these performers compete in non-timed sports. Remember, your inner saboteur exploits downtime, even if that period is a matter of seconds. Unless you have a trained mind, humans don't do downtime very well. Thoughts creep in quickly, doubts multiply, and a crippling self-consciousness emerges.

In an effort to cope, the performer often urges himself to try harder - and then harder still. But this only serves to intensify an already heightened level of arousal. All of a sudden, the performer reeks of panic.

Excessive anxiety can disintegrate any skill, but when those skills are well-engrained techniques, shaped by years of practice, performers will report the experience as one of the most frightening and surreal of their careers. They often feel "taken over by something bad inside my mind", as one golfer put it to me after walking off a course mid-tournament. Well, he was right of course; it *was* something bad inside. His mental monster had lashed out and disassembled his technique.

## Jane

I remember an actress I worked with, who described one of the most crippling episodes of toxic anxiety I'd ever heard of in a performance setting. As with the snooker player, golfer, tennis player and darts player, Jane's anxiety attacked the tools of her trade.

Jane (not her real name) had an audition one afternoon and the closer she got to it, the more anxious she became.

Initially, her increased arousal was invigorating and she felt up for the challenge. But then she began to think! Not about her audition recital, but about the outcome. Her self-talk became full of 'what ifs' and 'ah-buts', and she created a sense of dread about the audition. With an hour to go, she was going to ring in and cancel. Fear of failure, and thoughts of making a fool of herself, prompted this flight response. But to her credit she decided to fight her fear and turned up at the theatre with fifteen minutes to spare.

Time to relax, surely? No, not for Jane – she didn't know how to.

Instead, she burrowed so far down the rabbit hole of anxiety that her physical symptoms had a catastrophic impact. Indeed, she thought she was having a stroke.

She couldn't speak (not great for an audition), felt detached and experienced tingling in her face and down both arms. In the end, she sat down on the stage, like a deer frozen in the headlights of an oncoming car. It was this experience that prompted her to contact me, but not before an ambulance took her to hospital.

She had a comprehensive medical exam that day and was released after three hours, with a clean bill of health. It was "Just stress", the young doctor at A&E told her. Jane was none too pleased with the breeziness of his opinion.

After all, she'd just been to the dark side of anxiety and the word 'just', didn't belong there.

## Thoughts, Feelings and Behaviour Interact

On examining Jane's interpretation of her audition ("It was so important to me Mark – life and death it was. I needed that part"), and of her symptoms ("Oh God, I'm going to die here"), it was obvious an interplay was occurring between her thoughts, feelings and behaviour.

She had created for herself, a cocktail of effects that gave her no chance of performing that day. Through her negative and defeatist self-talk, she'd turned her amygdala on full blast. And the more it rang, the more she worried about her lack of readiness.

Then her voice went.

For several hours that day in May 2007, Jane moved from being a 22 year-old aspiring actress, motivated and ambitious, to a young woman under threat, frightened and lost.

Never underestimate the impact of an untrained mind. It's a plaything for your mental monster.

## OTHER PHYSICAL EFFECTS OF ANXIETY

**"My stomach's full of vomiting butterflies!"**
**Homer Simpson**

Further physical signs of excessive anxiety, include: a pounding and racing heart; surges of adrenaline; increased sweating; chest tightness; light-headedness; feeling detached or unreal; frequent urination and defecation; queasiness and indigestion; dry mouth; difficulty swallowing; and, tension headaches. Not that many then!

As an interesting aside, evolutionary theorists contend that frequent trips to the toilet is an adaptive survival response, since urinating (or otherwise) lightens the body and allows you to run from the threat with greater speed, or to fight it with enhanced agility! Who'd have thought it?

They would explain a reduced sex drive in similar terms. If you are in the midst of a physically dangerous situation, you must of course attend fully to the threat to stay alive. Keep your eye on the ball, as it were. Stopping off to make love wouldn't be good for your health. The cavemen who did that didn't live too long!

Today, we see these symptoms amongst stressed, depressed and anxious people. Many of my counselling clients will report reduced libidos and digestive problems, as features of their mental health difficulties.

They are often surprised to hear that these symptoms had their genesis in ancient times.

# COGNITIVE EFFECTS

Alongside the physical consequences of toxic anxiety, is a range of cognitive or mental effects. Chief amongst these, from a performance perspective, are impairments to your:

- Thinking and perception
- Confidence
- Focus
- Decision-making

## • Thinking and Perception

There is a powerful and reciprocal relationship between the content of your thoughts and the physical symptoms of anxiety. To illustrate, let's return to Jane, the actress described above.

Jane held very high expectations of her audition. She pitched its importance at the level of life and death. Unsurprisingly, this triggered her amygdala to invoke the fight-or-flight response. The closer the audition came, the greater her nervousness and she became besieged by rapid-fire thoughts of failure. This heightened her already excessive anxiety and confirmed her fears about failure. Her subsequent capitulation on stage was inevitable.

If you tell yourself that the forthcoming audition, or match, or presentation, is so significant as to be pivotal to your happiness and indeed to your survival, then any amygdala worth its salt, will do its thing.

And it did for Jane – she survived! So, well done to Jane's amygdala! But it was *sayonara* to a good performance, which was the purpose of her attending the audition in the first place.

In Pathway 2, we covered the *ABCDE technique* for defeating negative thoughts and interpretations. However, if you have opened the book at this page, let me briefly recap on the acronym, using Jane's case as a guide.

**A** is the activating event, the trigger. For Jane, her trigger was the audition. **B** represents the beliefs, thoughts or interpretations held by Jane about the event. We know she perceived the audition as being extremely important, not just in itself, but also to her future well-being.

As Jane interpreted the audition in this way, her anxiety started to increase. She felt weak, experienced 'pins and needles' in her limbs and face, her head became sore and, alarmingly, she had difficulty swallowing and speaking.

She sat in quiet servitude to these growing symptoms. These emotional and behavioural sensations and reactions were the consequences (**C**) – *not* of the audition – but of Jane's *interpretation* of the audition.

This distinction is so important to grasp.

Jane's extreme construal of her forthcoming audition and her negative perception of her readiness to do well was the basis of her capitulation that afternoon.

A sub plot, if you will, of Jane's ABC was that her increasing anxiety became another activating event all on its own. Her dry mouth, an inability to swallow or speak effortlessly, the rush-upon-rush of adrenaline and tingling around her body, triggered a set of defeatist and terrifying thoughts:

> **"I can't do this. I can't. I'll flunk it so badly. I'm just not ready. I'm not good enough. Word'll get out about how useless I am...Oh no, I'm on next."**

> **"Oh my good God, I'm tingling all over...I can't speak, I CAN'T speak... I can't breathe...Oh my God, I'm having a stroke!"**

You can see that it was all over for Jane before it even began.

These vicious circles, or negative wheels-within-wheels, were propelled by Jane's anxiety, which grew as she stepped up her defeatist and extreme interpretations. Anxiety, 'what if' thinking, worry, doubt, uncertainty, fear and inadequacy chased each other round and round the playground of her mind.

However, after a few sessions working together, Jane had learned to square these vicious circles. She developed a strong ability to identify and dispute her negative thoughts and interpretations and to generate much more helpful self-talk. She realised it was *her* perception of situations that governed her emotional state. That actually *she* was in charge of it all. She was not, as she once thought, a passive casualty of uncontrollable arousal.

To strengthen her emotional control even further, Jane learned how to relax, using very simple techniques. She also employed imagery as part of her preparation regimen. To enhance her imagery sessions, Jane would visit an audition venue a few days before the due date and, if she could, she would gain access to the stage.

Here, she would act out her audition script and back it up through imagery. All of these techniques and strategies galvanised her sense of control.

And the happy ending to this case is that Jane outperformed *eighty-six* other hopefuls to nail a part in a well-known play. She travelled with the company all around the UK and, to this day, Jane continues to do extremely well. Any anxiety Jane now feels is of the useful variety. It tells her she's ready to perform.

By the way, the D and E of the ABCDE acronym refer to *Disputation* and *Effects*. Dispute your negative interpretations, replace them with useful alternatives and practice with a purpose. Then you will begin to experience the profoundly positive effects of your newfound thinking skills.

It's as easy as ABC...and D&E!

# • **Confidence**

It goes without saying that as your anxiety increases, your belief in your ability to perform with excellence, diminishes.

Instead of recalling vivid instances of great performances, and telling yourself that you can master the task-at-hand, you are consumed by the very antithesis of confidence and self-belief – a doubting and anxious mind and a feeling of not belonging.

You become proficient at finding reasons why you *won't* play well. For each reason found, your anxiety moves up a notch, until your body tightens like a tourniquet around your performance – and you choke.

# • **Focus**

Let me ask you this. When your body is racked with unsettling sensations and your mind with negative thoughts, where does all your attention go?

Exactly, it goes straight to those inner feelings and thoughts. Which isn't good when you're about to take a free-throw or penalty, or receive a serve.

As your energy flows where your attention goes, then excessive anxiety will leech your mind of concentration. Remember, concentration, like blood, is a limited commodity.

Over-arousal will drain you dry of this precious resource, leaving your performances anaemic.

Anxiety can also drag your focus to the future through the medium of *what if* thinking. If your mind is drifting to the result or to what other people will think of you if you lose, or to that mistake you *don't* want to make, then your concentration is all over the place. And not where it needs to be - in the present moment, at the job-in-hand. You may be intensely self-conscious and worrying that the world is watching and judging your every move. This type of anxiety is claustrophobic and crippling.

## Time Travel for Masochists

Actually when you think about it, anxiety, or more specifically, worry, is a form of time travel for masochists. Though you feel the symptoms in the present, it is all about a *predicted* event - some future catastrophe ready to overwhelm you!

But remember, the future doesn't exist. Therefore, neither does the catastrophe. But guess what?

By imagining it, you are training your attention on it. So of course, your brain will do all it can to make it happen – it takes your negative imagery as an instruction. It accepts that as you're focusing on it, it must be important.

By the way, you cannot get out of it, simply by telling yourself NOT to do what you've just imagined, or thought about.

## Don't Think of George Clooney

I had the privilege of working with the Northern Ireland Women's senior international football team. It was a great experience, as it always is when you work with a highly motivated group. Their manager, Alfie Wylie, lives and breathes football and his passion is infectious and his coaching superb.

So, there I was, delivering a workshop, and had reached the section on thinking skills and how the brain processes language and self-talk. I asked the players what they were focusing on and thinking about in anticipation of the forthcoming game against the Czech Republic. A few examples were offered and in a couple of instances responses were prefixed with, "I don't want to..."

This is a very common thinking style. We engage in it all the time, under the illusion that it is a positive thing to do. "I don't want to play badly in front of our home crowd. I don't want to mess-up my first touch, or to be off the pace...Don't want to... Don't want to... Don't want to..."

But, as I explained to the team that evening, if you focus on what you *don't* want to happen, your brain simply ignores the 'don't' bit, and converts the remainder of the self-talk into an instruction. Your mind's focus then goes there.

To illustrate this phenomenon, I asked the Northern Ireland squad to NOT THINK OF GEORGE CLOONEY. To ripples of laughter, the point was made.

They realised that, you cannot NOT think of something.

You try it. Don't think of your mother, your father, your boyfriend, your girlfriend, your car, even your cat. What about the result of your last match...that mistake you made. Can you *not* think of these please! It's impossible isn't it? You actually end-up attracting the very thing you *don't* want.

Even an internet search works this way. Try typing in DON'T WANT WEBSITES OF ARSENAL FC. (No offence meant to any 'Gooner' reading this). Now, what happens? No websites of Wenger's wonders? No. To the contrary –

about 2,000,000 results emerge, all of which are *about* Arsenal; not *not* about Arsenal!

# • Decision-making

Over-anxiety can also hinder decision-making. As tension multiplies, doubt and uncertainty emerge and attention focuses inwards. Bear in mind too that anxiety can also escalate, when things are looking *good*.

A golfer I worked with last year was 5-under par after sixteen holes, on the last day of an important PGA tournament. He was topping the leader board and all seemed well and under control. But then, out of left field, he became hyperaware of his situation. "Flippin' heck", he thought, "I could win this. I mustn't drop any more shots." He left these thoughts unchallenged, thereby giving away his control over his emotional state.

What happened next was predictable.

Not only was there a mental and physical tightening, but the golfer also became distracted from a game plan that had been working perfectly well. His decision-making process was infiltrated by his anxiety. As his perception of his situation had altered, his shot-selection process altered to match the mood. He began to play very cautiously. Yet for sixteen holes, he had done none of this!

You will also find in situations like this, that many players will speed up. They want it all over with quickly – the anxiety and anticipation is just too overwhelming. But whether you decide to play it safe or to submit to an urge to speed up your routine, you have abandoned what was working.

Anxiety wins, you lose. The monster nabs you again!

## The Half-Lives of Physical and Cognitive Anxiety

While the physical symptoms of anxiety generally dissipate once competition begins, cognitive anxiety can make unwelcome cameos at various times throughout the game.

Entering from stage left, the cognitive anxiety gremlin can come out with, *"You stupid ass, you shouldn't have missed that"*, or *"That's it now, it's over. You're beaten!"* This is *your* self-talk of course, so drop the assumption that you have no choice in the matter.

If you say such self-defeating things to yourself, there is no-one else to blame but yourself. So do something about it! Pathway2 offers detailed instruction on how to combat unhelpful self-talk.

# BEHAVIOURAL EFFECTS

Okay, let's examine the behavioural features of toxic anxiety. When intense anxiety is holding court in your mind and body, you will find yourself acting in ways not typical of the true you. You may find yourself engaging in impulsive and reckless acts, such as speeding in your car, abusing drugs and seeking out confrontation.

On the other hand, your reactions may be much more subdued. You may withdraw from friends and family and avoid situations you once approached with excitement.

As explained above, your libido may decrease and relationships at home can become strained. You may find your hair-trigger agitation and irritability winning you no friends. Not great for household harmony and team camaraderie. From the athlete's perspective, the most significant behavioural effect of intense anxiety is, of course, UNDERPERFORMANCE.

## Pathway Pitstop 6.2

### My Anxiety Reactions

Spend a few minutes recording your anxiety responses, in terms of the three categories, just described. Recall instances, before and during competition, and name and claim the reactions as *physical, cognitive* or *behavioural*. It is important that you recognise the difference between these categories. Knowledge is power, after all, and a starting point for change.

You should also note how you tend to deal with the differing forms of anxiety. What strategies work best for each type? What category of anxiety is the most difficult for you to control? For instance, can you more readily manage the bodily sensations of anxiety, than you can intrusive thoughts and images?

# SOURCES OF ANXIETY: YOUR EMOTIONAL FAULT-LINES

Take the golfer above - he reached the seventeenth tee box on the last day of a regional tournament, glimpsed the leader board and started to do something he hadn't done for the previous sixteen holes – he started to interpret his situation in a destructive way.

His thoughts turned to the outcome and he became burdened by the enormity of the possibility of winning. This hyper-awareness set off the type of self-consciousness that generates 'What if?' thinking.

He began to worry what other people would think of him, if he didn't win from such a strong position. He became stifled by fear of failure and his sense of personal mastery and control left him. He said to me later, that he felt psychologically naked - a wonderful description of feeling mentally exposed at a critical time during performance.

Anxiety attacked his body, and his golf game deteriorated. He dropped three shots over the final two holes and finished in third place. But an important lesson was learned. He had recognised an emotional fault line. The source of his toxic anxiety was NOT that he was leading the tournament with two holes left. Rather, the source was his own INTERPRETATION of his leading the tournament with two holes to play.

Using the techniques described later in this chapter, this golfer learned to stay composed and stopped judging, predicting and comparing. He wiped the opinion of others off his mental radar and began to take back control of his mind.

He learned that he was causing his own stress and anxiety. That it wasn't out there on the golf course, the leader board or the pundits' predictions. Instead, it was an inside job!

> *The components of anxiety, stress, fear, and anger do not exist independently of you in the world. They simply do not exist in the physical world, even though we talk about them as if they do.*
>
> **Wayne Dyer**

## YouMinus pounces at SW19

British women's number one, Elena Baltacha, appeared to succumb to the wily ways of her mental saboteur, during a first round defeat to Croatian Petra Martic, at Wimbledon 2010. Mind you, it never looked likely, as Baltacha was sailing through. She was one set to the good and serving for the match at 5-4, when she began to experience bodily tension and anxiety, just as our golfer did.

> **"I'll be honest – I was actually quite tight at 5-4 up. I was nervous. Up until that point I was in control. I tried to stay as relaxed as I could but I got slightly tight"**
>
> *Daily Mail, 22.06.10*

It's no coincidence that these sensations arrived when they did. On the verge of winning and going through to the second round, it's possible that Baltacha became overly aware of the importance of her service game. After all, it was the gateway to that rare event – a British player going through to the second round at Wimbledon. Aside from Andy Murray, there has been a dearth of British players making it beyond the very early rounds at the SW19 venue.

I'm only speculating, but this or something similar, may have entered Baltacha's mind as she prepared to serve-out. As a result, she prised her focus away from the process of serving and returning, placing it instead on the outcome of the match.

When the opportunity to win is not taken, as in the Baltacha example, it is often the case that sports performers become self-critical and irritable. It's as if by missing the chance to close out victory, the opportunity to do so has gone forever.

But often, it's still there and with everything to play for.

And this is how it was with Baltacha.

While Martic did break back and went on to win the second set, there was still an entire final set to play for. No catastrophe had happened. All square, anyone's game. But is this how Baltacha interpreted it? Well I don't know of course, but there are strong indications that she didn't, as it all went downhill from there for the British number one.

She appeared to be frustrated and was heard remonstrating with herself. With confidence affected and focus compromised, the match was soon in the Croatian's hands.

Martic won the deciding set 6-3.

Tellingly, after the match, Baltacha hinted at the influence of other people's expectations on her mental game. It seemed that they may well have weighed heavily, particularly at the crucial moment.

> **"I mean, obviously when you get to Wimbledon, yeah, of course you're gonna feel nervous. You know, you're a Brit. You're expected to do things."**
>
> *asapsports.com*

*Wimbledon-itis*, as I call it, seems to afflict many of the home players. It appears that they are affected by the hype, hope and expectation thrown their way year after year. Well not so much affected by the hype, hope and expectation, as by their *interpretation* of these things.

If a player takes the hype with a pinch of salt, and maintains his focus on the controllables, then he is likely to play his best game. However, the player who takes the hype to heart will be placing an unnecessary layer of interference on his performance.

I would like to add an epilogue to the Elena Baltacha story. While her match against Martic provides a neat illustration of how a performer can sabotage their own efforts, it must be emphasised that the likeable Baltacha is a tough individual. She has moved up the world rankings to a top 50 spot and has done so, in spite of a severe health problem. No mean feat.

After the Martic match, she took a mature, pragmatic and solution-focused approach the loss:

> **"From whatever happened today, I'm going to go home, I'm going to learn, that's it. You move forwards. You can't have things your own way all the time... I'm human – I'm not a machine. Sometimes things like that happen...I'm going to be honest about why I got nervous and we're going to try to get a solution for it that can stop it from happening in the future."**
>
> *asapsports.com*

Such honesty is refreshing and there are clear signs that Baltacha is not that far away from making even more progress in her career.

Right, it's time for another Pitstop exercise; one that will help you to identify the triggers to your unsettling, emotional reactions.

## Pathway Pitstop 6.3

### My Anxiety Triggers

Let's take a step back for a moment and nail down those situations you find stressful; times when your anxiety is acute and interferes with your preparation and performance. What we're doing is beginning with the 'A' of the ABC Model.

### Situations That 'Make' Me Really Anxious

Situation 1 _____

Situation 2 _____

Situation 3 _____

This is a terrific awareness exercise, as it opens up your emotional landscape to scrutiny and therefore remedy. It is a bit like selecting the little gold man, of *Google Maps Street View* fame, and placing him amongst the streets, alleyways and cul-de-sacs of your emotional world, with the aim of earmarking the toxic landmarks for demolition.

Knowing your toxic landmarks/most stressful situations is one thing, but assuming that the situations *cause* the anxiety is another thing all together. I think you know the mantra by now: **Situations do not *cause* your emotions.**

The situations you've just described above are meaningless, until you give meaning to them. You will find if you tunnel down deeply enough, that the real threats triggering your anxiety are threats to your ego.

So for example, if you recorded *Making An Error* as a situation that 'makes' you anxious, then I would suggest that the real cause of your anxiety is not the error, per se, but your concern that by making a mistake you will be mocked, feel embarrassed and appear useless to others.

A further way to establish that it isn't the mistake in itself that 'makes' you anxious or upset, is to notice how you react to errors in practice, when the stakes are not as great. While you may feel annoyed, you will not want the ground to swallow you up as you would do in front of a stadium-full of spectators, or if the national coach was watching.

You may also notice that you are much more relaxed, confident and focused prior to a training session, than you are on match day. Clearly, the heart of emotional control lies in the *thoughts and expectations* you have *about* certain situations.

## HOW TO CONTROL YOUR EMOTIONS

We now know that your unhelpful emotions, the type that affect your preparation and performance, are very much down to you. And how do we know this? Because you create and enflame them; particularly, through your defeatist self-talk and negative appraisals.

Not great, huh?! But actually it's a very strong position to be in! After all, if you create your unhelpful emotions, then you have the power to control them. There are many ways to achieve this and the rest of this Pathway is devoted to showing you how.

As depicted below, there are three levels of intervention available to you to tame your troubling emotions.

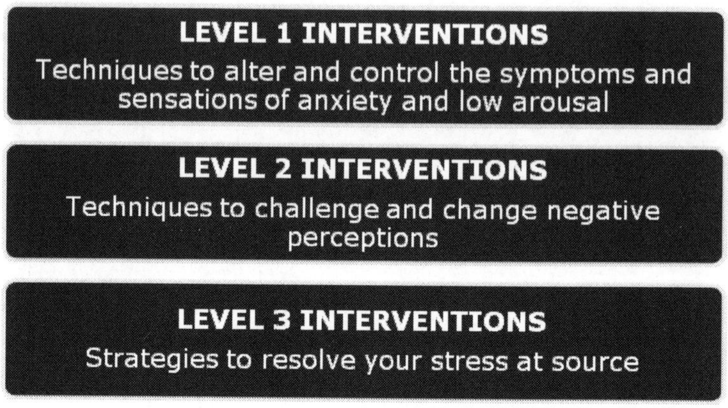

> **LEVEL 1 INTERVENTIONS**
> Techniques to alter and control the symptoms and sensations of anxiety and low arousal

> **LEVEL 2 INTERVENTIONS**
> Techniques to challenge and change negative perceptions

> **LEVEL 3 INTERVENTIONS**
> Strategies to resolve your stress at source

**Figure 7:** The Three Levels of Intervention (*After Jones and Moorhouse, 2008*)

Before we embark on these three areas, I need to put forward an important caveat. The techniques and strategies that litter the rest of this chapter, are *only* as effective as your awareness of WHEN you need to use them.

If you do not know your own ideal performance state, then you do not know when your arousal is either too high or too low and needs adjusting. It is vital, therefore, that you carry out Pathway Pitstop 6.4 in the following section, after which we'll move on to the techniques of emotional control.

# Personal Ideal Performance State (PIPS)

It is essential that you identify and tune-in to your 'just right' emotional bandwidth, the one most conducive to your performance. It is personal to you and sits somewhere along the arousal continuum, between low and high intensity. I refer to it as your PIPS; it is your emotional Nirvana, and you must find it. Here are examples from three of the world's best athletes:

✓ **Tommy Bowe** – Ospreys', Ireland and Lions' wing.

> **"[My PIPS is] when I am relaxed and excited about the game ahead. I will feel confident about myself and slightly anxious, but looking forward to getting out on the pitch"**
> *Personal communication, 01.04.10*

✓ **Paul Brady** – World Number 1, Handball.

> **"This [my PIPS] has changed a lot for me over the years. In the earlier part of my career I would have been very intense and over-hyped for weeks before a major match or tournament. As my career has progressed, I have learned to relax much more and to take each day as it comes. Sometimes when I think about an upcoming tournament, I can feel myself getting ahead of myself so I need constant reminding to stay in the moment"**
> *Personal communication, 04.06.10*

(And then there's Jimmy's PIPS!!)

✓ **Jimmy Connors** – Tennis legend.

> **"I psyched myself up into a state where I felt something close to hatred towards my opponent, a state where I detested the idea of someone making his name at the expense of Jimmy Connors"**
> *tennispsychology.com*

From these three examples alone, you can see that each performer's PIPS is personal to him. It cannot be copied – it is the emotional fingerprint an athlete leaves on great performances. It is his optimal state for competition - his *just right* state – and no-one else's.

So it is with *you* and *your* PIPS.

The following exercise is incredibly important, so set aside enough time to complete it.

## Pathway Pitstop 6.4

### Identifying Your PIPS

To discover your PIPS, you need to study your previous performances. Specifically, you need to scrutinise two types of displays: the ones you'd love to reproduce every week; and, those you'd never wish to repeat again.

Comparing your best and worst performances, will provide you with significant clues as to your optimal mental state for competition.

You may find for instance, that before **your poor performances**, you were restless, overly anxious and preoccupied with *not* failing. That you were pacing up and down the locker room, in an effort to assuage your crushing nervousness; but to no avail.

And that when it was time to step out into the sporting arena, you wondered if your legs would hold up as they were so unsteady. Then, as the performances themselves unfolded, your mind was anything but quiet. Thoughts about such extraneous matters as, what your coach was thinking, and how it would be awful to make a mistake on live TV entered your head and took away your focus from the task-at-hand. Your self-consciousness on these occasions made it impossible to perform anywhere close to your peak.

But when you look back over **your top performances**, you see a completely different picture. For example, you may find that prior to these displays you tended to feel excited, nicely nervous and up for the challenge. Your emotional state was not intrusive and you were confident about delivering a high level performance.

This mentality then formed the basis for a focused and committed display; a performance that was in the flow, enjoyable and which whizzed by so quickly, you were sorry when the final whistle went.

From all of this analysis, you should now be able to pin-down your personal ideal performance state, and complete the following sentence:

**I'll know I have reached my PIPS whenever I feel:** _____

_____

Right, you're in a very strong position here with an emotional heads-up. Now you know how you'd like to feel before kick-off, throw-in or tee-off. For this reason, the central part of your preparation will be to reach your PIPS for competition. But how do I do this Doc, I hear you say?

Well, you need to put a Preparation Chain in place (see Pathway Pitstop 4.9, Chapter 7).

This is a pre-competition regimen that ensures you hit your 'just right' state, every time. It contains effective emotion- and arousal-management techniques and tools that fall into three distinct categories of intervention. Let's have a closer look at these.

## Level 1 Interventions

### Controlling Symptoms & Sensations of Over- and Under- Arousal

Before competition, your arousal will be at one of three levels:

**↑Too High**

**↓Too Low**

**♂ Just Right**

The 'Just Right' or *Goldilocks* state is your PIPS. By completing Pathway Pitstop 6.4, you will now have a handle on your ideal performance state. And by virtue of knowing your PIPS, you will also be aware when it is absent.

This will prompt you to make adjustments to your arousal level; either raising it or lowering it.

But this begs the question, 'Do you know HOW to raise and reduce your level of arousal?' Can you find your way back to your PIPS?

If you don't know how to, or are unsure what techniques are available, then the following sections will really help you.

**Table 3:** Techniques to reach your Ideal State

| Techniques to use when: | |
| --- | --- |
| Your arousal is **TOO HIGH** | Your arousal is **TOO LOW** |
| Abdominal breathing | Mood Music |
| Meditation | Physical activity |
| The Ticker-tape Technique | Breathing Technique |
| PMR | Imagery |
| Imagery | Motivational DVDs |
| | Positive self-talk |

# ■ What To Do When Your Arousal Is TOO HIGH

Our breathing or more specifically how we breathe, has a powerful influence on the quality of our emotional state at any one moment. For the athlete, breathing offers a gateway to state control.

Before and during performance, many athletes will unknowingly breathe in a way that exacerbates anxiety and increases muscle tension and tightness. This breathing is typically short, shallow and uneven.

Breathing for emotional control needs to come from the stomach and not the chest, and should be slow, deep and even. This aids the flow of oxygen throughout the body and brain, and augments nerve messaging and muscle functioning - which is good for performance.

Okay, what's your typical breathing style? And does it improve your emotional state or make it worse? Not sure? Then carry out the following exercise.

### Pathway Pitstop 6.5

**Identifying Your Breathing Style**

When I am teaching breathing control to performers, I initially ask them to place one hand on their tummy and one hand on their chest, and to take a few good breaths. As they do this, I instruct them to notice which hand moves the most – the 'tummy' hand or the 'chest' hand.

So, now it's your turn. Sitting or standing, take several breaths – breath-in and let it out - and note what happens on the inhalation. Which expands more, your stomach or your chest? In other words, which fills up with air?

Well done if it is your stomach. You are breathing in a healthy and helpful way. But, if your chest expanded on the inhalations, then welcome to the club. You are with the majority who respire incorrectly. And, when the pressure is on, breathing in this way only serves to compound an already anxious and tense body. You are not optimising the oxygen available to you.

However, it is very easy to overcome this bad habit and to learn how to breathe in a manner conducive to living and performing.

As with many dysfunctional habits, breathing incorrectly was learned along the way. Just as we set aside the wonder of our imaginations towards the end of childhood, we also abandoned another birthright – breathing from the abdomen.

# Technique 1: Abdominal breathing

## The 4-2-4 Technique

Let's get those hands back on the tummy and chest. Sit for this one, as if you're in the locker room, prior to a big game.

- Breathe in slowly and deeply to the count of four, and make sure your abdomen rises and your chest hardly moves at all. Hold this breath for two seconds, before then exhaling slowly to a count of four, and, as you do so, notice how your body relaxes. By the way, purse your lips as you breath-out to gain maximum benefit from the technique.

- If we take this as one repetition, then you should perform twelve such repetitions right now.

- Practice abdominal breathing every day, for 21 days. Set aside ten minutes daily and practice, until you no longer need to incorporate your hands to gauge the appropriateness of your breathing. Within three weeks you should be automatically breathing in the correct way and starting to benefit greatly during times of over-arousal and bodily tension.

Now, how easy was that? With practice of this simple technique, you will have a powerful tool for rapidly reducing tension. Leonardo DaVinci was right when he said that "Simplicity is the ultimate sophistication".

# Technique 2: Meditation

## It's not just for Mystics

More and more athletes, actors and artists are engaging in meditation as a preparation for performance.

> 'Catch Lakers center Andrew Bynum throughout most of the day leading up to tip-off and you'll see him sitting on a chair meditating. He'll surely engage in these sessions with the team... but Bynum's pre-game meditation also happens on his own time, with a session after his pre-game lunch and shortly before the opening tip so he can visualize what's in store for later that night'
>
> *Los Angeles Times, June 9, 2010*

Many ill-informed people have considered meditation to be some sort of mystical activity belonging to the Eastern reaches. But over the past few decades meditation has become mainstreamed and is widely used here in the West. I'm sure you are familiar with the term *Transcendental Meditation,* or TM for short. It's thousands of years old, improves your brain functioning and is extremely beneficial to your physical and emotional health.

> "With continued practice of the TM program, you can become less and less anxious, developing a stable inner quietness than can be a buffer against otherwise stressful experiences."
>
> *Dr Steele Belok, www.tm.org*

Now, what would an *inner quietness* do to your performance?

Wouldn't it be great to lessen the white noise of an overanxious mind and body, as you get ready for competition? Well, the following Pitstop shows you how.

## Pathway Pitstop 6.6

### How To Meditate

It is important to prepare for meditation. You should schedule a set time each day to engage in the technique. You should also:

- Meditate in a quiet setting, where you will be left alone.
- Meditate in a relaxing position, sitting upright, with knees gently bent and feet flat on the floor
- Meditate with arms resting on your upper leg, with your palms facing upwards.
- Meditate in comfortable clothing and footwear.
- Meditate when your stomach is empty; before breakfast, for instance.

### Protocol for a mentally-cleansing meditation

- Aim for a five minute period of meditation.
- Once seated in a comfortable position, shut your eyes and dismiss any thoughts from your mind. In fact 'watch' them go by, but stay in the moment.
- Concentrate on your breathing. From the earlier Pathway Pit Stop, you will have learned how to breathe correctly from the abdomen. Focus on your breaths in and breaths out and notice how your tummy expands and contracts.
- As you breathe out, say a word that has meaning to you in the circumstances. Many simply say "re-la-x" in their minds as they exhale slowly. It is also very useful to picture all the tension leaving your body as you exhale. Form an image that works for you.
- If distraction tries to force its way in, refrain from forcing it away. Simply observe your anxiety, negative thoughts or regrets, as you would the clouds in the sky. Neither dwell on them, nor judge them. They are merely chemical events in your brain, nothing more than that. Stay focused on the rhythm of your breathing, as it is *real* and *current*. Give each

breath the respect it deserves: they are, after all, a sign that you're alive right now. Worries are fantasies; as woolly as the clouds. Watch them go by.

- Maintain this routine for the full five minutes or so. Once finished, take a few moments to take in the situation and to orientate yourself, before getting up and on with your day.

This type of meditation is particularly beneficial to the athlete. It is mindful and teaches a performer to stay in the present moment and to let potential distraction float away (also see *Ticker-Tape Technique* below). The value of meditation for you and your performance is clear. Firstly, it enables you to regain control of an over-stimulated mind and body and secondly, it offers a pathway to effective focus.

**Remember, learning to focus on your breathing is learning to focus in the present.**

Although I have provided a quick overview of the key elements of meditation in this Pitstop, you should really shape your own meditation practice. For example, I've suggested a five minute session, but there's no hard and fast rule for this.

There are many forms of meditation out there that could inform the content of your sessions. Why don't you find a local class where someone steeped in the art of meditation can teach you?

A great starting point in your research would be to read Jon Kabat-Zinn's 2004 book, *Wherever You Go, There You Are: Mindfulness Meditation for Everyday Life*.

## Meditation changes the brain

In the summer of 2010, researchers from the Dalian University of Technology in China informed the world that a particular meditation technique - *Integrative Body-Mind*

*Training* - can generate actual and positive physical changes in the brain. And rapidly!

This is how the research was reported in the media:

> **'Just 11 hours of learning a meditation technique induces positive structural changes in brain connectivity, by boosting efficiency in a part of the brain that helps a person regulate behavior in accordance with their goals...**
>
> **...A type of magnetic resonance, called diffusion tensor imaging, allowed researchers to examine fibers connecting brain regions before and after training. The changes were strongest in connections involving the anterior cingulate, a brain area related to the ability to regulate emotions and behavior'.**
>
> *Science Daily, 18.08.10*

No doubt about it. This form of meditation would greatly benefit all performers, as the ability to control one's emotions and behaviour is central to the attainment of sporting goals and high level performance.

## Technique 3: Ticker-tape it!

When you're weighed down by negative thoughts and symptoms of anxiety, it is all too easy to get involved with them.

You start to question their presence ("Why am I so nervous today?") or you feel they'll adversely affect your imminent performance ("I can't go out there feeling like this; I'll mess things up big time").

From such involvement, you can end up generating even more anxiety for yourself and, before you know it, you've spiralled downwards at an alarming rate.

A method that I have named the *Ticker-Tape Technique* encourages athletes to simply observe their thoughts and feelings, rather than to engage with them in the manner just described.

It's like noticing the 'news ticker' moving across the bottom of the television screen relaying the latest share prices, for example.

What I'd like you to do now is to imagine a screen in front of you. It's blank - apart from the line of ticker-tape running along the bottom, from left to right.

Moving across this ticker are your thoughts, emotions and physical sensations, simply passing by like various boxes on a conveyor-belt.

One particularly innovative client used to visualise his negative thoughts and feelings as different animals. He'd watch them amble across his imaginary screen like they were entering Noah's Ark.

So be creative!

The key to the success of this exercise is to deliberately observe your thoughts and feelings without engaging with them.

I guess it's a bit like staring back at the school bully who expected you to cry, plead or run away!

## Technique 4: PMR

> "Progressive relaxation is a new method to bring quiet to the nervous system, including the mind."
> *Dr Edmund Jacobsen*

Progressive Muscle Relaxation (PMR) is yet another great weapon against unhelpful anxiety and bodily tension.
Developed by Edmund Jacobson, in the mid-1920s, it reduces stress, loosens up tight muscles and will help you to attain an emotional state conducive to your performance in training and competition.

In addition, PMR has been shown to aid a good night's sleep, improve focusing ability and help assuage the severity and frequency of panic attacks.

Although it is a response to bodily tension and stress, there is a benefit mentally too. You'll find that through continued practice, PMR will reduce the tendency to obsess, worry and fret.

## Rationale

We know that our muscles tense when we're over-aroused and anxious. So it stands to reason that learning to relax the muscles will reverse this process, or prevent it from happening at all.

PMR builds on this rationale. It's as simple as this:

**Muscular tension and relaxation *cannot coexist*.**

In the same way that an expectant female can't be pregnant and not pregnant at the same time, so a muscle cannot be tense and relaxed simultaneously.

PMR enables you to feel the difference between tension and relaxation, by moving you through the main muscle groupings of your body and asking you to tense and relax them in a preplanned order.

This is the *progressive* bit of PMR.

## Pathway Pitstop 6.7

### How to carry out PMR

Schedule your PMR session for 20 minutes. As with learning all relaxation techniques, you should begin practising in a quiet setting, far from the madding crowd. Get comfortable lying down.

Ensure you uncross your arms and legs. Take several deep, abdominal breaths to quieten the mind, and then proceed to move through your body, tensing and relaxing the key muscle groups. You will do this in a methodical fashion, moving up from your feet to your face.

*Caveat*

*When tensing or squeezing a muscle group, do it firmly, but not so forcefully that you induce a cramp or strain the muscle. When releasing a muscle group do so quickly and benefit from the sudden sensation of relaxation. Stay with this sensation for about 15 seconds, before moving on to the next muscle group.*

***Please note:*** take out contact lenses before starting PMR.

### From Feet To Face, Muscle Group-By-Muscle Group:

- Curl your toes downwards around an imaginary perch. Hold for 10 seconds, then release them abruptly, and stay with the ensuing relaxed feeling for 15 seconds. You will do this Hold-Release-Relax sequence for all of the muscle groups in the exercise.
- Keeping your legs straight, point your toes and feet towards you. Hold, release and relax.
- Clench your thigh muscles. Hold, release and relax.
- Squeeze your buttocks together tightly. Hold, release and relax.
- Arch your back up and away from the floor. Hold, release and relax.
- Suck-in your stomach, tense the muscles. Hold, release and relax.
- To tighten your chest muscles, take a deep breath and hold for 10 seconds. Then release, slowly this time, and relax.
- Make a fist with both hands and clench them. Bend your arms at the elbow, bring them up and in towards your upper

chest and tighten your bicep muscles. Hold the pose. Release and relax.

- Shrug your shoulders up to your ears...hold, release and relax.
- Bring your chin into your chest. Hold, release and relax.
- Push the back of your head 'into' the floor. As you hold, notice its weight. Release, and relax.
- Open your mouth as widely as you can. A mixture of Edvard Munch's *The Scream* and Batman's foe *The Joker* should do the trick! Hold, release and relax. Allow your mouth and jaw to slacken.
- Squeeze your eyes shut. Notice the inner kaleidoscope. Hold, release and relax.
- Raise your eyebrows, as if you've had a facelift too many. Hold this surprised look for the 15 seconds, then release and relax.

Once you have completed this sequence from feet to face, count back slowly, from 5 to 1, to allow any remaining tension to leave your body.

Then gather yourself up and re-engage in your day. Or, as *Little Britain's* Kenny Craig would put it, "You're back in the room".

## Scanning your body in the locker room

Once you've mastered PMR, you will have a clear and practical understanding of the difference between muscle tension and relaxation.

You will become skilled at locating where the tension is in your body. Without needing to go feet-to-face, you can scan your body and tighten, hold, release and relax ONLY those muscle groups where the tension exists.

This rapid relaxation response is ideal when time is tight, such as in the changing room prior to a match, when your somatic anxiety is likely to be building.

# Technique 5: Imagery

As the mind and body are essentially one, you can use mental imagery to promote relaxation in the body. Pathway 5 explains how the brain accepts vivid imagery as real. As a consequence, you have at your disposal a wonderful facility - the ability to take your mind to other places. This is a great advantage to have, when relaxation is your goal.

## Pathway Pitstop 6.8

### Using Imagery

At the outset, you should read Chapter 8, if you haven't done so already. To use imagery effectively, it is important to follow the instructions found in Pathway 5, and to engage in regular practice. Imagery is a skill.

Using imagery to calm an overanxious mind and tense body is a personal affair. Personal in respect of the content of your images. For instance, you may have favourite places you visit from time-to-time to unwind and to feel at peace – forest parks, lakeside cabins, hillside cottages, and beautiful beaches. You will have childhood memories of cosy tree houses and secret hideaways. One athlete I work with, places himself in the back seat of his father's *Ford Granada*. He always enjoyed long trips with his parents, and felt a cosy comfort in his own back seat den.

When anxious and jelly-legged before kick-off, he travels back there. He re-experiences the cocoon-like comfort of these childhood car journeys. His imagery is so vivid that he can hear his Mum and Dad chatting in the front, smell the pine-fresh deodoriser, feel the seat underneath, and see his Action Man tucked into the pocket at the back of the passenger seat. Imagining in this way always brings his tension down several notches, to a more appropriate emotional state.

Clearly, you must set about developing your own scene. The rule of thumb is to use whatever works for you. Make your senses work overtime and engage all five to help capture the entirety of the scene. One extra suggestion is to develop an imagery scene that involves a lane, road or path leading to a particular place. For example, a trail that takes you through a leafy glen down to a beautiful lake. As you make progress along the path, you can feel more and more relaxed as the lake comes into view.

Once you have scripted your scene in a way that stimulates your senses, you need to practise it.

Sitting or lying down, close your eyes and take several deep breaths to clear your mind, in readiness for the images. Then picture the scene in vivid detail. Feel the heat of the sun on your back, or the tickle of the breeze on your face. Hear the lapping of the waves, or the cooing of the woodpigeon.

Smell the creosote on the fences, taste the salt in the air. See the cobalt sky through the trees; feel and hear the autumn leaves crunch under your step. Wherever you are, BE THERE!

As you live the scene, feel the relaxation spread throughout your body. Stay there for several minutes, breathing slowly and deeply, and attain the calmness you crave. As you leave the scene, and ready to open your eyes, feel assured that your relaxed state will stay with you. Count down from 5. Then open your eyes and return to the present, relaxed, refreshed and composed.

## Take a bow left hemisphere

There is always a time and a place for left brain involvement. Here's a great little technique that exploits its love of words, sequencing and detail. If arousal is kicking-off a bit, then why not do your 'A-to-Zs'? Reduce over-arousal by naming football teams beginning with each letter of the alphabet – Arsenal, Birmingham City, Chelsea, Derby County and so on.

If soccer is not your bag, then try female names, countries or capitals. Identify a few topics that would stretch your mental powers sufficiently to distract your anxious mind.

Incidentally, I recall a peculiar A-to-Z moment with 'Jim', a 40-something golfer I worked with several years ago. We met at his local club one morning and before heading to the first tee, Jim asked for some advice. He wanted a few simple techniques to use to keep his mind from wandering in-between shots. Particularly between his drive and second shot and when he was walking from green to tee box.

I underlined the need for Jim to switch-off from golf between shots, and to relax his focus. Along with taking in the scenery, humming a tune, chatting to his caddy, I suggested he go A-to-Z on girls' names. He said he liked this and would try it immediately.

After hitting his drive on the first, Jim and I set off down the hill to his ball. An enthused Jim began his A-to-Zs out loud. "Alison, Barbara, Catherine, Debra..." However, he tailed off on the edge of 'E' and stood rooted to the spot, some way from his ball.

"What's the matter Jim?" I asked. "I-I-I feel so angry Mark. I'm sorry. I need to take a time-out". "Of course. But what's wrong? Are you feeling sick - can I help in any way?". "No Mark. I'm beyond help with this one. You see, Edith's the name of my ex-wife. And she's bleeding me dry for maintenance at the moment. 'E' was next on my A to Z, and in popped Edith..."

You never stop learning from your clients!

## Two-Way Communication

Up until now, you have been provided with several terrific techniques that capitalise on the strong communication channel between mind and body. You have been presented with *body-to-mind* strategies and *mind-to-body* strategies to reduce your arousal level to your ideal state. But, as with all aspects of your sport, you *must practice* these techniques on a regular basis.

## Remember, it's personal to *YOU*

As your PIPS is unique to you, your means of attaining it will also be idiosyncratic. Many athletes I work with, pick'n'mix the strategies that can raise or lower their anxiety levels to the 'just right' state for competition.

One such athlete is the world's best handball player, Paul Brady. In the quote below, he sets out his regimen for the week leading up to a match, and the techniques he uses to attain his PIPS before taking to the court:

> **"I usually adopt various different strategies when dealing with pre-match nerves depending on the circumstances. During the week leading into a big match/tournament, I try to stay as relaxed as possible and to put things in perspective if I am feeling overly anxious. I reframe my thinking and try to remind myself to <u>enjoy the challenge</u> that lies ahead. I convince myself (most often unsuccessfully!) that it is only a game at the end of the day, even though it doesn't feel like that at the time. On the day of a match, I again try to stay as relaxed as possible by focusing on a few key points:**
> - **Breathing - slow, deep breaths**
> - **Keep on the balls of my feet**
> - **Listen to my IPod**
> - **Go over key points in my mind again and again"**
>
> *- Personal communication, 04.06.10*

Former middle distance runner, Seb Coe, now Lord Coe, was one of the UK's most successful athletes. Speaking to the BBC, he described his typical pre-race routine - one that maximised his readiness to perform.

> **"My routine was to sleep before an event. I took the view that if I wasn't thinking about the race, then I wasn't expending energy. If a race was at eight or nine o' clock at night, I'd be asleep by mid-afternoon right up until six o' clock. I'd get up, warm up and run. It wasn't a routine that was suggested to me, it was something that worked for me from a young age."**
>
> *Raise Your Game, BBC SPORT website*

## ■ What To Do When Your Arousal Is TOO LOW

> **"The last time I felt flat before a competition was Russia 2006, before I started any mental training. I did nothing to pick myself up at the time. I fought rubbish."**
>
> **Lisa Kearney**, *Elite Judoka*

Although it's less common, some athletes do feel flat before performance and need to find ways to lift their arousal levels. We've all felt like this at times. Maybe it's the result of poor sleep, a loss of focus and purpose, or burnout. It could just be a temporary blip that can be dealt with by speedy intervention.

Or it could be a sign of depression. Do you find yourself feeling low no matter what the situation is? Are you withdrawing from your usual pleasurable activities? If you are, then I suggest you seek advice from your general practitioner.

Okay, so how can you lift your arousal level when you feel flat and not up to competing? How can you achieve your PIPS under these conditions?

# Technique 6: Mood Music

A useful way to elevate your emotional state is by listening to music. Now, as with all arousal-management techniques, it's a very personal thing. Music that will lift my mood and energise me, may not float your boat whatsoever!

I grew up with the music of the 1980s and really can't see *Kajagoogoo* raising anyone's spirits these days. Can you?

## Pathway Pitstop 6.9

### Compile Your Mood Music Top 10

I'm sure you already know about the power of music. It's a potent tool that communicates with body and mind in a way that leads to emotional change.

I only have to hear *Crazy Nights* by Kiss and I'm up and running and ready to go. Except at my age there's often nowhere to go to!

Seriously though, I do have a list of tracks that I listen to while travelling to seminar venues or clubs. I only do this if my energy is a bit low and I need a mental shake-up.

You should do the same.

Compile a *Mood Music Top 10* to raise your energy and while you're at it, identify the tracks that tend to relax you, useable for those times when your arousal soars.

To assemble your Mood Music Top 10, it is important to begin with say 15 to 20 tracks that you know have a positive effect on your emotional state. Then set about evaluating the specific effectiveness of each track, or track combination, by asking yourself a few questions: When I listened to Track X, Y or Z what emotional changes did I experience? Were they positive and did a good performance ensue? Is there an optimal time to listen to music before competition?

By following this selection process, you can whittle the 20 or so tracks down to the ten that are the most useful.

## Music: the legal performance-enhancing drug

Dr Costas Karageorghis, Head of the Music in Sport Research Group at Brunel University, knows that music can stimulate, as well as sedate:

> **"[Music] is considered by some athletes to be a legal drug with no unwanted side effects... Music with a fast tempo can be used to pump you up prior to competition, or slower music can be used to calm your nerves and help you focus."**
>
> *Raise Your Game, BBC Sport website*

One of my greatest experiences in sport was working with the Fermanagh Senior Gaelic Football team in 2004. They reached the semi-finals of the All-Ireland Championship that year, only losing (after a replay) to Mayo, who subsequently got steamrollered by Kerry in the final. I refer to this experience a lot in my seminars as a fantastic example of an alleged sporting underdog using mental preparation and skills to punch above their weight - and to confound every pundit, bookie and armchair critic around.

In relation to emotional control, I can still recall the Fermanagh team's CD of inspirational and upbeat tracks. We had U2's *Beautiful Day* and Eminem's *Lose Yourself*, to name but two.

> ♪ **Look, if you had one shot, or one opportunity**
> **To seize everything you ever wanted- One moment**
> **Would you capture it or just let it slip?** ♪
> *Lose Yourself, **Eminem***

Al Pacino's *Inch By Inch* team talk from *Any Given Sunday* was also on the CD. Pacino played football coach, Tony D'Amato in the movie. Now if you haven't heard this speech, then you're in for a treat as it pushes all the right motivational buttons. Actually, if you can, set the book down for a few minutes, dog-ear your page and go straight to *YouTube*. Type in: *Al Pacino Inches Speech, Any Given Sunday*. And enjoy!

## Me and Simon Le Bon

In 1999 and 2000, I underwent three operations on a lower back problem. As I recovered and began driving again, I would dose myself up with some painkillers to ease the discomfort from getting back behind the wheel.

Even driving short distances were very uncomfortable. I would drive tentatively, sitting at an angle on one hip and gripping the steering wheel with white-knuckles. But then, one frustrating afternoon as I drove the eight miles to my parents' house, I pulled over to the hard shoulder and after a minute or two's fumbling in the glove compartment found my *Duran Duran* CD. In a 'physician heal thyself' moment I put the CD on, located Track 7 – *Hungry Like the Wolf* – turned the volume up to shake-the-windows level and started singing.

Before I knew it, I had also sung and possibly mimed to *Girls on Film, Planet Earth* and *Union of the Snake*. I had also arrived at my folks' house without any pain at all. I moved with greater ease out of the car and my mood had noticeably elevated.

Even my mother said, "You're in better form today son. Not as grumpy as usual". Diplomacy was never my mother's strong point! But she was right of course, as I had become a bit irritable with life after three operations and almost a year off work!

The message here is a strong one. **Music is a miraculous mood shaper**. Use it.

There are other ways to raise your mood to where you want it to be.

# Technique 7: Physical activity

Engage in vigorous short bursts of activity. For example, running on the spot and stretching.

# Technique 8: Breathing Technique

Take short, shallow breaths to invigorate your physiology and mental state.

# Technique 9: Imagery

Use imagery to place your mind in stimulating situations. Create images that increase your arousal level. If you're a forward in football, you could visualise yourself sprinting into the box to meet a cross and heading in a superb goal. You could hear the crowd cheer, and feel the emotional impact of the moment. Shape this technique to your own sport.

# Technique 10: Use Motivational DVDs

Depending on the time available to you, you could watch and listen to an inspirational video. Many teams I have worked with have compiled their own footage and mix it with arousing music. I strongly recommend this motivational tool.

Images of excellence and team spirit can do wonders for the psyche, lifting it up to a higher state of readiness. Timing is everything when using this tool.

# Technique 11: Positive, constructive self-talk

Become your own inner motivator; your own Tony D'Amato. Talk to yourself in a way that cajoles you to respond physiologically. Reflect on earlier successes and bring them strongly into focus. Be there again; feel the rush of adrenaline as you do so.

> **"While I try to make sure I'm not flat in the first place, when it does occur I remind myself of how hard I have trained...I sit down and write out the reasons why I deserve to win or why I should be motivated to win"**
>
> **_Paul Brady_**

Many teams have collective rituals they follow before competition. There's the ubiquitous huddle in the changing room or out on the pitch and there are the more elaborate routines such as the _Haka,_ guaranteed to raise an antipodean pulse or two.

## Smorgasbord of Strategies

Essentially, this Pathway offers you a platter of strategies from which you can choose and shape the ones that work best for you. After all, you're the boss.

As always, the techniques you opt for need to be practised and used regularly for you to gain the maximum benefit from them.

Writing for the Belfast Giants' website, ice hockey star, Bobby Robins, provides an articulate and personal insight into the nuances of his pre-match routine. He has honed a meticulous regime that works for him. It enables him to attain an emotional state, just right for a night on the rink.

## Bobby Robins' Routine

**"But two hours before a game, all you have are your thoughts. And they are slow, detailed, churning thoughts. Each player has his own way of dealing with this two-hour window of high stress.**

In two hours from this moment, you know you will be in a war zone, where grown men are flying around a frozen oval, wearing body armour, and toting curved metal weapon spears in their hands.

Some people kick around the soccer ball. Some people blast their earphones, and rhythmically nod their heads to the beat. Some crack jokes, and tell farfetched stories inside a cloud of chuckles. Some stand in a steaming shower and stare down at water droplets bouncing off beige tile. Some read the paper and catch up on business matters, celebrity gossip, or the happenings around the rest of the league.

I prepare my weapon.

I tape my stick with such precision, following the exact lines and details I have done every day for the past twenty years. I unroll that black tape slowly, and methodically press down layer after layer until the entire blade is covered.

I fill in every crease and seam with wax. I am diligent and pious, as I inhale that sweet smell of black cloth tape. I ask our equipment manager to bless the stick, and he takes it from my hands and performs whatever magic he knows, and he guarantees goals and stick-handling wizardry.

Sometimes it works, sometimes it doesn't. At this point I usually turn to one of my teammates who looks unusually stressed and worrisome, and I perform the Fifteen Count Manual of Arms.

It's an old military movement, back from my military school days, and consists of fifteen precise movements of the rifle—or in this case, my Easton Synergy Hockey Stick, Drury Pattern, Medium Flex.

Sometimes I add an extra twirl of the weapon, catching it in the rigid Present Arms position, and then perform an "about face" and soldierly march away, without saying a word, back to my locker stall, where the only things waiting are musty equipment, still damp from the morning skate, and thoughts and thoughts and thoughts. Maybe at this point I will move to the floor and stretch. And while I'm there bending my arms and legs, I hear the countdown begin, "thirty minutes".

The stretching evolves and now I'm standing and doing jumping jacks and swinging my legs and leaping about, and "fifteen minutes". It's time now.

I put on my pads, the same way, and every day, left to right. Then the thoughts become louder. The dreaded "what if's". And I go through every possible terrible situation that can happen in a hockey game, and I'm knocking on wood, and desperately trying to focus on nothing other than tying my skates.

And I look around at all the stern faces in the room. We are all about to engage in battle. And I meet the eyes of some of other players who are looking around, and you simply give a slight nod, and flash fiery pupils.

"Ten minutes."

The music is aggressive on the stereo, loud angry music, and it is at the ten-minute mark in the countdown where the players start bellowing positive phrases.

"Here we go boys" and "smart plays, lotta talk out there" and random swearing and grunts, all the while the countdown happening, and you feel a rising surge of adrenaline pumping through your veins, and each surge blocks out some of the lingering thoughts or doubts, and your courage grows, and you hurry to finish up that last strap of your equipment, or adjustment of your jersey.

"Now you are walking through that tunnel, and it is so bright, and you see a mass of faces and colors, and when the steel of your skates first touch the ice surface, the slate is wiped clean, and some sort of purity sets in, and there you are, fearless and thoughtless, and only reacting, and with a slight smirk on your face, you get to experience this heightened retreat, where for the next three hours you feel, undoubtedly, that you are exactly where you are supposed to be."

**Bobby Robins**, *belfastgiants.com*

# Level 2 Interventions

## Challenging and Changing Your Negative Perceptions

> "An emotion is suggested and demolished in one glance by certain words."
>
> **Robert Smithson**

I hope you agree that Pathway 3, Chapter 6, provided you with amazing and life changing information about the power of interpretation. Interpretation is the portal to how you experience life, let alone sport.

The meaning you give to an event, including bodily sensations, dictates how you are going to feel and behave. The event itself does not cause your reactions. The example I continuously preach, is that a mistake doesn't make you angry or frustrated. Rather, it is *your interpretation* of the error that generates your subsequent negative responses.

This means *you* have a choice. It's *your* interpretation after all. The control is yours.

This knowledge can be utilised to ameliorate the impact of increasing stress and anxiety. When you feel overwhelmed by those disconcerting symptoms of stress – the nauseous stomach, the wobbly legs, the racing heartbeat – always remember, **you have a choice**. You can interpret these sensations as *either* a sign of your impending capitulation, *or* you can decide to view them as a clear indication of how important the match is to you.

Your body is readying itself for combat and that's a good sign!

If you interpret the bodily reactions negatively, guess what happens?

That's right, the sensations worsen. But interpret the feelings as a positive indicator of your readiness to compete, and guess what? They begin to release their grip on your mind.

This *reframing technique* is employed by top performers worldwide. Gaining control of your thinking and interpretive ability, is a vital mental game tool for life and sport.

It's the ultimate in empowerment.

Pathway 3 covers this in great detail and provides stunning strategies that will give you full authority over your emotional and mental states.

Very few of us were ever taught to control our emotional state through the power of our thoughts. Our education system seemed to have left that bit off the syllabus!

But thanks to this book, you now have the knowledge.

Work hard on your thinking skills, as many of us have cultivated styles of thinking and interpretation that mess with our minds and tease our emotions.

These types of thinking distortions have also been examined in Pathway 3, but they're worth an encore here.

## Pathway Pitstop 6.10

### The Mental Monster's Henchmen

Go back to Pathway 3 and study the *The Gremlin 6-a-side team*. These thinking distortions are dreadfully unhealthy. They serve no useful purpose, but they do feel real. Do not forget that your brain believes what you tell it.

So if, for instance, you think in an 'all-or-nothing' way, I can assure you that your brain won't give you a dig in the ribs reminding you to wise up and that your interpretation is wrong. It will just go along with your inner chatter.

Revist Pathway 3, read the descriptions of the six main types of faulty thinking, and record examples of when and where you have employed them. For example, you may discover that you engage in these thinking distortions when the pressure begins to step-up before a big game.

You may also note that these negative thinking styles can actually make a benign situation malignant.

# 'What if' thinking makes a Meerkat of Brandon's mind

I recall Brandon, a young up-and-coming 200m runner, telling me that, "all was fine, until I started to dwell on my 'what ifs'...I could hardly make the starting line after that!".

So, what had he done? Well, he simply thought of a few *what ifs?* and BANG! - his stomach turned over, his legs went weak and a distinct urge to avoid the race overwhelmed him. His lack of emotional control floored him completely:

> **"Mark, it's at times like that, that I wonder who's really running my mind...I can tell you, it didn't feel like me."**

But of course Brandon had been running his mind all along – only in a very negative way! As he had created a pretty powerful YouMinus, it was little wonder that he felt like sprinting back to the locker room!

Through his 'what if?' thinking Brandon was in fact preparing to make mistakes, lose concentration and to underperform. The very things that he DIDN'T want to happen out on the track.

At the very least, he was telling his brain to WATCH OUT!

By scanning his environment for threat, he attracted those things that he feared. It's the 'Don't think of George Clooney' Paradox that we covered earlier in the chapter.

Brandon's meerkat-like behaviour left him anxious, helpless and always on 'red alert'.

Not good for peak performance!

So even though he would train hard during the week, the work he put in was regularly undermined by his poor mental game. In view of this, I immediately put him on the Six Pathways programme.

And within three months we had a complete turnaround in his mental outlook. Remarkable progress was made.

Indeed, I am delighted to say that Brandon went on to have a very successful season for his school and County and achieved goals that once appeared to be well beyond his reach.

You see, Brandon realised that his interpretation of events was one of the key routes to emotional control. By working tirelessly on Pathway 3 strategies, he became expert at flipping negatives on their head.

For example, he learned to reframe his anxiety as 'excitement in disguise' and his nervousness as an indication of his readiness to perform well.

As personal development expert, Tony Robbins, explains:

> **"If we perceive something as a liability, that's the message we deliver to our brain. Then the brain produces states that make it a reality. If we change our frame of reference by looking at the same situation from a different point of view, we can change the way we respond in life. We can change our representation, or perception, about anything and, in a moment, change our states and behaviors. This is what reframing is all about"**
> **Anthony Robbins**, *Unlimited Power,1986*

And this is what Brandon did on a regular basis, and with performance-changing consequences. He's in very good company of course. The best in world sport have been using the reframing technique to control their emotions for years.

# Level 3 Interventions

## Resolving Your Stress at its Source

I would like to clarify something here. When I use the term *sources of stress*, I am not contradicting the Frankenstein Factor. I'm not suddenly declaring, after everything I've said, that something in your sporting world can indeed *cause* you to feel anxious or frustrated; or any other emotion, for that matter.

Absolutely not!

**You** remain the ultimate source of your own emotional state, good or bad.

A missed putt, pass or tackle cannot cause you to feel anything. You **choose** to be troubled by these things. As you cannot rewind time and execute the skill correctly, you have to find a way to park the error. Level 2 interventions enable you think constructively at such moments and to release the mistake from your mind. But Level 3 strategies are slightly different. They deal with situations that *do* exist and that are current or live.

So, if you've had a blazing row with your girl- or boyfriend, mother, father, coach, or teammate, you have a couple of strategies open to you.

1) Interpret the situation differently: i.e. in a way that reduces your angst, sadness or anger - and then get on with your life, with no regrets. You can also let go of an argument by using the same sort of strategies that help you to park a mistake during competition.

2) As a row with someone else involves *someone else*, you have one extra strategy open to you. You can go to that person, in real time, and sort it out. Doing this is important when you're unable to think your way out of your annoyance. You should then think yourself *into* speaking with the other person or people involved. This is an example of what I call a *Level 3er technique.*

I mean, how many of us have worried about something, let it fester for a while and then once we've resolved it at source, wonder why we didn't do it earlier? *"What was I fussing about? He was absolutely grand about it. He didn't feel one bit insulted by my joke about his haircut. Yet I've worried all week about losing his friendship!"*

There are two reasons why we don't face the source of our angst head-on and deal with it there and then:

- **We believe it's not possible**. "If I ring her to apologise, she'll just hang-up"; or "Someone like me would never gain access to the Chairman - so no point trying"; or "The gaffer wouldn't thank me for asking him about my future".

- **We are often vetoed from doing so by our fragile egos**. How many wars could have been prevented if the protagonists overcame their stubbornness and fear of losing face? How many relationships disintegrate due to unnecessary obstinacy, when a simple meeting of open minds could have paved the way to reconciliation? And, how many cancers could have been detected early, but for the ego-protecting behaviour of the (typically male) patient?

This is the power of a threatened ego. I'm sure you have felt similarly compromised. Instead of simply approaching a situation and dealing with it, you weigh-up the loss to your ego from doing so:

- **"She'll think I'm oversensitive, weak and unmanly."**

- **"The doctor will think I'm wasting his time."**

- **"He started it. So it's up to *him* to apologise to *me*"**

## Pathway Pitstop 6.11

### Bore Down To The Source Of Your Stress

Is anything troubling you right now, that you have written-off as unsolvable at its source? If yes, note it down in your journal. Then beside it, record your supporting evidence. "I have written-off going to the source of my stress (name or describe the source) because_____"

Once you have noted the evidence, hold it up to scrutiny. Is the evidence based on fact or conjecture? Are you afraid of embarrassing yourself or of exacerbating the situation? Is losing face or appearing weak in the mix? Is it less threatening to your ego to manage the stress and anxiety using Level 1 and 2 interventions? Perhaps trying to solve the problems at their source is too up close and personal for you? Maybe you're the type of person who shuns confrontation? Would you rather suffer that bit longer than put yourself through the short-term discomfort and awkwardness of meeting up with someone who has trashed you, overlooked you or failed to explain his actions to you?

Be honest with your answers.

Don't rob yourself of a potentially swift solution, just because your ego needs protecting.

# Case Study Update – Grant

## Grant Makes Progress Along Pathway 6

### Solution to Grant's Pathway Problem

In Chapter 3 you met Grant, the **28 year-old professional ice hockey player** who moved from his native Canada to the UK, in the early 2000s. He uprooted his family and moved to a UK Superleague club. They signed him up because their top player had left unexpectedly to return to Finland.

Grant, a former NHL draft pick, was seen as the next big thing for his new club - the all-conquering hero from the home of ice hockey.

But as you know from the case, Grant had difficulty coping with the move and dealing with the high expectations placed on his shoulders. He became very anxious before games and found that his focus had shifted to the consequences of a poor performance rather than remaining on the process of playing great hockey. A once composed, organised and confident player, he had begun to implode emotionally.

If you could do with a quick reminder of his case, then by all means turn to Chapter 3 now.

Having rated his ability to manage his emotions as a mere **two out of ten** on the Pathways Profiling system, Grant was clear on one thing: "I need to do something about this quick, or I'll be back off to Canada..."

Thankfully this drastic action wasn't necessary, as Grant worked hard at regaining control over his mental and emotional states. He made rapid progress on the Pathways Programme and started to achieve brilliant results.

## Sport Psychology Intervention

When I met Grant, he hadn't been playing anywhere near his best for a while and was getting less and less ice time. The situation became critical and Grant felt cornered. Not only was he playing poorly, but he was also concerned that his wife and kids were unhappy in England.

I remember our first session, when we met at Grant's apartment. His wife had taken the kids to McDonald's that day. After exchanging a few words about the weather, the decor and how I liked my coffee, we sat down at his breakfast bar. The moment I asked him how he was feeling, he broke down. This 6'4" man-mountain was distraught at his situation and he felt culpable:

> **"I've let everyone down. Janice is unsettled and the kids don't seem all that happy either. Then there's me and my performances right now. I'm playing so bad, have done since I came here. I haven't settled either, you know. The team's**

**expecting big things of me, so are the supporters, the media...It all seems too much! I just can't seem to play, to just go out on the blasted ice and play my game. Yet at home, I was steady and consistently good. Didn't have all this crap in my head and all these pressures from other people..."**

Although I felt sorry for Grant, he didn't want sympathy - he wanted a way out of the situation. He was beginning to drown in these unchartered waters and had become increasingly anxious before games. He just wanted the mental anguish to stop and allow him to play his best hockey. But he had become heavily preoccupied with "playing well at last" and garnering public acclaim.

So for Grant, **winning people over had become as important as winning matches!**

The opening psych. session helped him tremendously. Not only was Grant able to release some pent-up emotion, but he also discovered why he was anxious and irritable; why his performances had deteriorated; and why he felt the urge to escape it all.

I often find that clients benefit greatly from seeing, in black and white, the audit trail behind their current difficulties. And for Grant, the trail had begun in England.

**"I was in good form. Life was grand and my game was at its best ever, before I came over here."**

From this, we began the process of tracing the development of his mental game difficulties. As Grant talked, I wrote down the key moments in his narrative. These moments included those times when he clearly interpreted situations in a very negative way. For instance, on the morning of his first match for his new team, he (foolishly) read a few comments on a hockey web forum.

These were critical of him and seemed to water the seed of doubt that had been lurking inside the recesses of his psyche. Instead of sidestepping these comments, Grant ingested them.

He also recalled feeling extremely anxious before taking to the ice for his debut. This was not like him. Only a few weeks earlier he was playing regularly in a strong North American league.

Back then, he seldom experienced unhelpful nerves, let alone the type of corrosive anxiety he felt in anticipation of his first appearance in the UK Superleague.

Not surprisingly, Grant went on to have a wretched debut. He performed very poorly that night and in front of an expectant home support.

I also noted that he'd become increasingly consumed by factors outside of his control, thereby overlooking those factors that were within his gift. Grant had clearly misappropriated his focus to aspects of his sport that were irrelevant to his game on the ice.

At this point, I set a homework assignment for him to complete in two day's time, when I planned to meet up with him again. I asked him to fetch a blank sheet of paper, draw a line down the middle, and head up the two columns 'Factors RELEVANT to my game' and 'Factors IRRELEVANT to my game'. By carrying out this task, Grant soon realised that he had been approaching his preparation *the wrong way round*.

The audit trail technique provided a rationale to Grant's current difficulties, while the homework task emphasised that he had indeed been focusing on issues extraneous to his role as a hockey forward.

To develop his insight even further, I asked Grant to revisit two of his best performances during the previous season. I wanted him to work out *why* he had performed so well on those occasions.

To provide a structure to this task, I encouraged him to identify and record:

- How he had felt at training, during the week leading up to the games.
- His routines the night before and during game day.
- The routines he used in the locker room and when warming up on the ice.
- His level of pre-game confidence.
- His mental and emotional states before face-off (i.e. his readiness to play).
- Where his focus was, when playing (i.e. was it primarily on the task-at-hand, or elsewhere?).
- How well he dealt with mistakes and other distractions.
- How he managed breaks in the game, including downtime between periods.
- How he interpreted his performance after the game was over (e.g., did he give himself credit for good passages of play and log these to his memory bank? Or did he tend to dwell on the negative moments?).

At this point in the intervention, I noticed that Grant was answering many of his own questions. He was regaining a foothold and a sense of control. He realised that he had stepped away from his routines, was wasting his focus on irrelevancies, and that he had allowed his domestic situation to permeate his game.

Grant reintroduced himself to his old routines, drawing up a schedule of the usual activities that worked well when playing back at home. I asked him to place these activities on a timeline, stretching from the night before right through to face-off.

I spoke at length with Grant to establish what his personal ideal performance state actually was. Having already analysed his high level displays, he was able to pinpoint the specifics of his PIPS:

> **"I know that when I've had great ice, I'd been sorta nervous before stepping out on the rink. I had butterflies alright, but that was okay. It would be odd if they weren't there. Now recently I've felt overwhelmed by like millions of butterflies with swords. So yeah, some nerves are grand, and then I have to feel slightly aggressive too, you know. Not looking for a fight, but feeling up for it all, ready, confident. When I'm like this, it's strange, but I know I'll play well..."**

Grant re-engaged with his former self and in doing so, started to act in a more professional manner.

I also suggested to Grant that he have a gentle chat with his wife, Janice, to see how she was really coping and if the children were as unhappy as he thought. This was a valuable move.

It turned out that Janice was worried about her husband's transformation from "Mr Cool and Calm to Mr Uptight and Ratty", and that Grant had misread her behaviour as an indication of her unhappiness with the move.

In truth, Janice was content with the transition, but concerned about Grant. She also reassured him that the kids would be fine and, as with most young children, they were oblivious to what was going on. They had new friends now and were coping well enough with everything.

Grant's next step was to set up one-to-one meetings with his coach and agent. These conversations went better than he thought they would and eased his mind about the situation. His mental fog lifted and he set about focusing on his match preparation with a newfound clarity.

He overturned his fear of failure and instead set about *wanting success*. Success for him was performing as well as he could. To ensure this, he needed to stick to his role, deal with distractions when they came, have strategies to deal with the unanticipated and, above all, to commit to three periods of 'in-the-moment' hockey.

I encouraged Grant to go back to basics by asking him, "What is your role as an ice hockey forward for this team?" I stressed that it's impossible for any of us to perform at our peak in a role we do not understand (let alone know inside-out). He agreed and set about recording the elements of his job on the ice. He also considered what his role should be during periods of downtime.

Although Grant had used visualisation before, he had abandoned it over recent weeks. It was essential therefore that he reconnected with his *inner simulation trainer* and use it to rehearse his role.

He set about this with vigour, realising that his imagery system was a pathway to great hockey. Not only would the mind's eye help him practice his skill-sets and moves on the ice, but it would also increase his confidence.

## Distance travelled

Literally within days, Grant was a changed man and a significantly better hockey player! The speed of the turnaround amazed many, including Grant himself.

My initial meeting with Grant was on a Monday, my second on Wednesday; we spoke by phone on the Friday and by 10pm on the Saturday night he had scored his first hatrick for the team. He was also voted Man-of-the-Match.

An intensive week's mental training had been rewarded.

We had a quick chat together after the game and it was great to see Grant cracking a few jokes again. He was back in love with hockey. His mind had returned 'home'.

> "It was awesome out there Mark - and all because of your help... I followed your instructions and kept to my routine. Bed early last night, up at eight, took a walk round the block, had breakfast, watched a DVD and played with my kids. When my thoughts were negative, full of that s\*\*t about other people, I either talked back to them or distracted myself... You said these worries were like vultures that saw my career as prey. Well that's how I see them now and there's no way I'm going to be picked at...
>
> ...I had a good routine at the stadium and in the locker room I chatted to some of the younger guys, gave them a pat on the back, you know, and, well, I hadn't done that for weeks. I'd started to hide away a bit. Didn't think that I was in a position to give anyone advice.
>
> But I did what you said and ended up back in time, behaving as I did on those days when I played well.
>
> As the nerves and thoughts kicked-in, I used the breathing to relax me and put some secure images through my head. Just to give me perspective...

**...As face-off approached, I pumped Eminem's Lose Yourself through the earphones to psyche myself up. Boy - I felt ready. First time in a long time! After that, no real problems. Just played my game, I guess"**

Over the next few weeks, Grant was central to his team's winning streak of six games unbeaten. Nine goals and many assists later, Grant was himself again. His YouMinus had been overcome.

He was no longer overpowered by the stench of expectation, no longer under the jackboot of anxiety and no longer out of control.

Re-rating his position along Pathway 6 was an easy exercise. Two months after we first met, Grant assessed his capacity to control his emotions at **9.5** out of 10 (a jump from a baseline rating of 2).

## Key Points from Pathway 6

■ Mentally tough athletes know themselves well. So it is no surprise that they have insight into their personal ideal performance state (PIPS). They understand what works best for them; and have a toolbox of highly effective techniques to regulate their arousal levels to this *just right* state every time.

■ Your monster exploits the relationship that exists between your thoughts, feelings and behaviour to keep you trapped in a circle of fear, anxiety and avoidance. By placing your focus on 'what ifs?' the monster stokes up powerful and debilitating emotions, such as toxic anxiety.

- Anxiety is a double-edged sword. It can enliven and motivate you, or it can sap all the vitality and ability out of you.

- You want your inner alarm (the amygdala) to 'ring' when an actual threat exists, not a perceived threat. Otherwise you could be on red alert constantly, with your survival response hijacking your brain.

- Toxic anxiety manifests itself in acute physical, cognitive and behavioural effects. It pollutes your preparation and performance and, unless addressed, will destroy your sporting career.

- It is important that you locate your emotional hotspots (e.g., the morning of a game, the last few minutes before kickoff, preparing to take a penalty) and monitor your physical sensations, thoughts and behaviour for negative changes and signs of growing toxicity. Once identified, you need to find ways to bring your emotional state to heel at these times.

- There are three main ways to improve your emotional control:
    1. Control the physical sensations of over-anxiety and low arousal.
    2. Dispute and amend negative perceptions.
    3. Tackle stress at its source.

- It is important to understand that, when all is said and done, stress and anxiety is in the mind of the thinker. Therefore, the source of all your worries and unease come from inside you – your monster!

- Pathway 6 will take your emotional control to a whole new level. At last *you* will be in charge. You'll have identified your PIPS and be able to attain it, on-demand, by using powerful techniques and strategies.

# Afterword

## From Monster-Munched to Mental Mastery: A Summary

**The mind is a superb instrument,
if used rightly.**
*Eckhart Tolle*

**When there is no enemy within,
the enemies outside cannot hurt you.**
*African Proverb*

In your quest to progress from being monster-munched to having mental mastery, this book has guided you through five phases, starting off with the truth; which is surely the best place to begin any pursuit.

- **Phase One:** The Truth

- **Phase Two:** The Programme

- **Phase Three:** The Assessment

- **Phase Four:** The Plan

- **Phase Five:** The Action

## THE TRUTH

*Facing Frankenstein* has introduced you to your true opponent in sport – YouMinus, your mental monster or inner saboteur. Now that your eyes are wide open, you can't delude yourself anymore.

Revealing the best kept secret in society today, the book has explained that your mind has been ill-shaped and manipulated during your formative years, and that this has given birth to a destructive human phenomenon, called the *Frankenstein Factor*.

Having learned that you've been spun a great big lie about life and the nature of reality, you have now come to understand the role of the Frankenstein Factor in your inability to reach your sporting potential.

You now know that, if left unchallenged, your mental monster will devour your preparation and performance from the inside-out, until all that remains are the bones of your once promising career. You'll be monster-munched! And I can tell you, many a sporting wunderkind's early promise has been blown away in this fashion.

### The Myth of the External Cause

For the first time, you've come to realise that sport itself isn't psychologically demanding after all. That there is *nothing* in your sporting environment or experience that can cause you anxiety or stress. That there are no sporting stressors; only *your thoughts* about situations. So, the need for a mental game is therefore a human thing, not a sport thing.

You know this now. I think World handball champion, Paul Brady, puts it best when he describes the book in the following way:

> **"'Facing Frankenstein' woke me up to the fact that sport psychology has got nothing to do with the psychology of sport, but everything to do with the psychology of being human."**

You have discovered that the journey from monster-munched to mental mastery is one of winning back control of the single most effective and fantastical piece of kit in the known universe - the human brain. Your brain is the gateway to greatness, should you choose to use it constructively. It is the genie in your genes, ready and willing to grant your wishes, to help you realise your sporting dreams. In Part Two of the book, you were provided with the means to shape your brain for sporting success.

## THE PROGRAMME

### Mental Toughness: Where Six Pathways Meet

The book has not only brought you face-to-face with your sporting nemesis, but also it has provided you with a powerful programme of training to help you defeat it.

*The Six Pathways to Mental Toughness* programme is used by the best to be the best. It is expressly designed to win back those brain systems commandeered by YouMinus. In this way, it has liberated your mind from your monster's grip, in the most effective and efficient way possible. It has enabled you to overcome the Frankenstein Factor and to eliminate the self-sabotaging habits that have held you back, thus far.

## THE ASSESSMENT

Becoming mentally tough is a journey BY DESIGN. You cannot leave it to chance. As a result, you mapped out your personal route to mental toughness.

You began by assessing your mental game, using the *Pathways Profiling System*, and then you prioritised the work you had to do. You started with the mental skill that, once acquired, would have the greatest impact on your preparation and performance. To sharpen your focus and resolve, you named and claimed your destination in precise terms (i.e. you described the specific mental skill you wanted to develop), before setting out HOW you were going to get there and by WHEN. This, as you'll remember, was your 'Achievement Plan'.

## THE PLAN

To bridge the gap from monster-munched to mental mastery, you detailed the specific steps you were going to take. These steps were then translated into well-designed and motivating goals. By using the PUMAA system, you set the coordinates for your journey. After all, you didn't want to end up back where you started.

Importantly, you not only planned your journey to mental toughness, but also you prepared for each of your individual mental skill sessions. I must admit, I have found that many athletes fail to prepare adequately for these sessions. Accordingly, their enthusiasm wanes as they lose sight of what they were aiming for.

## THE ACTION

Overcoming your mental monster was never going to be a lunchtime procedure. There is no mental toughness equivalent of Botox. This book has taught you that the mental game is one of skill development; of forming repeatable mental habits that enable you to unleash your talent in competition; and that there are simply no shortcuts to such mental control. You have accepted this and are now committed to the Six Pathways programme.

### World-Class Mental Toughness

To get the most out of the programme, you know to apply the principles of *deliberate practice*. This unique training system allows you to journey from monster-munched to mental mastery in a Ferrari, rather than a Skoda. It also ensures that you arrive in Monaco, rather than Margate!

## The Bottom-line

By overcoming your mental monster, you will be able to prepare for and compete in your sport, unshackled by fear, anxiety and doubt. You will begin to like and trust yourself again (even when adversity calls) and you will stop beating yourself up. Instead, you will show self-compassion. What's more, your performance will be characterised by poise, perseverance and a quiet, yet focused mind.

## Welcome Home

By winning back control of your brain you will, in effect, be returning home to your natural state. You now know that you were *not* born into some sort of mental prison of low self-esteem, worry and limitation. Rather, it was society and the education system that 'placed' you there. And then you did the rest, keeping yourself incarcerated through poor mental habits. You'll also know that the most destructive of these is *worry*, particularly worrying about what other people think of you.

But when you defeat your inner monster, you will immediately reconnect with the boundless potential you entered the world with. The layers of mental interference will begin to peel away and you will find, stretching out in front of you, a vista of endless possibility. Grab this opportunity NOW, for you and your sporting career. It's time to return home my friend. Good luck and enjoy the journey!

With best wishes,

Mark

# Appendices

## Worksheets

## Appendix 1: **Pathways Profile Chart**

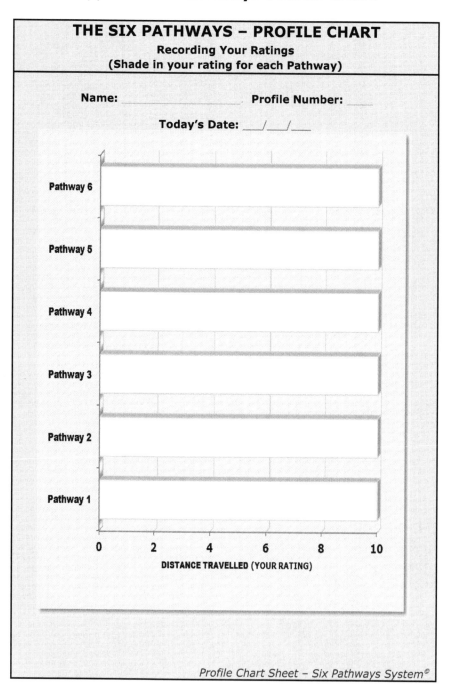

## Appendix 2: **'ABC' Worksheet**

| **A**ctivating Event | **B**eliefs | **C**onsequences |
|---|---|---|
| *Describe the trigger situation* | *Record your negative thoughts/interpretation of the situation at 'A'* | *Record your emotions, bodily sensations & behaviour* |
| | | |

## Appendix 3: 'DE' Worksheet

| Disputing | Effects |
|---|---|
| *Challenge your negative thoughts about 'A' and record your alternative interpretations in this column* | *Record how your new thinking about the situation makes you feel and act* |
| | |

## Appendix 4: **Distractions Worksheet**

| My Usual Distractions | Current Strategies to Manage the Distraction |
|---|---|
|  |  |
|  |  |
|  |  |
|  |  |
|  |  |
|  |  |
|  |  |

## Appendix 5: **Attentional Demands Worksheet**

| Times when I need a **broad-external focus**: | Times when I need a **narrow-external focus**: |
|---|---|
| | |

| Times when I need a **broad-internal focus**: | Times when I need a **narrow-internal focus**: |
|---|---|
| | |

# Appendix 6: **Web**

## References

http://www.boxingscene.com/

http://www.bbc.co.uk/wales/raiseyourgame/

http://www.bbc.co.uk/wales/raiseyourgame/sites/dedication/lessonsfromthelegends/

http://www.bbc.co.uk/blogs/tomfordyce/

http://www.mentalgoaltending.com/

http://www.hoganstand.com/

http://www.guardian.co.uk/

http://www.express.co.uk/home

http://www.soccerbase.com/

http://www.eircom.net/

http://www.bbc.co.uk/comedy/onlyfools/christmas/1996_3.shtml

http://global.quiksilver.com/

http://www.pgatour.com/

http://www.pursuitofexcellence.ca/

http://www.psy.fsu.edu/faculty/ericsson/ericsson.exp.perf.html

http://www.belfastgiants.com/

http://www.channel4.com/

http://www.channel4.com/programmes/the-simpsons/episode-guide/series-4/episode20

http://www.tennispsychology.com/

Dr. Mark S. Elliott

http://www.nhl.com/

http://www.asapsports.com/

http://www.wtatennis.com/page/Home/

http://www.youtube.com/

http://www.guardian.co.uk/

http://www.irishrugby.ie/

http://www.kysportpsych.com/

http://www.tm.org/

## Appendix 7: **Print Media**

### Newspapers/Journals/Magazines

*The Daily Mirror*

*The Belfast Telegraph*

*The Telegraph*

*The Daily Mail*

*The Sunday Times*

*The Independent*

*The Larne Times*

*The Guardian*

*The Los Angeles Times*

*The Magazine*

*Highball Magazine*

*Science Daily Magazine*

*Sportszone Magazine*

### Books

Colvin, G., *Talent Is Overrated: What Really Separates World-Class Performers from Everybody Else* (Portfolio, 2008)

Coyle, D., *The Talent Code: Greatness Isn't Born. It's Grown. Here's How* (Bantam, 2009)

Dispenza, J., *Evolve Your Brain: The Science of Changing Your Mind* (Health Communications, 2009)

Dweck, C., *Mindset: The New Psychology of Success* (Random House, 2006)

Ericsson, A., Charness, N., Feltovich, P., and Hoffman, R., *Cambridge handbook on expertise and expert performance* (Cambridge University Press, 2006)

Jones, G. and Moorhouse, A., *Developing Mental Toughness: Gold Medal Strategies for Transforming Your Business Performance* (Spring Hill, 2008)

Kabat-Zinn, J., Wherever *You Go, There You Are: Mindfulness Meditation for Everyday Life* (Piatkus Books, 2004)

Martin, I., *Green and White Army: The Northern Ireland Fans* (Appletree Press, 2008)

Robbins, A., *Unlimited Power* (Simon & Schuster Ltd, 1986)

Sampras, P. and Bodo, P., *A Champion's Mind: Lessons from a Life in Tennis* (Crown Publishers, 2008)

29306517R00282

Printed in Great Britain
by Amazon